DEMOCRACY and LEADERSHIP

Irving Babbitt

DEMOCRACY
and
LEADERSHIP

IRVING BABBITT

Foreword by Russell Kirk

Liberty Fund

This book is published by Liberty Fund, Inc., a foundation established to encourage study of the ideal of a society of free and responsible individuals.

The cuneiform inscription that serves as our logo and as a design element for Liberty Fund books is the earliest-known written appearance of the word "freedom" (*amagi*), or "liberty." It is taken from a clay document written about 2300 B.C. in the Sumerian city-state of Lagash.

6th printing (2024), printed on demand by Lightning Source, Inc.

Library of Congress Cataloging in Publication Data
Babbitt, Irving, 1865–1933
    Democracy and leadership.

    Reprint of the 1924 ed. published by Houghton Mifflin, Boston.
    Bibliography : p. 367.
    Includes index.
    1. Democracy. 2. Political science. 3. Humanism. 4. United States—Politics and government. I. Title.
JC423.B18   1978   321.8   78-11418
ISBN 0-913966-54-1 (hardcover edition)
ISBN 0-913966-55-X (softcover edition)

ISBN-13 978-0-913966-55-6 (softcover edition)

Liberty Fund, Inc.
11301 North Meridian Street
Carmel, Indiana 46032
libertyfund.org

Such legislation [against private property] may have a specious appearance of benevolence; men readily listen to it, and are easily induced to believe that in some wonderful manner everybody will become everybody's friend, especially when someone is heard denouncing the evils now existing in states, . . . which are said to arise out of the possession of private property. These evils, however, are due to a very different cause — the wickedness of human nature.

ARISTOTLE: Politics, 1263b, 11

Society cannot exist unless a controlling power upon will and appetite be placed somewhere, and the less of it there is within, the more there must be without. It is ordained in the eternal constitution of things, that men of intemperate minds cannot be free.

BURKE: Letter to a member of the National Assembly

The fundamental article of my political creed is that despotism or unlimited sovereignty or absolute power is the same in a majority of a popular assembly, an aristocratical council, an oligarchical junto, and a single emperor — equally arbitrary, cruel, bloody, and in every respect diabolical.

JOHN ADAMS: Letter to Thomas Jefferson (November 13, 1815)

Den einzelnen Verkehrtheiten des Tags sollte man immer nur grosse weltgeschichtliche Massen entgegensetzen.

GOETHE: Sprüche

CONTENTS

FOREWORD

By Russell Kirk

"The first thing to note about this book is that it constitutes one of those rare applications of a general intelligence to the sphere of politics." So Herbert Read, an anarchist, wrote of Babbitt's *Democracy and Leadership* when it was published in 1924. Babbitt's motive in this book, Read continued, was that of his other works: "the reestablishment of humanistic standards in place of the utilitarian, humanitarian, or romantic confusions so prevalent everywhere today."

Read found fault with Irving Babbitt for Babbitt's hostility toward the Soviet Union and for Babbitt's not seeing Christianity "relatively enough"—the latter rather an odd criticism, when one considers Babbitt's uneasiness with organized churches and his refusal to pass in his books beyond the realm of ethics to the realm of religion. (To his friend Paul Elmer More, Babbitt once exclaimed, "Great God, man, are you a Jesuit in disguise?") Yet Read was a kindly critic, by the side of the latter-day

liberals and socialists who then were dominant in intellectual circles. Much of Babbitt's life was spent in con-
troversy—including public debates—with the disciples
of Rousseau, Marx, and Dewey, whom he cudgeled in his
writings.

Babbitt left no disciples, Harold Laski wrote in his
American Democracy. But this is a proof of Laski's superficiality where American thought was in question. It is
true that Babbitt, during the hue and cry which the Left
raised against him, more than once told his students to
remember what he said, if they liked, and to employ his
ideas, if they chose to, but not to quote him directly: for
that would bring anathema upon them. Yet there have
been men of eminence who have been proud to quote
Babbitt, ever since he commenced lecturing at Harvard;
T. S. Eliot's is the greatest name among these. University
and college presidents like Nathan Pusey and Gordon
Keith Chalmers have been his disciples; some of the
better-known Catholic writers and some of the more able
Protestant clergymen have acknowledged their debt to
him; and his books still are sought after.

Babbitt initially was surprised at the fierce animosity
his books provoked among naturalists and men of the
Left. Those persons recognized in him and in Paul Elmer
More their most intelligent and courageous opponents;
and their hatred, hardened into dogmas of negation, lin-
gers on. A quarter of a century ago, long after Babbitt's
death, James T. Farrell denounced Babbitt as the arch-
priest of "traditionalism"; but it became clear to readers
of Farrell's essay that the novelist-critic simply did not
know what Babbitt actually believed. Arthur M. Schles-

inger, Jr., has referred to Babbitt as the defender of the "genteel tradition"; but Schlesinger either misunderstood Babbitt or misapprehended George Santayana's term "genteel tradition." Peter Gay, with more forthrightness than elegance, has declared that Babbitt's "essential vulgarity" was displayed by Babbitt's attacks on the character of his opponents, notably Rousseau. Now I do not know that it really is vulgar to criticize the character of a writer long dead, or that the private life of a social reformer is totally irrelevant to his public professions. More to the point just now, however, is my sneaking suspicion that many such people who heap vituperation upon Babbitt have not read Babbitt at all, but merely some hostile summary of his work in a book like Oscar Cargill's *Intellectual America*, adorned with quotations badly severed from their context.

For those who have read Babbitt, and know something of the man's life, it is amusing to find him described as vulgar: for he was the antithesis of vulgarity. Not that he was a "Brahmin," another absurd charge sometimes made, in the same breath, by his adversaries: he was a farm boy, a reporter in Cincinnati, and a cowboy in Wyoming, well before he became a Harvard professor. But he lived with a high dignity that was reflected in his very dress, and disdained easy success or popularity, and flattered nobody.

James T. Farrell made the blunder, repeatedly, of referring to him as "Dr. Babbitt"—when no man was less Herr Doktor Professor. Babbitt held the Germanic doctoral degree in merciless contempt, and fought with equal fervor against the degradation of the American college into a luxurious center for dilettantes and against the false specialization of the Ph.D.

Babbitt was born in Ohio in 1865 and died in Massachusetts in 1933. For a thinker so much discussed in his own day, Babbitt's literary production was not large: in addition to *Democracy and Leadership,* he published five other books—*Literature and the American College, On Being Creative and Other Essays, The Masters of Modern French Criticism, The New Laokoon,* and *Rousseau and Romanticism.* Also he translated the *Dhammapada,* and posthumously there was published a collection of his periodical pieces, *Spanish Character and Other Essays,* with a bibliography of his writings. No biography of this talented and manly Harvard professor of French literature has been written; but there exists a collection of brief memoirs by his friends and disciples, *Irving Babbitt, Man and Teacher,* edited by Frederick Manchester and Odell Shepard.

Babbitt was a principal leader of the intellectual movement called American Humanism, or the New Humanism, which for a generation filled the serious journals of the United States and Britain with friendly or hostile criticism, and which remains a living force in any American educational institution worthy of the name—although usually professed, in any university, only by a staunch minority. The American Humanists contended against the Marxist, Freudian, Instrumentalist, and Naturalist schools of opinion.

John Dewey and his associates, in 1933, alarmed at the growing interest in the American Humanists, made a disingenuous attempt to capture the word "humanism" by issuing what they called "The Religious Humanist Manifesto." Now Dewey's friends, with few exceptions, were not religious men; and when once Dewey himself was asked why he employed in his writings certain religious overtones quite inconsonant with his naturalistic system, he replied that to cut away at once the last vestiges of religious sentiment might wound some people unnecessarily; they must be accustomed more gradually to the divorce. The "humanism" which the Deweyites endeavored to promulgate has survived as a militant secularism; the word "religious" has gone by the board. But Dewey's humanism has little or no connection with the ancient continuity of thought and education which Babbitt, More, and their colleagues expounded.

What did Babbitt and the other American Humanists believe? To put matters very briefly, genuine humanism is the belief that man is a distinct being, governed by laws peculiar to his nature: there is law for man, and there is law for thing. Man stands higher than the beasts that perish because he recognizes and obeys this law of his nature. The disciplinary arts of *humanitas* teach man to put checks upon his will and his appetite. Those checks are provided by reason—not the private rationality of the Enlightenment, but the higher reason which grows out of a respect for the wisdom of our ancestors and out of the endeavor to apprehend order in the person and order in the republic. The sentimentalist, who would subject man to the forces of impulse and passion; the pragmatic materialist, who would treat man as a mere edified ape; the leveling enthusiast, who would reduce human personality to a collective mediocrity—these are the enemies of true human nature, and against them Irving Babbitt directed his books.

It is the humane tradition and discipline which keep us civilized and maintain a decent civil social framework, Babbitt argued. As Lynn Harold Hough wrote, Babbitt believed that "he lived in a world where undisciplined and expansive emotion was running riot." The modern world was dedicating itself to the study of subhuman relationships, which it took for the whole of life; it was sinking into unreason. "If by science you meant the discovery and the use of every truth you could find in every realm," Hough put it, "nothing would have pleased Babbitt more than to be regarded as the exponent of the scientific mind. But he believed that the naturalistic scientist ignored truths even more important than those which he discovered, and so he set men going wrong." Babbitt meant to restore an understanding of true humanism, that modern culture might know again the greatness and the limitations of human nature.

Against the humanist, Babbitt set the humanitarian. The humanist, by an act of will, strives to develop the higher nature in man; but the humanitarian believes in "outer working and inner laissez faire," material gain, and emancipation from moral obligations. What the humanist desires is a working in the soul of man; what the humanitarian hungers for is the gratification of all appetites in an equality of condition impossible to realize. Bacon symbolized for Babbitt the utilitarian aspect of humanitarianism, the lust for power over society and nature. Rousseau symbolized for him the sentimental aspect of humanitarianism, the treacherous impulse to break what Edmund Burke had called "the contract of eternal society" and to substitute for moral self-restraint the worship of one's reckless self.

As Paul Elmer More wrote, the central sentence in the whole of Babbitt's writings is this: "The greatest of vices, according to Buddha, is the lazy yielding to the impulses of temperament (*pamāda*); the greatest virtue (*appamāda*) is the opposite awakening from the sloth and lethargy of the senses, the constant exercise of the active will. The last words of the dying Buddha to his disciples were an exhortation to practice this virtue unremittingly." To egoism and appetite, which oppress our time, Babbitt opposed humanism, with its strict ethical disciplines. Humane studies are those which teach a man his dignity and his rights and his duties. They teach him that he is a little lower than the angels, but infinitely higher than the beasts.

In *Democracy and Leadership*, his only directly political book, Irving Babbitt applies these principles of humanism to the civil social order. "He starts from the axiom that man is the measure of all things," Herbert Read wrote in his review, "and is thus led to reject all deterministic philosophies of history, whether it be the older type found in Saint Augustine or Bossuet, which tends to make of man the puppet of God, or the newer type which tends in all its varieties to make of man the puppet of nature." He summarizes the principal political philosophies; contrasts Rousseau with Burke; describes false and true liberals; distinguishes between ethical individualism and destructive egoism; stands up for work and duty—and does much more. But the contents of this succinct and energetically written book I leave to the reader. It is the labor of a sage—that is, of a man whose moral imagination transcends the neat rules of formal philosophers.

Those who read this sincere and thoughtful book— this book which calls for a democracy of elevation, with just leaders—may find it difficult to understand the fury with which some writers of his time, and later, attacked that kindly big man Irving Babbitt. But as I suggested earlier, some of his more mordant critics may not have read Babbitt at all, really. One such was Ernest Hemingway, who had been told that Babbitt believed in human dignity—as indeed he did believe. Hemingway declared snarlingly that he would like to see how dignified Babbitt would be at the hour of his death, dissolving into slime. Yet as a matter of fact, Babbitt died with high dignity, wasted away by the painful disease of colitis; he continued to meet his Harvard classes, uncomplaining, almost until the day of his death. It was Hemingway, unable to confront the prospect of old age, who died in a very different fashion—by his own hand.

T. S. Eliot, whose early mentor Babbitt had been, wrote several tributes to the great scholar and polemicist. Eliot's chief quarrel with his old master arose out of Eliot's own passage to Christian faith. "We must regret deeply," Eliot wrote in his obituary in *The Criterion*, "that Babbitt's attitude toward Christianity remained, in spite of his sometimes deceptive references to 'religion,' definitely obdurate." But Eliot knew well what he and many others owed to the Humanist leader. "After a life of indefatigable, and for many years almost solitary struggle," Eliot observed, "he had secured for his views, if not full appreciation, at least wide recognition; he had established a great and beneficent influence, of a kind which has less show than substance, through the many pupils who left him to become teachers throughout America; and he had established a strong counter-current in education." All who had come under his influence, even if they went too far for Babbitt or not far enough, Eliot concluded, would "acknowledge to him a very great debt, and revere his memory in affection, admiration, and gratitude."

Much that Irving Babbitt grimly predicted, in politics and morals and education, has come to pass since 1924, and so some minds have waked today to Babbitt's hard truths. Will and appetite have had their way unchecked in a great part of the world; humanism fights a rearguard action in America; democracy sinks beneath tribulations, and leaders with imagination are few. Whether some humane restoration can be worked may depend upon the existence of a remnant which can understand Babbitt's sentences and endeavor to clothe them with flesh. However that may be, *Democracy and Leadership* remains one of the few truly important works of political thought to be written by an American in the twentieth century— or, for that matter, during the past two centuries. This new edition of an original and resolute book will inform and hearten some readers who—what with nearly all of Babbitt's works being out of print—may have confounded Irving Babbitt with Sinclair Lewis' character George Babbitt. There exists some reason to suspect that the novelist's employment of that particular surname was malicious; certainly many shafts of malice were directed against a good man and a great teacher.

Yet the troubles of our time fulfill Irving Babbitt's theses; and it seems quite probable that Babbitt's name, contrary to his expectation, may loom large among thinking people in the last two decades of the twentieth century, and longer than that.

PREFATORY NOTE

Parts of this book were used in a series of four lectures that I gave at Kenyon College on the Larwill Foundation in March 1920. I called the series "Democracy and Imperialism." In April 1922 I gave four lectures at the Leland Stanford University on the West Foundation. This series, which I entitled "The Ethical Basis of Democracy," contained some of the same material as the Kenyon series, altered, however, in form and with considerable additions. Finally, I drew on certain chapters of the volume for a course of public lectures delivered at the Sorbonne (March–May 1923) under the title "Les Ecrits politiques de J.-J. Rousseau." I desire to thank the authorities of these institutions for various courtesies extended to me in connection with the giving of the lectures.

I. B.

CAMBRIDGE, MASSACHUSETTS
   February 1924

INTRODUCTION

According to Mr. Lloyd George, the future will be even more exclusively taken up than is the present with the economic problem, especially with the relations between capital and labor. In that case, one is tempted to reply, the future will be very superficial. When studied with any degree of thoroughness, the economic problem will be found to run into the political problem, the political problem in turn into the philosophical problem, and the philosophical problem itself to be almost indissolubly bound up at last with the religious problem. This book is only one of a series in which I have been trying to bring out these deeper implications of the modern movement. Though devoted to different topics, the volumes of the series are yet bound together by their common preoccupation with the naturalistic trend, which goes back in some of its main aspects at least as far as the Renaissance, but which won its decisive triumphs over tradition in the eighteenth century. Among the men of the eigh-

teenth century who prepared the way for the world
in which we are now living I have, here as elsewhere in
my writing, given a preeminent place to Rousseau. It is
hard for any one who has investigated the facts to deny
him this preeminence, even though one should not go so
far as to say with Lord Acton that "Rousseau produced
more effect with his pen than Aristotle, or Cicero, or
Saint Augustine, or Saint Thomas Aquinas, or any other
man who ever lived."[1] The great distinction of Rousseau
in the history of thought, if my own analysis be correct,
is that he gave the wrong answers to the right questions.
It is no small distinction even to have asked the right
questions.

Rousseau has at all events suggested to me the terms
in which I have treated my present topic. He is easily
first among the theorists of radical democracy. He is also
the most eminent of those who have attacked civilization.
Moreover, he has brought his advocacy of democracy
and his attack on civilization into a definite relationship
with one another. Herein he seems to go deeper than those
who relate democracy, not to the question of civilization
versus barbarism, but to the question of progress versus
reaction. For why should men progress unless it can be
shown that they are progressing toward civilization; or
of what avail, again, is progress if barbarism is, as Rousseau affirms, more felicitous? If we thought clearly
enough, we should probably dismiss as somewhat old-
fashioned, as a mere survivor of the nineteenth century,
the man who puts his primary emphasis on the contrast

---

[1] See *Letters of Lord Acton to Mary Gladstone*, p. xii.

between the progressive and the reactionary, and turn our attention to the more essential contrast between the civilized man and the barbarian. The man of the nineteenth century was indeed wont to take for granted that the type of progress he sought to promote was a progress toward civilization. Some persons began to have doubts on this point even before the war, others had their doubts awakened by the war itself, and still others have been made doubtful by the peace. An age that thought it was progressing toward a "far-off divine event," and turned out instead to be progressing toward Armageddon, suffered, one cannot help surmising, from some fundamental confusion in its notions of progress. One may be aided in detecting the nature of this confusion by the Emersonian distinction of which I have made considerable use in my previous writing—the distinction, namely, between a "law for man" and a "law for thing." The special praise that Confucius bestowed on his favorite disciple was that he was "always progressing and never came to a standstill." What Confucius plainly had in mind was progress according to the human law. What the man of the nineteenth century meant as a rule by the term was no less plainly material progress. He seems to have assumed, so far as he gave the subject any thought at all, that moral progress would issue almost automatically from material progress. In view of the duality of human experience, the whole question is, however, vastly more complex than the ordinary progressive has ever suspected. Progress according to the natural law must, if it is to make for civilization, be subordinated to some adequate end; and the natural law does not in itself supply this end.

As a result of the neglect of this truth, we have the type of man who deems himself progressive and is yet pursuing power and speed for their own sake, the man who does not care where he is going, as someone has put it, provided only he can go there faster and faster.

If progress and civilization do not mean more than this, one might be justified in sharing Rousseau's predilection for barbarism. The reason he gives for preferring the barbaric to the civilized state is in itself extremely weighty: the barbaric state is, he maintains, the more fraternal. The fraternal spirit is the fine flower, not merely of genuine philosophy, but of genuine religion. One should be ready to make almost any sacrifice in order to attain it. My endeavor has, however, been to show that Rousseau's fraternity is only a sentimental dream. The psychic impossibility involved in this dream is obvious, one may even say, glaring. For example, Walt Whitman, one of the chief of Rousseau's American followers, preaches universal brotherhood among men each one of whom is, like himself, to "permit to speak at every hazard, Nature without check with original energy";[2] in other words, Whitman proposes to base brotherhood, a religious virtue, on expansive appetite.

I have tried here and elsewhere to show that democratic fraternity, as a Rousseau and a Whitman conceive it, and progress, as the utilitarian conceives it, are, however much they may clash at certain points, nevertheless only different aspects of the same naturalistic movement. This movement may be defined in its totality as humani-

---

[2] See *Song of Myself.*

tarianism. I ventured the assertion several years ago that something is omitted in this movement, and that the something may turn out to be the keystone of the arch.[3] The error that results from this central omission assumes many forms. I choose almost at random a very crude form—the form in which it is finally reaching the man in the street. A writer in a widely circulated magazine, *Photoplay*, devotes several editorial paragraphs to denouncing the people who say "don't"; they are, he complains, mere destroyers, the enemies of every generous creative impulse. Only in so far as one gets rid of the don'ts does one fulfill the saying of the Teacher, "I am come that ye shall have life, and that ye shall have it more abundantly." Mr. Henry Ford would no doubt dismiss such utterances as part of the great Jewish plot to destroy Gentile civilization. It was not, however, a Jew, but Madame de Stael who declared that everything expansive in human nature is divine. This notion of a divine expansiveness has a long history in the Occident anterior to Madame de Stael, a history that in some of its phases goes at least as far back as the Neoplatonists.

In any case the assertion that one attains to more abundant life (in the religious sense) by getting rid of the don'ts sums up clearly, even though in an extreme form, the side of the modern movement with which I am taking issue. This book in particular is devoted to the most unpopular of all tasks—a defense of the veto power. Not the least singular feature of the singular epoch in which we are living is that the very persons who are least will-

---

[3] See *The Masters of Modern French Criticism* (1912), p. 188.

ing to hear about the veto power are likewise the persons who are most certain that they stand for the virtues that depend upon its exercise—for example, peace and brotherhood. As against the expansionists of every kind, I do not hesitate to affirm that what is specifically human in man and ultimately divine is a certain quality of will, a will that is felt in its relation to his ordinary self as a will to refrain. The affirmation of this quality of will is nothing new: it is implied in the Pauline opposition between a law of the spirit and a law of the members. In general, the primacy accorded to will over intellect is Oriental. The idea of humility, the idea that man needs to defer to a higher will, came into Europe with an Oriental religion, Christianity. This idea has been losing ground in almost exact ratio to the decline of Christianity. Inasmuch as the recognition of the supremacy of will seems to me imperative in any wise view of life, I side in important respects with the Christian against those who have in the Occident, whether in ancient or modern times, inclined to give the first place either to the intellect or to the emotions. I differ from the Christian, however, in that my interest in the higher will and the power of veto it exercises over man's expansive desires is humanistic rather than religious. I am concerned, in other words, less with the meditation in which true religion always culminates, than in the meditation or observance of the law of measure that should govern man in his secular relations. Moreover, I am for coming at my humanism in a positive and critical rather than in a merely traditional manner. To this extent I am with the naturalists, who have from the start been rejecting outer authority in favor of the immediate and experimental. One should have only respect for the man of science in so far as he deals in this critical fashion with the natural law—and no small part of human nature itself comes under the natural law. The error begins when an attempt is made to extend this law to cover the whole of human nature. This is to deny not merely outer authority, but something that is a matter of immediate experience, the opposition, namely, of which the individual is conscious in himself, between a law of the spirit and a law of the members. Deny or dissimulate this opposition and the inner life tends in the same measure to disappear. Carlyle's contrast between the Rousseauism of the French Revolution and true Christianity is also the contrast between humanitarianism in general, in either its sentimental or its utilitarian form, and any doctrine that affirms the higher will. "Alas, no M. Roux!" Carlyle exclaims. "A gospel of brotherhood not according to any of the four old Evangelists and calling on men to repent, and amend *each his own* wicked existence, that they might be saved; but a gospel rather, as we often hint, according to a new fifth Evangelist Jean-Jacques, calling on men to amend *each the whole world's* wicked existence and be saved by making the Constitution. A thing different and distant *toto coelo*."

My own objection to this substitution of social reform for self-reform is that it involves the turning away from the more immediate to the less immediate. In general I have sought in my attack on the utilitarian-sentimental movement to avoid metaphysical and theological assumptions, and to rely on psychological analysis supported by an immense and growing body of evidence. My human-

ism is in this sense not only positive and critical, but,
what will be found to come to the same thing, individualistic. Under existing conditions, the significant struggle
seems to me to be not that between the unsound individualist and the traditionalist, nor again, as is currently assumed, that between the unsound individualist and the
altruist, but that between the sound and the unsound
individualist. To be a sound individualist, one needs, as
I take it, to retain one's hold on the truths of the inner
life, even though breaking more or less completely with
the past.

It may help to a fuller understanding of my present
attempt to deal in a fashion at once critical and humanistic with the problem of the will in its bearing on the
political problem if I say a few words at this point about
certain previous stages in my argument. In the opening
chapters of *Literature and the American College* I seek
to discriminate between the humanist and the humanitarians of either the utilitarian or the sentimental brand.
These two sides of the movement I sometimes term the
Baconian and the Rousseauistic after the names of the
men who seem to me to have prefigured them most completely in their writings and personalities. The humanitarian is not, I pointed out, primarily concerned, like the
humanist, with the individual and his inner life, but with
the welfare and progress of mankind in the lump. His
favorite word is "service." The current tendency to regard
humanism simply as an abbreviated and more convenient
form for humanitarianism can only be the source of the
most vicious confusions.

In *The Masters of Modern French Criticism* I attempt

to carry a stage farther my defense of a critical humanism. Though the basis of the inner life is the opposition
between a lower and a higher will, the higher will cannot, after all, act at random. It must have standards.
Formerly the standards were supplied by tradition. The
man who accepted Christian tradition, for example, was
in no doubt as to the kind and degree of discipline he
needed to impose on his lower nature. He thus achieved
some measure of moral unity with himself and also with
other men who accepted the same discipline. If the individualist, on the other hand, is to have standards, he
must rely on the critical spirit in direct ratio to the completeness of his break with the traditional unifications of
life. He is confronted at the outset with the most difficult
of philosophical problems—that of the one and the many.
For it is obvious that standards cannot exist unless there
is an element of oneness somewhere with which to measure the infinite otherwiseness of things. The special
theme of *The Masters* is the problem of the one and the
many and the failure of Sainte-Beuve and other eminent
French individualists to deal with it adequately and so to
achieve standards in a modern fashion. The results of the
critical endeavor of the past century may be summed up
most completely, perhaps, in the word relativity. The
failure of criticism to attain to any center of judgment set
above the shifting impressions of the individual and the
flux of phenomenal nature is a defeat for civilization itself, if it be true, as I have tried to show, that civilization
must ultimately depend on the maintenance of standards.
In *The New Laokoon* I have sought to exhibit the anarchy
that has supervened in literature and the arts with the

progressive decline of standards. Superficially, this anarchy seems above all an anarchy of the emotions. On closer scrutiny, however, emotional anarchy itself turns out to be only a sign of something subtler and more dangerous—anarchy of the imagination. In *Rousseau and Romanticism*, a book that is closely connected in argument with *The New Laokoon*, the problem of the imagination receives special treatment. I come here to another distinctive feature of the type of humanism I am defending. I not only have more to say of will and less of reason than the humanist in the Greco-Roman tradition, but I also grant a most important role to imagination. If one does not, like Diderot, dismiss as "artificial" the conflict between a natural or expansive will and a specifically human will or will to refrain, if, on the contrary, one insists on this conflict as a primordial fact of consciousness, one will be led, I believe, to the further conclusion that the outcome of this "civil war in the cave" will be determined by the attitude of the imagination; that the imagination, in other words, holds the balance of power between the higher and the lower nature of man. In the light of history (one need not go any farther back than the Great War) man's pretense to be governed by reason in any ordinary sense of the word seems a bad jest. The critical observer is forced to agree with Napoleon that, not reason, but "imagination governs mankind." It does not follow that mankind need be governed, as it has been very largely during the past century, by the Napoleonic quality of imagination.

The complaint has been made that the word imagination has been used in so many senses that it has ceased to have any meaning. My own understanding of the term may perhaps be made clearer by a brief historical survey. The Latin word (*imaginatio*) from which our word is derived is itself a rendering of the Greek phantasy or fancy (φαντασία). Fancy means literally "what appears"; in other words, either the various impressions of sense, or else a faculty that stores up these impressions and is therefore closely related to memory. Greek philosophy gave a rather low rating to "fancy" or appearance in comparison with reality, which it inclined to identify with reason or mind. To the Stoic in particular it seemed both feasible and imperative that reason should hold sway over all the impressions that beat upon the gateway of the senses and make a severe selection among them. "How easy a thing it is," says Marcus Aurelius, "to put away and blot out every 'fancy' [i.e., impression] that is disturbing or alien, and to be at once in perfect peace." The disparagement of fancy in this sense is already found in Plato. He hopes to attain a truth that is "firm and not pulled around this way and that by our 'fancy'."[4] A chief source of Christian humility, on the other hand, was the conviction that man is unable by his own resources to achieve any such truth, the conviction, above all, that mere reason cannot prevail over the deceits of the senses. Pascal, for example, gives to the word imagination about the same

---

[4] *Cratylus*, 386 E. It goes without saying that no philosopher affords better examples of the higher uses of the imagination (in the extended sense that we have come to give to the word) than Plato. As for the Platonic theory of the imagination in this extended sense, it is not altogether easy to grasp, even after every allowance has been made for changes in terminology.

meaning that the Stoic gave either to it or its Greek equivalent, and like the Stoic he disparages imagination; only to this disparagement he adds the disparagement of reason. What he opposes to an imagination that is only a "mistress of error" and to a reason that is impotent to resist this error is the "heart," by which he means the illumination of the higher will in the form of grace. This inner revelation has itself the support of outer revelation. Here, he holds, one may find at last a firm footing of truth and reality. He does not admit that imagination has any part either in outer revelation or in the life of the "heart." He has this much at least in common with Plato that he believes it possible to draw a firm and fast line between imagination (or mere appearance) and reality. Strict psychology, however, scarcely warrants any such sharp discrimination between the true and the illusory. It forces one rather to conclude with Joubert that "illusion is an integral part of reality." This conclusion, however damaging it may be to mere dogma, does not force one to forgo standards. But in that case one needs to attend to another possible meaning of the word imagination, the second main meaning, one is tempted to say, that the word has actually had in Occidental thought. The word in this other meaning stands less for what one perceives, either inwardly or outwardly, than for what one conceives. Conceit, it should be remembered, was in older English usage not only a complimentary term, but one of the synonyms of imagination. The process by which the term has come to have its present unfavorable meaning of vain imagining has its adequate historical explanation into which I need not here enter. Now to "conceive" is, in an almost etymological sense, to gather things together, to see likenesses and analogies and in so far to unify what were else mere heterogeneity. The imagination, says Coleridge somewhat pedantically, is the "esemplastic" power—the power, that is, that fashions things into one. The passages in which Coleridge expounds this view of the imagination afford, perhaps, the lost example in English of what I have called the second main meaning of the word. For an instance of the other main meaning we may turn to Addison's papers on the imagination in the *Spectator*. Addison not only tends to reduce imagination to outer perception, but, encouraged by the Latin rendering of the Greek "fancy," to narrow outer perception itself to visual perception.

If we mean by imagination not merely what we perceive, but what we conceive, it follows inevitably that the problem of the imagination is closely bound up with that of the One and the Many and therefore with the problem of standards; for it is impossible, let me repeat, to achieve standards, at least along critical lines, unless one can discover in life somewhere an abiding unity with which to measure its mere variety and change. Because "illusion is an integral part of reality," we are not justified in assuming that every unity that the imagination may conceive must therefore be dismissed as illusory. A somewhat paradoxical person might indeed affirm that, even though one did not raise directly the question of reality at all, it would still be possible to have standards; that one might measure men accurately enough for most practical purposes simply by the quality of their illusions—and their disillusions. However, in spite of the fact that abso-

lute unity and reality must ever elude us and that the
absolute in general must be dismissed as a metaphysical
dream, we may still determine on experimental grounds
to what degree any particular view of life is sanctioned
or repudiated by the nature of things and rate it accordingly as more or less real. God, according to Synesius,
communicates with man through the imagination. Unfortunately the devil communicates with him in the same
way and the test of these communications is not, strictly
speaking, in the imagination itself. To determine the
quality of our imaginings, we need to supplement the
power in man that perceives and the power that conceives
with a third power—that which discriminates. All divisions of man into powers or faculties are, I am aware,
more or less arbitrary, but, though arbitrary, they are
inevitable, if only as instruments of thought; and the
threefold division I am here employing will, I believe,
be found practically one of the most helpful.

In emphasizing the importance of the power in man
that discriminates, I mean this power, working not abstractly, but on the actual material of experience. I may
perhaps best sum up my whole point of view by saying
that the only thing that finally counts in this world is a
concentration, at once imaginative and discriminating,
on the facts. Now the facts that one may perceive and
on which one may concentrate are not only infinite in
number, but of entirely different orders. This is one
reason why material progress, so far from assuring moral
progress, is, on the contrary, extremely difficult to combine with it. This progress has been won by an almost
tyrannical concentration on the facts of the natural law.

Man's capacity for concentration is limited, so that the price he has paid for material progress has been an increasing inattention to facts of an entirely different order—those, namely, of the human law. The resulting spiritual blindness has been an invitation to Nemesis. One may have some inkling of the nature of this Nemesis from the Great War and other similar symptoms that have been multiplying of late in our Western societies.

It goes without saying that the partisans of "progress" have not admitted their spiritual blindness. They have accepted as valid substitutes for the traditional standards and the moral unity that these standards tended to promote certain new unifications of life that display great imagination, indeed, but an imagination that has not been sufficiently tested from the point of view of reality. These new schemes for unifying men flourished especially in connection with the so-called romantic movement. It is therefore no small matter that the leaders of this movement can be shown to have erected deliberately a cult of the creative imagination on the ruins of discrimination. Any one who takes seriously the creations of this type of imagination, an imagination that is not disciplined to either the natural or the human law, but is, in Young's phrase, free to wander wild in its own realm of chimeras, falls into mere conceit or vain imagining. Conceit has always been the specifically human malady, but never, perhaps, more so than today. The outstanding trait of the men of our period may seem in retrospect to have been the facility with which they put forth untried conceits as "ideals." We have all grown familiar with the type of person who is in his own conceit a lofty "idealist," but when put to the test has turned out to be only a disastrous dreamer.

Though man is governed by imagination, fortunately it does not follow that he must be governed by conceit. There remains the distinction between the mere visionary and the man of vision. This distinction acquires its full importance only when related to the question of leadership. A main purpose of my present argument is to show that genuine leaders, good or bad, there will always be, and that democracy becomes a menace to civilization when it seeks to evade this truth. The notion in particular that a substitute for leadership may be found in numerical majorities that are supposed to reflect the "general will" is only a pernicious conceit. In the long run democracy will be judged, no less than other forms of government, by the quality of its leaders, a quality that will depend in turn on the quality of their vision. Where there is no vision, we are told, the people perish; but where there is sham vision, they perish even faster. The worst difficulties of the present time arise, I am sometimes tempted to think, even less from lack of vision than from sham vision. Otherwise stated, what is disquieting about the time is not so much its open and avowed materialism as what it takes to be its spirituality.

Among the visionaries who have usurped the credit that belongs only to the man of vision, Rousseau seems to me to have been, at least in these recent ages of the world, the most conspicuous. The Nature to which he invites us to return is only a conceit. This conceit encourages one to substitute for the vital control, which is the true voice of man's higher self, expansive emotion. Ideally this substitution is to be marked by a triumph of the fraternal spirit. Actually, as I have sought to prove, the outcome of yielding to a mere expansive conceit of the emotions is not fraternity, but a decadent imperialism. I have made a considerable use of the word imperialism in this work and in a somewhat broader sense than is familiar to English and American readers. My justification lies in the fact that one finds behind every other form of imperialism the imperialism or push for power of the individual. In this respect, at least, I am in accord with Bergson, who declares that "imperialism is, as it were, inherent in the vital urge. It is at the bottom of the soul of individuals as well as of the soul of peoples."[5] By his cult of *élan vital* Bergson is in the direct line of descent from Rousseau. One must note, however, an important divergence between master and disciple that is all to the advantage of the latter. Bergson does not hope to base on *élan vital* a fraternity that must be sought rather in the exercise of *frein vital*. On the contrary, *élan vital* is, he avows frankly, imperialistic. According to the new Bergsonian beatitude, not the meek in spirit, but those who have the most vigorous vital urge are to inherit the earth. It is hard to overlook the affinity between this world-famed philosophy, as interpreted by its author, and the vulgar admiration for "punch."

My application of the epithet decadent to the type of imperialism that has been promoted by the glorification of instinct from Rousseau to Bergson calls for a word of

---

[5] See Bergson's introductory note to *Balzac et la morale romantique*, par E. Seillière.

comment. That there are various types of imperialism, even if we use the word, not in the psychological, but in the more familiar political sense, appears evident. For example, the imperialism that made the Romans masters of the world is not of the same kind as that which prevailed when they cringed beneath a Tiberius or a Nero. Yet it is possible to trace the process by which the older imperialism finally took on a decadent cast. The critical moment for Rome was the moment of triumph when the leaders of the state no longer felt the restraining influence of dangerous rivals like Carthage. At the same time they were beginning to grow individualistic in the sense that they were beginning to throw off the traditional controls. As a result of all this emancipation, "men's desires," in Montesquieu's phrase, "became immense." It has been usual to regard as the most significant symptom of this inordinateness the growth of luxury. "Luxury," says Juvenal, "more cruel than the foeman's arms, fell upon us, and is avenging the conquered world." A still graver symptom, however, was the appearance of leaders who were ever more and more ruthless in the pursuit either of their personal advantage or that of some class or faction. The new spirit that was undermining the Roman constitution manifested itself even less, as Cicero notes, in acts of injustice and cruelty to the vanquished peoples than in the rage of civil strife. It can scarcely be maintained of the Romans who thus precipitated the decadence that they exercised to any serious degree their *frein vital*, or will to refrain. The right opponents of these anarchical individualists, one may venture to affirm, were not the mere traditionalists, but the individualists who had qualified for true leadership by setting bounds to their expansive lusts, especially the lust of domination. Rome declined because she failed to produce individualists of this type in sufficient numbers. Certain analogies may be discovered between this Roman dilemma and the dilemma with which we are now confronted in America. We, too, seem to be reaching the acme of our power and are at the same time discarding the standards of the past. This emancipation has been accompanied by an extraordinary increase in luxury and self-indulgence. Persons who postpone everything else to their "comfort" and to commercial prosperity are probably more numerous in America today than they were in ancient Rome. Disturbing as this symptom may be, it is less so than the increasing role played in our national life by "blocs" with highly unethical leaders—leaders who seek to advance the material interests of some special group at the expense of the whole community. The actual gravity of this symptom may perhaps be exaggerated; if it should prove, however, to be something more than a passing phase, it portends the end of our constitutional liberties and the rise of a decadent imperialism. The more one ponders either the modern American or the ancient Roman situation, the more surely will one be led from imperialism in the political, to imperialism in the psychological sense. In other words, one will be forced, if one wishes to get at the root of the matter, to turn from the merely peripheral manifestations of the push for power to the inner life of the individual.

My views as to the relation between the Rousseauistic movement and imperialism may perhaps be still further elucidated by a comparison with the views on the same subject of two recent European writers, the German Oswald Spengler, and the Frenchman Ernest Seillière. Spengler has developed in his chief work, *The Downfall of the Occident*, the thesis that the Western world, especially Western European "culture," is now engaged in a sort of rake's progress that starts with Rousseau and his return to nature. The goal of this decadence, as Spengler describes it, is not unlike what I have termed a decadent imperialism. Moreover, we are not only on a descending curve, but it is a fatal curve. He has actually appended to the first volume of his book a table exhibiting the degree of degeneracy that the Occident will have attained about the year 2000. The whole conception not only implies a philosophy of history, but a philosophy of history that has, in my judgment, gone mad. This conception is based in any case on an utter denial of the quality of will in man on which I myself put supreme emphasis. In spite therefore of certain superficial resemblances in our respective views, Spengler and I are at the opposite poles of human thought. My own attitude is one of extreme unfriendliness to every possible philosophy of history (in the more technical sense of the term), whether it be the older type found in a Saint Augustine or a Bossuet, which tends to make a man the puppet of God, or the newer type, which tends in all its varieties to make of man the puppet of nature. *The Downfall of the Occident* seems to me a fairly complete repertory of the naturalistic fallacies of the nineteenth century; it is steeped throughout in the special brand of fatalism in which these fallacies culminate, and as a result of which the Occident is actually threatened with "downfall." One is justified in my opinion in dismissing Spengler as a charlatan, even though one be forced to add that he is a charlatan of genius. The immense sale of his books in Germany, if it is indicative of a real influence, is a depressing symptom.

The second writer I have mentioned, M. Seillière, merits a very different judgment. In about a score of volumes he has been tracing with great psychological finesse the influence of Rousseau on the literature and life of the past century. This influence he associates with what he calls an irrational imperialism. In short, the results of his survey are on the negative side very similar to my own. On the positive or constructive side, on the other hand, M. Seillière and I diverge sharply. What he opposes to an irrational imperialism is a rational imperialism; by which he means "the social army on the march towards the conquest of power by the coordination of individual efforts."[6] In his general position, as revealed in such utterances, he seems to me to strike back through the utilitarians to Hobbes and ultimately, in some respects, to Machiavelli. The essential contrast for me is not, as for M. Seillière, that between a rational and an irrational imperialism, but between imperialism and that quality of will in man which is, in every possible sense of the word, anti-imperialistic. M. Seillière, again, seems as much bent on running together Stoical and Christian ethics as I am on separating them and insisting on their final incompatibility. Stoicism in both its ancient and its

[6] *Balzac et la morale romantique*, p. 42.

modern forms I regard, at least in its total trend, as false
and impossible; whereas I hold that at the heart of genuine Christianity are certain truths which have already
once saved Western civilization and, judiciously employed, may save it again.

I wish also to say a few words at the outset regarding
certain possible misapprehensions of my method. The
most serious of these misapprehensions may arise if one
looks either in this volume or in the previous volumes of
the series (with the partial exception of *The Masters of
Modern French Criticism*) for rounded estimates of individuals. I have not attempted such estimates. Still less
have I attempted rounded estimates of historical epochs—
for example, of the nineteenth century. It is even less
sensible, perhaps, to indict a whole century than it is,
according to Burke, to indict a whole people. I am attacking, not the nineteenth century in general, but the naturalistic nineteenth century and its prolongation into the
twentieth century, along with the tendencies in the previous centuries, from the Renaissance down, that prepared
the way for naturalism. My treatment of this whole
naturalistic trend has seemed, even to critics who are not
altogether unfriendly, to be negative, extreme, and one-
sided. I hope I may be pardoned if I reply briefly to each
of these three charges.

As to the charge that my treatment of naturalism is
one-sided, there is a sense, it must be admitted, in which
it is not only one-sided, but one-sided to the last degree.
There is, however, a humanistic intention even in the
one-sidedness. I dwell persistently on the aspect of human
nature that the naturalists have no less persistently ne-

glected in the hope that the way may thus be opened for a more balanced view. Moreover, what the naturalists have neglected is not something that is on the fringe or outer rim of human experience, but something, on the contrary, that is very central. The naturalistic effort during the past century or more has resulted in an immense and bewildering peripheral enrichment of life—in short, in what we are still glorifying under the name of progress. I have no quarrel with this type of progress in itself, I merely maintain that no amount of peripheral enrichment of life can atone for any lack at the center. Furthermore, though I assail the naturalists for what seems to me a vital oversight, I have, let me repeat, at least one trait in common with them—I desire to be experimental. I seek to follow out the actual consequences of this oversight, to deal with it, not abstractly, but in its fruits. If certain readers have persisted in seeing in my books something that I myself have not sought to put there, namely, rounded estimates of individuals and historic epochs, the misapprehension has no doubt arisen from the very abundance of my concrete illustrations.

As to the charge that I am negative, I have already said that the element in man that has been overlooked by naturalistic psychology is felt in relation to his ordinary self negatively. If instead of taking the point of view of one's ordinary self, one heeds the admonitions of the inner monitor, the result is two of the most positive of all things: character and happiness. This is the great paradox of life itself. For being negative in this sense I am not in the least apologetic. There is, however, another sense in which I may seem negative and about this

I feel somewhat differently. The type of criticism that prevailed about the beginning of the nineteenth century proposed to substitute the "fruitful criticism of beauties for the barren criticism of faults." I may be accused of reversing too sharply this maxim even by some who admit that the proper remedy for the lax appreciativeness of the modern movement is a criticism that displays a tonic astringency. I am constantly calling attention to the defects of certain eminent personalities, it may be urged, and at the same time have little or nothing to say of their virtues. My method is even in this respect, I believe, legitimate, provided that it be properly understood, though I myself cannot help regretting that it should make me appear so constantly unamiable.

The charge that I am extreme touches me even more nearly than the charge that I am negative and one-sided; for I aim to be a humanist and the essence of humanism is moderation. There is, however, much confusion on the subject of moderation. A man's moderation is measured by his success in mediating between some sound general principle and the infinitely various and shifting circumstances of actual life. The man who is thus rightly mediatory attains to one of the most precious of virtues—urbanity; though one must add that probably no virtue has been more frequently counterfeited. When an intellectually and spiritually indolent person has to choose between two conflicting views he often decides to "split the difference" between them; but he may be splitting the difference between truth and error, or between two errors. In any case, he must dispose of the question of truth or error before he can properly begin to mediate at all. Otherwise he will run the risk of resembling the English statesman of whom it was said that he never deviated from the straight and narrow path between right and wrong. Some of the casuists whom Pascal attacked had managed to assume a moderate attitude toward murder! One may fancy oneself urbane when in reality one is in danger of being numbered with the immense multitude that Dante saw in the vestibule of Hell—the multitude of those who are equally "displeasing to God and to the enemies of God." To be sure, it is not always easy in any particular instance to distinguish between the humanist and the mere Laodicean. Thus Luther denounced Erasmus as a Laodicean, whereas to us he seems rather to have shown real poise and urbanity in his dealings with the religious and other extremists of his time.

At all events the differences of doctrine I debate in the following pages are of a primary nature and so not subject to mediation. Between the man who puts his main emphasis on the inner life of the individual and the man who puts this emphasis on something else— for example, the progress and service of humanity— the opposition is one of first principles. The question I raise, therefore, is not whether one should be a moderate humanitarian, but whether one should be a humanitarian at all. In general I commit myself to the position that we are living in a world that in certain important respects has gone wrong on first principles; which will be found to be only another way of saying that we are living in a world that has been betrayed by its leaders. On the appearance of leaders who have recovered in some form the truths of the inner life and repudiated the errors of naturalism may depend the very survival of Western civilization. The truths of the inner life may be proclaimed in various forms, religious and humanistic, and have actually been so proclaimed in the past and justified in each case by their fruits in life and conduct. It is because I am unable to discover these truths in any form in the philosophies now fashionable that I have been led to prefer to the wisdom of the age the wisdom of the ages.

CHAPTER 1

The Types of Political Thinking

According to Aristotle, a government, if is to endure, must reflect the *ethos* or body of moral habits and beliefs of the governed. There is no abstract and ideal political form, as the French Jacobins inclined to believe, that may be imposed to advantage on all communities. If we attempt to apply the Aristotelian principle of the necessary relation between the government of any particular community and its ethos to the governments that have actually existed in the past, our first impression is of an endless diversity in political forms as in everything else. But if we penetrate beneath this bewildering surface variety, we shall discover, as I have tried to show elsewhere, that human experience falls, after all, into a few fairly distinct categories. The view of life that prevails at any particular time or among any particular people will be found, on close inspection, to be either predominantly naturalistic, or humanistic, or religious; and it will also be found that political forms tend to vary accordingly.

If, for example, a people is deeply religious, a government with a more or less strongly marked theocratic element is probable. Fustel de Coulanges has shown how closely allied the government of the ancient city-state was at the outset with traditional religious forms, and then how government tended to change when the hierarchy that traditional religion had established, first of all in the family and then in the state, was gradually undermined by individualistic and egalitarian tendencies. The yielding of religious control to an anarchical naturalism led in the political order to the triumph of naked force and to the decline of ancient civilization. As Christianity prevailed over this effete paganism, a new religious ethos gradually took shape and, corresponding to it, arose a theocratic conception of government that was to prevail throughout the medieval period. During that period Europe enjoyed, in theory and to no small extent in practice, a genuine religious communion. The church had succeeded in creating symbols that in a very literal sense held sway over men's imagination and united them from the top to the bottom of society in the same spiritual hopes and fears. Every one might, as Villon relates of his aged mother, enter the great cathedral and see depicted on one hand the torments of the damned and on the other the bliss of paradise, and, like her, he would normally be filled by the former images with fear and by the latter with joy and gladness. As a result of this imaginative control exercised over all classes, the church did not need the support of physical force: purely spiritual penalties, especially excommunication, sufficed. Henry IV at Canossa is usually taken to typify the extreme triumph of the theocratic idea.

The church is no negligible factor even today. When Cardinal Mercier visited America, it was reported in the press that engineers and firemen knelt on the platform of the Pennsylvania Railway Station in New York to receive his blessing. Here is at least some survival of the older loyalty, a loyalty utterly different in essence from that of these same men to their unions. Still, if one compares the power of the church today with its power in the Middle Ages, one becomes aware of a change in the ethos, not of this or that country merely, but of the whole of the Occident. The older religious control has been giving way for several centuries past to individualistic and centrifugal tendencies, and the danger is now manifest that in the absence of any new integrating element, what may triumph in our modern world, as it finally triumphed in the ancient world, is the principle of naked force.

The theocratic conception of government always implies a divine grace or sanction somewhere; but as to the channel through which this grace is received important differences of opinion are possible. In the Middle Ages, for example, some held that the only channel of grace was the church and so tended to subordinate the emperor, the head of the temporal order, to God's vicar upon earth, the pope. Others maintained that the emperor derived his sanction, not through the pope, but immediately from on high. This latter form of the theo-

cratic conception is best set forth, perhaps, in Dante's
De Monarchia. Dante desires cooperation and ultimate
unity of the two powers, secular and spiritual, but without confusion.

Dante and other political theorists of the Middle Ages
who acepted the theocratic idea, but wished at the same
time to keep separate the things of God and the things
of Caesar, showed themselves in so far true Christians.
We need to remember, however, how much in the Christian tradition itself goes back ultimately, not to Judea,
but to Greece and Rome. There is no small element of
truth in the common assertion that Saint Augustine
is the Christan Plato and Saint Thomas Aquinas the
Christian Aristotle. Yet we need to emphasize at this
point certain important differences between the Platonic
and Aristotelian type of political thinking and the type
that prevailed during the medieval period. In a certain
sense, Aristotle and Plato are in their true spirit nearer
to us than to the men of the Middle Ages. The medieval
view of life rests on a belief in a supernatural revelation.
This in turn is made the basis of an absolute outer authority; whereas Plato and Aristotle belong, as I have said,
to an age of free critical inquiry. They are, in short, true
"moderns." For, as I have tried to show elsewhere, to be
critical and individualistic in one's outlook on life and
to be modern come to very much the same thing. In
seeking to make of Aristotle a prop of outer authority,
Saint Thomas and other men of the Middle Ages were
therefore using Aristotle in a very un-Aristotelian way;
and the confusion continued when the men of the Renaissance, on breaking with tradition in favor of a more

individualistic and experimental attitude, inclined to re-
pudiate Aristotle as the chief source of the scholastic
logomachy. Bacon, for example, practically never gets
behind the scholastic Aristotle to the real Aristotle.

Plato, then, differs from the medieval thinkers in
dealing critically with the political problem in the *Republic* and elsewhere. He arrives, however, at a conception that is on the whole theocratic; so that if one
looks, not to the method, but to the conclusions, one is
forced to agree in part with those who assert that the
Middle Ages already begin in Plato. Add the all-important
distinction between the things of God and the things
of Caesar and the class of Guardians in the *Republic*
would work out into something very similar to a monas-
tic order. It is hard, again, not to see in the Nocturnal
Council and the House of Reformation of the "Laws"
a first adumbration of the Inquisition. In general Plato's
growing sense of the dependence of man on God fore-
shadows Augustine and the reign of grace. Aristotle, on
the other hand, remains the chief example in the past
of a thinker who has treated in a way at once critical and
humanistic the problems of government. Before writing
his *Politics*, he had made detailed studies of the history
and constitutions of one hundred and fifty-eight city-
states, and in general rests his conclusions upon a great
body of actual political experience. One may disagree
with these conclusions—I disagree with them in essential
particulars—but the method itself for any one who
aspires to be modern would seem to be impeccable. Even
when we differ from Aristotle, we should differ from him
on Aristotelian grounds. We have been enlightened con-

cerning certain problems by an enormous mass of experience in both the East and the West that he did not have at his command. We have been enlightened by the Christian experience above all and the great new principle it brought into the Occident, namely, the separation of the temporal and spiritual powers, and all the consequences that flow from this principle either directly or indirectly, especially the idea of individual liberty that ultimately rests on this distinction, and of which neither Aristotle nor Plato has any adequate conception.

We have been enlightened since the time of Aristotle not merely by the Christian experience; we also have more or less available an enormous mass of experience unknown until recently to the Occident—that of the Far East, especially India and China. Here again we find political institutions that reflect views of life that are predominantly either naturalistic, humanistic, or religious. Perhaps no country has ever been more religious than India. India has always been the home of religion, good, bad, or indifferent; and so one is not surprised to find the theocratic view of life set forth more uncompromisingly perhaps than in any other book of the world in the *Laws of Manu*. The precepts of this work have probably never been applied in their full rigor, but they have always been of great aid to the Brahmin caste in maintaining what would seem to us a veritable spiritual tyranny. In controlling men by an appeal to their religious hopes and fears without any need of physical compulsion, the Brahmin caste has perhaps been even more successful, and that down to our own day, than the church of medieval Europe. It has been alleged that the Montagu Act

(1919), designed to give a greater measure of self-govern-
ment to the Hindus, would in practice simply play into
the hands of the Brahmin theocracy.

Buddhism, another product of ancient India, is interesting from the point of view of our present topic for two
reasons: first, because Buddha, even more perhaps than
Plato or Socrates, worked out a positive and critical view
of life; second, because he displayed this positive and
critical spirit in the field of religion. His kingdom, like
that of Jesus, and unlike that of Plato, is not of this
world. He does not seek, like the Plato of the *Republic*,
to achieve ideal good in the secular order and with the
aid of political institutions. Buddha did not set out to
reform society directly, but established a religious order
in which caste and other like distinctions did not exist.
Later Buddhism, especially Buddhism of the so-called
Great Vehicle, is a vast and complex movement that
departs widely from the positive and critical spirit of
the founder. Lamaism, the very corrupt form of the
doctrine that prevails in Tibet, marks an extreme of
theocratic interference with the secular order. In a country like Burma, where something of the older and more
individualistic form of the faith still survives, the distinction between spiritual and temporal is fairly well maintained. In general the rival pretensions of church and
state have led to less frequent and less serious political
clashes in Buddhist than in Christian lands. It is, indeed,
this aspect of Christianity that more than any other seems
to justify Christ's saying that he brought not peace, but
a sword.

India has never seen an important humanistic move-

ment. The nearest approach to it, perhaps, is the doctrine
of the middle path that Buddha proclaimed in the religious life itself. It is difficult to imagine a more complete
contrast in this respect than that between India and
China, which in its central tradition, of which Confucius
is the chief exponent, has always been humanistic. The
bathing ghats at Benares suggest something almost as
remote from ordinary Chinese psychology as from our
own. Confucius is less concerned with the other world
than with the art of living to the best advantage in this.
To live to the best advantage in this world is, he holds,
to live proportionately and moderately; so that the Confucian tradition of the Far East has much in common
with the Aristotelian tradition of the Occident. In one
important respect, however, Confucius recalls not Aristotle, but Christ. Though his kingdom is very much of
this world, he puts emphasis not merely on the law of
measure, but also on the law of humility. He was humble both in his "submission to the will of Heaven" and
in his attitude toward the sages of old. He aspired at
most to be the channel through which the moral experience of his race that had accumulated through long centuries and found living embodiment in these sages should
be conveyed to the present and the future; in his own
words, he was not a creator but a transmitter. A man
who looks up to the great traditional models and imitates
them, becomes worthy of imitation in his turn. He must
be thus rightly imitative if he is to be a true leader. No
one has ever insisted more than Confucius on a right
example and the imitation that it inspires as the necessary
basis of civilized society. This insistence would seem

justified by the force of his own example which has molded, for seventy generations or more, the ethos of about a fourth of the human race—and that with little or no appeal to the principle of fear either in this world or in the next. The Confucian influence seems, indeed, to offer more warrant than anything in our Occidental experience for the belief that man may after all be a reasonable animal.

In dealing with the political problem, Confucius is inevitably led to brush aside, as of slight account, everything except the question of leadership. "The virtue of the leader," he says, "is like unto wind; that of the people like unto grass. For it is the nature of grass to bend when the wind blows upon it."[1] Now the true leader is the man of character, and the ultimate root of character is humility. This Confucian conception has such a central soundness that I shall need to return to it later. At the same time, Confucianism, like all great doctrines, has its characteristic weaknesses. The chief of these, we scarcely need to be reminded, is that the present seems to be held in a perpetual spiritual mortmain by the past. A purely traditional humanism is always in danger of falling into a rut of pseudoclassic formalism. Confucius himself had a deep and genuine perception of what is specifically human in man which he defines as a principle of inner control; this principle, however, at least if we accept as ancient and authentic all that is in the *Li-Ki*, or Book of Rites, is from the start too much associated with outer forms and,

---

[1] Cf. Aristotle, *Politics*, 1273a: "Whenever the chiefs of the state deem anything honorable, the other citizens are sure to follow their example."

at times, with the rules of etiquette. Some of the prescriptions are not much more closely related to the decorum
which is at the center of every truly humanistic doctrine
than the information, which has also been piously handed
down to us, that Confucius ate ginger at every meal, and
that he always changed countenance in a thunderstorm.
We desire a spirit that is more free, flexible, and imaginative, such as is found in Greek humanism at its best.
We are also likely to feel something more modern and,
therefore, more congenial to us in the highly untradi-
tional and individualistic Buddha. Still Confucius, though
traditional, is not dogmatic; he is not even systematic.
His extreme reticence about ultimate things that so irri-
tated his translator, the Christian dogmatist Dr. Legge,
seems, now that we are coming more and more to appre-
ciate the psychological method of dealing with certain
problems, a merit rather than a defect. As a result of all
that is summed up in Confucianism, China has, perhaps,
in spite of all its corrupt mandarins and officials of the
past and present, planted itself more consistently than
any other country on moral ideas, and this fact is not
unrelated to its long survival. The Greeks have disappeared; for the Greeks of today can be regarded only
in a very qualified sense as the descendants of the Greeks
of the age of Pericles: whereas the descendants of the
Chinese of the age of Confucius are still with us to the
number of several hundred millions. Their civilization
has numerous and grave peripheral faults. At the same
time, it is likely to have a secret strength as long as the
Chinese refuse to "drop their pilot," as long as they hold

fast, in other words, in spite of pressure from the West, to what is best in the Confucian tradition.

I have been considering thus far, in both East and West, various religious and humanistic views of life, whether on a traditional or a positive and critical basis, and the corresponding types of political thinking. It remains to consider the naturalistic view of life and its political implications. The naturalist no longer looks on man as subject to a law of his own distinct from that of the material order—a law, the acceptance of which leads, on the religious level, to the miracles of other-worldliness that one finds in Christians and Buddhists at their best, and the acceptance of which, in this world, leads to the subduing of the ordinary self and its spontaneous impulses to the law of measure that one finds in Confucianists and Aristotelians. The rise of the individualistic and critical spirit and the resulting break with the medieval and theocratic ideal, from the Renaissance on, might have assumed a religious or humanistic character; it has actually been in the main naturalistic. One important outcome of this naturalistic trend has been the growth of the national spirit. The Protestant religion itself, if one takes a sufficiently long-range view, appears largely as an incident in the rise of nationalism. If one wishes, however, to study, in its purest form, the new nationalistic spirit that was destined finally to destroy the religious unity of medieval Europe, one needs to turn to Machiavelli. He will probably remain the best type in either East or West of the unflinching political naturalist. To understand Machiavelli, one needs to study him in his relation to traditional religion. Christianity, especially in its Pauline and Augustinian forms, has always tended to oppose a stark supernaturalism to a stark naturalism; so that when an austere Christian, such as Pascal, considers man in his fallen estate, man unsupported by divine grace, he quickly arrives at conclusions regarding the secular order and its political problems that are, if possible, more Machiavellian than those of Machiavelli himself. One seems to have no alternative except to get rid of ethics in getting rid of theology. Moreover, the church, as an actual institution, had such a monopoly of the higher life of man that to seek, like Machiavelli, to give the state a basis independent of the church was to run the risk of giving it a basis independent of morality. Furthermore, Machiavelli was, within certain limits, an extraordinarily shrewd observer. His views reflect the failure of Christianity to control men's actual deeds, either in his own time or in the medieval past with which he was familiar. His intention, as he proclaims it, is "to follow up the real truth of a matter rather than the imagination of it, . . . because how one lives is so far distant from how one ought to live, that he who neglects what is done for what ought to be done sooner effects his ruin than this preservation."[2] The statesman should, therefore, be sternly realistic. As a matter of fact, any one who neglects men's ideals and fine phrases and attends solely to their actual performance is always likely to seem a bit Machiavellian. There is, for example, a strong Machiavellian element in this sense in Thucydides.

---

[2] *The Prince*, chap. 15.

The conclusions to which Machiavelli was led by his special type of realism are familiar. The rules of ordinary morality may hold in the relations between man and man, but have only a secondary place in the relations between state and state; what prevails in these latter relations is the law of cunning and the law of force. The ruler who wishes to succeed should, therefore, blend harmoniously in himself the virtues of the lion and the fox.[3] The true essence of any doctrine is revealed finally in the kind of personality in which it becomes incarnate. Machiavelli, as is well known, saw the perfect incarnation of his own conception in Cesare Borgia. He relates, in one place, the detestable treachery by which Borgia trapped and then had strangled several of his political enemies, and then says elsewhere: "When all the actions of the duke are recalled, I do not know how to blame him, but rather it appears to me, as I have said, that I ought to offer him for imitation to all those who, by fortune or the arms of others, are raised to government."[4] One should mark especially the meaning that Machiavelli attaches to the word virtue. He begins an account of the medieval tyrant Castruccio Castricani, in which the main traits that emerge are ruthlessness and cruelty, by praise of his "virtue." The virtue of the Machiavellian political leader plainly has very little in common with humanistic virtue and nothing at all with religious virtue. Christian virtue in particular has its foundation in the law of humility. The man who takes on the yoke of this law

---

[3] *Ibid.*, chap. 19.
[4] *Ibid.*, chap. 7.

enters, at the same time, into a realm of free conscience; he has ceased to be subject to any mundane state and has become a member of a heavenly commonwealth or City of God. This divided allegiance seemed to Machiavelli a source of weakness and effeminacy. Humility should give way to patriotic pride. The ruler above all should have no conscience apart from the state and its material aggrandizement. Any one who consents to become a passive instrument in the service of any corporation, political, commercial, or religious, to the point of practicing a morality different from that which should rule the individual, is in the Machiavellian tradition. Machiavelli is the ancestor of the German who puts the fatherland "over all," and of his equivalent the one hundred percent American, and in general of those who are so patriotic that they are ready to back their country right or wrong. He embodies, more completely than any one else, what is usually defined as the realistic tradition in European politics. Yet one cannot grant that either Machiavelli or his spiritual descendants, the *Realpolitiker*, are thoroughgoing realists. The Nemesis, or divine judgment, or whatever one may term it, that sooner or later overtakes those who transgress the moral law, is not something that one has to take on authority, either Greek or Hebraic; it is a matter of keen observation. Without asserting that there is no such thing as reason of state and that public and private morality should coincide precisely at all points, nevertheless, one may affirm that it is chimerical to set up a dual code in the Machiavellian sense, to suppose that men can, as a rule, be ruthless in the service of country and at the same time upright as individuals.

To be merely a naturalistic realist, to combine, that is, a clear perception of the facts of the material order with spiritual blindness, leads practically to imperialistic dreaming. Machiavelli relates how at the time he was composing *The Prince* he was wont, after a day spent in petty occupations on his small property at San Casciano, to pull off his peasant clothes and don court attire in the evening, and then, retiring into his study, escape from the trivialities of the present to the imperial glories of ancient Rome. This particular land of heart's desire is still that of a certain number of Italians.

Perhaps the most important followers of Machiavelli, in actual practice, have been found among the Germans from Frederick the Great to Bismarck. For the student of political theory, on the other hand, the most significant line of development runs rather through England. Hobbes is possibly even more lacking in ethical perception, even more naturalistic in his conception of human nature, than Machiavelli himself. Strip man of the conventions that have been imposed upon him from without, says Hobbes, and what one discovers as his essence is "a perpetual and restless desire of power after power, that ceaseth only in death."[5] Hobbes reflects, to some extent, in his philosophy the cynicism and disillusion that had been engendered in many by the civil convulsions of seventeenth-century England. If one is to retain a rose-colored view of human nature, it is not well, it should seem, to see it at too close range in periods of great upheaval. La Rochefoucauld, who is also in the

---

[5] *Leviathan*, pt. 1, chap. 9.

Machiavellian tradition by his insistence on the egoistic element even in what appear to be man's fairest virtues, was influenced, we are told, in no small measure by his participation in the Fronde.

Though Hobbes is Machiavellian in his emphasis on the law of cunning and the law of force, he is, unlike Machiavelli, not merely systematic but metaphysical. He seeks to develop the postulates of naturalism into a logical and closed system. The difference between the two men is related to Pascal's distinction between the geometrical spirit and the spirit of finesse. Hobbes's extreme confidence in reasoning of the abstract or geometrical type (*la raison raisonnante*) strikes one as rather un-English, but in other respects he belongs to the great English utilitarian tradition, and points the way to Locke, who is himself, in essential respects, a dogmatic rationalist. For a striking fact about the English utilitarian is that, while professing to appeal from mere theory to experience, he repudiates that whole side of experience that belongs to the realm of the human law. Wishing to be thoroughly positive and critical, he inclines to identify this experience with the traditional forms in which it had become embedded and so to reject it as mere myth and fable; and herein he is at one with the traditionalists themselves who do not admit that the truths of the human law can be disengaged from certain special forms and, like the truths of the natural law, dealt with in a purely critical fashion. As I have tried to show elsewhere, the positivists have failed signally thus far to live up to their own program. Hobbes, for example, opposes to the dogmas and metaphysical assumptions of the traditionalists other assumptions that are almost equally metaphysical. One needs to consider what some of these assumptions are, for, in one shape or other, they have pervaded most political thinking from the time of Hobbes to our own day, even the thinking of those who at first sight seem most opposed to him.

One may take as the first of these metaphysical assumptions the conception of absolute and unlimited sovereignty. When anything absolute is set up, we may know that we are running into metaphysics; for precise observation of life does not give anything absolute. The only thing that approaches the absolute in man is his ignorance, and even that is not quite absolute. Hobbes's assertion of absolute and unlimited sovereignty recalls the medieval notion of sovereignty with a most important difference: it rests upon force and is in this sense imperialistic; it does not, like the sovereignty of the Middle Ages, have a supernatural sanction. For the medieval sovereign, whether pope or emperor, if not responsible to the people, is responsible to God, who is, finally, the only absolute and unlimited ruler. Furthermore, the individual in the state of Hobbes has no refuge from its despotic control in religion, or, what amounts to the same thing, in a domain of conscience set apart from the secular order. Hobbes subordinates the spiritual to the temporal, and, in his dealing with the rival claims of church and state, is, like Machiavelli, not only unmedieval but un-Christian.

Whence, one may inquire, does the sovereign of Hobbes derive a power so unlimited and irresponsible as to be subversive not only of liberty in the temporal

order, but also of the "liberty wherewith Christ hath
made us free." The reply is that the sovereign holds his
unlimited and irresponsible power, not by the grace of
God, but as a result of a contract with the people; and
here emerges another metaphysical assumption, that of
the social contract, which dominated to an extraordinary
degree the political thinking of several generations. This
involves, in some form or other, the assumption of a
state of nature, in which man is isolated and unsocial,
in opposition to a state of society where men escape from
their isolation on the basis of a convention or contract.
Just as Machiavelli is infinitely below Aristotle in setting
up two codes of morality, one for the state and one for
the individual, so Hobbes marks a great retrogression
from Aristotle in accepting this mythical contrast between
man in society and man as he is naturally. According to
Aristotle, it is natural for man, being as he is a political
animal, to live in society. Hobbes, also, as we have just
seen, by running together the things of God and the
things of Caesar, compromises the chief advance in
political thinking that has been made since Aristotle. As
a whole, his work may be described as an attempt to
justify metaphysically what would result practically in a
violent materialism.

To the social contract, unlimited sovereignty, and the
state of nature, we need to add natural rights if we wish
to complete the list of abstract and metaphysical conceptions that have dominated so much modern political
thinking. The rights that man possesses in the "state of
nature" would not seem very valuable, since his life in
this state, as conceived by Hobbes, is "solitary, poor,

nasty, brutish, and short"; and since, as a result of the dominance of self-love, every one is at war with every one else (*bellum omnium contra omnes*). From the point of view of theory, it is, however, important that man has in the state of nature unlimited liberty, in the sense that he has unlimited sovereignty over his own person, and can, therefore, transfer by the social contract this unlimited sovereignty to the state. Men also tend to be equal in the natural state, since the physically weak may, according to Hobbes, develop a cunning that will in the conflict of egoisms put them more or less on a level with the strong. The state of nature according to Hobbes may, then, be defined as liberty, equality—and war.

Natural rights and the freedom and equality that are supposed to be based upon them become increasingly important with the tendency that appears about the time of Hobbes to interpret more optimistically the state of nature. The origins of this tendency are complex. Perhaps the most important single influence was the revival of Stoical philosophy and the Stoical views regarding *jus naturale* and *jus gentium* that had been incorporated in Roman law. The underlying driving power behind the "return to nature" from the Renaissance down was the rise of the new astronomy and the growing triumphs of physical science. The success of the great revolt on naturalistic lines against the Christian and medieval dualism was due even less perhaps to scientific discovery, and to the type of progress that resulted, than to the positive and critical method by which the progress and the discoveries had been achieved, a method that was in direct conflict with the dogmatic and uncritical affirmations of

the traditionalists. In the political theorists of the sixteenth and seventeenth centuries, the naturalistic and
Stoical elements are combined in almost every conceivable
proportion with elements that derive from the traditional
supernaturalism. A mixture of this kind is especially
evident in the "De Jure belli et pacis" (1625) of Grotius,
the father of international law. The great nationalities,
that were arising with the breakdown of medieval theocracy, were plainly in a state of nature as regards one
another, so that it was even more important to determine,
in the case of the nation than in the case of the individual,
whether there can prevail in the state of nature any other
law than the law of cunning and the law of force. If one
is to refute Machiavelli and Hobbes, one must show that
there is some universal principle that tends to unite men
even across national frontiers, a principle that continues
to act even when their egoistic impulses are no longer
controlled by the laws of some particular state supported
by its organized force. Whether one starts with a state
of nature in which men are conceived as mere isolated
units, and then imagines a contract of some kind by
which they pass from a state of nature into society, or
whether one asserts with Aristotle that man is a political
animal, and that it is, therefore, natural for him to live
in society, one needs in either case to define with some
care the principle of cohesion among men. According to
the true Christian, the final counterpoise to egoism, in
virtue of which alone men may be drawn to a common
center, is submission to the will of God, a submission that
is conceived in terms of the inner life. The attempt to find

a bond of union among men in a "rule of reason," and the association of this rule of reason with nature, is, strictly speaking, not Christian, but Stoical. It is as natural for a man to serve other men, says Marcus Aurelius in his exposition of Stoical "reason," as it is for the eye to see. This doctrine of service, which the Stoic deems at once rational and natural, does not involve the inner life in the Christian sense. The final appeal is to something outside the individual—namely, to what Cicero, a main source of Stoical influence upon the modern world, calls the "common utility" (*utilitas communis*). The community that one serves may again, according to Cicero, be either one's country or mankind at large (*societas generis humani*). Stoical utilitarianism is in general highly rationalistic. English utilitarianism, on the other hand (and England is the chief source of utilitarian doctrine in modern times), puts far greater emphasis on the principle of pleasure, and in general on the instinctive side of man, an emphasis that is less Stoical than Epicurean. Cumberland, for example, seeks to refute Hobbes not merely by an appeal to right reason, but by asserting the presence in man of an instinct to promote the common good; thus to serve the community, says Cumberland, combining the new utilitarian conception with the older theology, is to fulfill the will of God.

One finds, however, in writers like Cumberland only the beginnings of the transformation in the very basis of ethics that has taken place in connection with the great movement, partly utilitarian, partly sentimental, that I have defined in its totality as humanitarianism. What is singular about the representatives of this movement is that they wish to live on the naturalistic level, and at the same time to enjoy the benefits that the past had hoped to achieve as a result of some humanistic or religious discipline. They have contradicted religion by asserting in substance that man, in order to rise above his selfish impulses, does not need conversion and the system of supernatural sanctions on which conversion has traditionally rested. They have also sought to refute the egoistic naturalists of the type of Machiavelli and Hobbes, who have maintained that the most fundamental impulse in man is the push for power. The rise of emotional ethics may be studied, especially in the England of the early eighteenth century, in connection with the deistic movement. The trend of deistic moralists like Shaftesbury and Hutcheson is all toward what we should call, nowadays, altruism and social service. With the decline of the doctrine of total depravity, the age of theology is beginning to give way to the age of sociology. The word beneficence gains currency about this time. The sympathetic man, the good-natured man, the man of feeling are emerging and are being held in ever-increasing estimation.

Those who believed in the intrinsic evil of human nature on either theological or naturalistic grounds were still numerous and aggressive. The divergent views concerning the goodness or badness of human nature were combined in almost every conceivable proportion in different individuals. They were so combined in Pope and Voltaire, for example, as to introduce into their writings a central incoherency. A curious attempt to combine the new expansiveness with an attack on the school of Shaftesbury and an affirmation of the egoistic element in man that reminds one of Hobbes and La Rochefoucauld and Machiavelli, is found in Mandeville's *Fable of the Bees*. With the growth of the new philosophy, man was encouraged to indulge more freely his natural desires. At the same time, scientific discovery was making increasingly possible the satisfaction of these desires. It was gradually developing a vast machinery designed to minister to man's material comfort and convenience and destined to culminate in the industrial revolution. Mandeville warned the English, who were entering an era of commercial and imperialistic expansion, that this expansion, with its concomitant growth of luxury, would, so far as the individual is concerned, be an expansion of vice and selfishness. The Stoical notion that mere "reason" can control the selfish passions, he refutes. The assertion of Shaftesbury, that there inheres in the natural man a "moral sense" or will to serve, that can prevail over the will to power, or instinct of sovereignty, as he terms it, he dismisses as "romantic and chimerical." He recommends ironically as a remedy a return to the Golden Age and its diet of acorns. The true remedy, he professes to believe, is the most austere Christianity and its renunciation of the lusts of the flesh. The real sting of his argument, however, is in the new turn that he gives to the Machiavellian idea of the double standard. The multiplication of wants, which is bad, considered from the point of view of the individual, may, if properly directed by government, make for the greatness of the state. Private vices are public benefits:

> Thus every part was full of vice.
> Yet the whole mass a paradise.
> . . . . Luxury
> Employ'd a million of the poor,
> And odious pride a million more;
> Envy itself and vanity,
> Were ministers of industry.

Mandeville concludes:

> Fools only strive
> To make a great and honest hive.

In Shaftesbury and Mandeville, we see clearly revealed, for perhaps the first time, the opposition between the romantic idealist and the Machiavellian realist. Much of Shaftesbury's doctrine stands in close relation to that of the ancient Stoics, notably Marcus Aurelius and Epictetus, so that there is truth in Mandeville's accusation that Shaftesbury "endeavored to establish heathen virtue on the ruins of Christianity." Shaftesbury, for example, does not go beyond Stoicism when he hopes, in Mandeville's phrase, to "govern himself by his reason with as much ease and readiness as a good rider manages a well taught horse by the bridle." But Mandeville is not entirely wrong in discovering in Shaftesbury a flattery of human nature beyond what the Stoics or other pagan moralists ever attempted. "He imagines that men without any trouble or violence upon themselves may be naturally virtuous. He seems to expect and require goodness in his species as we do a sweet taste in grapes and China oranges." On the basis of his natural goodness which displays itself in an instinctive affection of man for his own species, Shaftesbury was the first "to maintain virtue without self-denial." The word sympathy first became current largely as a result of its use by the Greek Stoics, but there is a wide gap between Stoical sympathy and the incipient sentimentalism of a Shaftesbury. So far from encouraging emotional effusion, the Stoic aimed at "apathy," and in his more austere moments would have us serve men, but refrain from pitying them.[6] The moral aestheticism that is beginning to appear in Shaftesbury, though it has no strict parallel in classical antiquity, is Epicurean rather than Stoical. The more advanced type of sentimentalist has, in order to display his "virtue," merely to palpitate deliciously.[7] As a matter of fact, the love or sympathy on which the romantic idealist puts so much emphasis is, as I shall try to show later, a sub-rational parody of Christian charity.

---

[6] See Seneca, *de Clem.*, ii, 4–6.

[7] The following passage from Rousseau (*Emile*, liv. 4) may serve as a sample of the fully developed emotional ethics of which the beginnings are found in Shaftesbury: "Cet enthousiasme de la vertu, quel rapport a-t-il avec notre intérêt privé? . . . Otez de nos coeurs cet amour du beau, vous ôtez tout le charme de la vie. Celui dont les viles passions ont étouffé dans son âme étroite ces sentiments délicieux; celui qui, à force de se concentrer au dedans de lui, vient à bout de n'aimer que lui-même, n'a plus de transports, son coeur glacé ne palpite plus de joie, un doux attendrissement n'humecte jamais ses yeux, il ne jouit plus de rien." This type of "enthusiasm" assumes at times a Platonic coloring, as in *Nouvelle Héloise*, pt. 2, letter 11. Plato, however, as Gomperz points out (*Griechische Denker*, ii, p. 411), "would have utterly despised the sentimentalism of Rousseau."

The moral sense of Shaftesbury and his disciple Hutcheson was developed by Hume and Adam Smith and other exponents of emotional ethics, and is not unrelated to the emphasis that the later utilitarians put on the principle of pleasure. Though Mandeville denied that sympathy of the humanitarian type can prevail over the "instinct of sovereignty," it is well to remember that he was himself an emotional moralist. He even recognizes among man's natural passions a passion of pity that may on occasion be violent. One has only to exalt this passion of pity and, at the same time, to take seriously Mandeville's occasional praises of ignorance and the simple life, to be in sight of the primitivistic solution of the problem of luxury and of civilization itself that Rousseau was to set forth in his two Discourses. Mandeville is on the side of decorum, and yet he admits that decorum is not only "artificial," but is, as Rousseau was to say later, only the "varnish of vice" and the "mask of hypocrisy." He affirms that vice in general is nowhere more predominant than where arts and sciences flourish, and that we shall find innocence and honesty nowhere more widely diffused than among the most illiterate, the "poor silly country people." "Would you banish fraud and luxury? Break down the printing-presses and burn all the books in the Island, except those at the universities where they remain unmolested."

What is being weakened by the realism of Mandeville, as well as by the idealism of Shaftesbury, is the sense of the inner life. And by the inner life, I mean the recognition in some form or other of a force in man that moves in an opposite direction from the outer impressions and expansive desires that together make up his ordinary or temperamental self. The decisive victories of both rationalistic and emotional ethics over the traditional dualism were won in the eighteenth century. At the same time, we must not forget that we have to do with the final stages of a secular process. The political reflex of this process is the passage from a Europe that was unified in theory, and to some extent in practice, by the Roman theocracy to a Europe made up of great territorial nationalities governed in their relations to one another by international law. As conceived by Grotius, international law rests largely upon naturalistic foundations. The publication of his work was followed in a few years by recognition of the new Europe in the Peace of Westphalia (1648). Within the bounds of each separate nationality, the essential aspect of this secular process is the passage from divine right to popular right, from the sovereignty of God to the sovereignty of the people. In the long period of transition, supernaturalist and naturalistic views are blended in almost every possible proportion. For example, Protestants, especially the Calvinists, and Catholics, especially the Jesuits, borrowed naturalistic concepts such as a state of nature, natural rights, and the social compact, but only that they might affirm more effectively the principle of divine sovereignty, with its theocratic implications, in the spiritual order.

Some, to be sure, saw the danger of thus making secular power seem to receive its sanction, not from above, but from below. Thus Filmer says in his *Patriarcha*: "Late writers have taken up too much upon trust from the subtle schoolmen who, to be sure to thrust down the king below the pope, thought it the safest course to advance the people above the king." A doctrine that was opposed to Jesuitical encroachments of this kind, and played an important role in the rise of nationalism, was that of the divine right of kings and of passive obedience. The strict subordination of the spiritual to the temporal power, urged by Erastus, had been encouraged by Luther himself. And Luther's own attitude was related to that of medieval theorists like Occam, who had sought to exalt the emperor and depress the pope. The monarchs, however, to whom the Lutheran inclined to give jurisdiction in matters religious (*cujus regio, ejus religio*), were not like the emperor universal; they ruled by hereditary right over certain limited teritories. The theocratic state of Calvin again is related to the medieval theory that exalted the pope at the expense of the emperor; but here also there is lacking the element of universality. Practically both the Lutheran and the Calvinistic state tend to run together the things of God and the things of Caesar, and to leave the individual without any *civitas dei* in which he may take refuge from the secular power. There is, then, this justification for the opinion of those who look upon Protestantism in all its forms as only an incident in the rise of nationalism.

A defense of divine right that should receive attention as an example, though a very imperfect one, of an important type of political thinking, is the work of Filmer I have just mentioned: *Patriarcha, or the Natural Power of Kings* (1680). The arguments in favor of the patriarchal view of government have indeed never been adequately set forth in the Occident. In spite of all that has been urged by Aristotle and others, we must, if we go by the actual experience of mankind, conclude that the patriarchal conception has enormous elements of strength. It has been the normal conception of great portions of the human race over long periods of time. Such a study as that of Fustel de Coulanges on the Greek and Roman city-state, and its derivation from the religion of the family, aids us to understand political and social institutions that still survive in countries like China and Japan. Unfortunately, Filmer does not apply an adequate psychological analysis to the patriarchal conception and uncover its deep roots in the actual facts of human nature. He is at once too naturalistic and too theological. By his very subtitle, he proclaims that the patriarchal power is "natural," and, at the same time, he seeks by somewhat grotesque speculations to prove that the actual power of kings is based on their direct descent from Adam.

Filmer seems to have missed the point seriously in seeking to show that the basis of patriarchal and royal power is natural. A more powerful and consistent champion of divine right is Bossuet in his *Politique tirée de l'Ecriture Sainte* (1709). He asserts, indeed, that all laws are founded on the first of all laws, that of nature, conceived as a law of equity and right reason. But in general he opposes to the oncoming naturalistic tide a thoroughgoing supernaturalism. Men are born, not free and equal, but subjects, first of all to their parents. Parental authority itself is the image of that of God, who is the only absolute sovereign. Parental authority serves, in turn, as a model for that of the king. The king's power does not depend upon the consent and acquiescence of his people. It is independent of the pope. But though absolute, it is not arbitrary; for it is controlled from above. Bossuet exalts the monarch in the secular order only to humble him in the sight of God and to lay upon him the weight of an almost intolerable responsibility. "Behold," he says, "an immense people brought together in a single person, behold this sacred, paternal, and absolute power; behold the secret reason which governs all this body of the state. You see the image of God in kings and gain from them the idea of royal majesty. And so, O kings, exercise your power boldly; for it is divine and salutary to mankind; but exercise it with humility. It is laid upon you from without. At bottom it leaves you weak, it leaves you mortal, it leaves you sinful; and burdens you in God's sight with a heavier reckoning." Kings, after all, he goes on to say, are but gods of flesh and blood, of clay and dust. Earthly grandeur may separate men for a moment, but they are all made equal at the end by the common catastrophe of death.

This exercise of the royal office in humble subordination to God was scarcely achieved even by a Saint Louis. As for Louis XIV, one is tempted to say that he took to himself the first part of Bossuet's doctrine (*l'état c'est moi*) and overlooked the humility. Bossuet, in asserting the immediate derivation of the royal power from God, goes back, like other champions of divine right, to the medieval theorists of the empire. But there was only one emperor whose sway was supposed to be universal, whereas there were a number of kings equally absolute in their pretensions, ruling by hereditary right over great territorial nationalities, and clashing, not merely in their secular ambitions, but also, as a result of the Reformation, in their religion. Practically the rulers of these nationalities were in the state of nature with reference to one another, whatever one may conceive the state of nature to be. Bossuet pushed his love of unity to the point of encouraging religious persecution, as manifested, for example, in the Revocation of the Edict of Nantes (1685). Yet his doctrine not only failed to provide an adequate offset to a centrifugal nationalism, it seemed by its insistence on the liberties of the French king and clergy (*les libertés gallicanes*) to make against unity in the church.

In asserting the Gallican liberties, Louis XIV and Bossuet were setting themselves against the main trend of the church since the later Middle Ages. The fourth article of the Declaration of the French clergy, made in 1682 and subscribed by Bossuet, declares that the judgment of the pope is not definitive without the consent of the church. But this type of limited and constitutional Catholicism had been compromised by the breakdown of the conciliar movement. Every significant change from that day to this has been in the direction of greater papal centralization. The theorist of this ultramontane type of Catholicism and the enemy of Bossuet and Louis XIV is Joseph de Maistre. His book on the pope (1819) looks forward to the final triumph of the doctrine of papal infallibility in the Vatican Council (1870). A main element in Christianity from a fairly early period is what one may term Roman imperialistic organization. This element de Maistre develops into a thoroughgoing papal imperialism. The supreme ruler by divine right is the pope. Temporal rulers, so far as they profess to be Catholic, should recognize his hegemony. This conception of rigid outer authority de Maistre proceeds to establish on the ruins of every type of individualism. In contrast to Bossuet, who was in the great central Christian tradition, so much so that one is tempted to call him the last of the fathers of the church, de Maistre, though a man of admirable character, reveals in his writings little sense of the inner life, not much more, it might be maintained, than the rationalists of the eighteenth century whom he was assailing. The subordination of the true Christian is based on humility and charity. The subordination at which de Maistre aims is primarily social. The chief need of society is order, and order, as de Maistre conceives it, must be achieved largely by fear and repression. The ultimate support of the whole social structure, as he tells us in a celebrated chapter, is the executioner. He champions the agencies of the church that are most frankly ultramontane and anti-individualistic—the Index, the Inquisition, and the Jesuits.

Bossuet pushes the doctrine of the divine right of kings about as far as it will go, and no one is ever likely to go beyond de Maistre in asserting the divine right of the pope. The reply to the absolute and unlimited sovereignty, whether of pope or king, based on divine right, was the assertion of the absolute and unlimited sovereignty of the people, based on natural right. The doctrine of popular sovereignty is found even in the Middle Ages, notably in Marsilius of Padua, and at the beginning of the seventeenth century is worked out along rather radical lines by Althusius. Practically, however, the most important precuror of Rousseau in the development of this doctrine is Locke. The first of his two *Treatises of Govern-*

ment (1690) has lost its interest along with the special form of the doctrine of divine right that he sets out to refute, that of Filmer's *Patriarcha;* the second treatise, however, remains a chief landmark of political thinking. To understand this work in its derivation, one needs to go back to the contrast between nature and convention established by the early Greek thinkers, and to the conception of a law of nature that grew out of this contrast, largely under Stoical influence, and became embodied in Roman law; finally one needs to trace through the centuries the process by which the Roman juristic conception finally became, in writers like Locke, the doctrine of the rights of man. The doctrine of natural rights, as maintained by Locke, looks forward to the American Revolution, and, as modified by Rousseau, to the French Revolution. Locke has to defend natural right not merely against the partisans of royal prerogative, but also against Machiavellian realists like Hobbes. For Hobbes, the state of nature is liberty, equality, and war. He would, therefore, in the interests of peace have the individual enter into a contract by which he renounces once and for all his liberty or unlimited sovereignty over his own person, and enjoy equality under a despot. For Locke, on the other hand, though he has an occasional primitivistic touch, the state of nature is liberty, equality, and reason. It is "a state of peace, good will, mutual assistance, and preservation."[8] In fact the law of nature is identical with the will of God[9] (or, as Pope was to say a little later, "The

---

[8] Bk. 2, chap. 3.
[9] *Ibid.*, chap. 11.

state of nature was the reign of God"). Locke, indeed, so
runs together the spiritual and the temporal order that he
speaks of an "appeal to heaven" when he means an appeal to force. He recognizes, however, certain disadvan-
tages in the state of nature, especially in its bearing upon
the safety of private property. If property is to be fully
secured, men need in addition to the natural law a positive
law to be administered by impartial judges who require
in turn the force of an organized state to give their decisions due execution. The first aim, therefore, of the contract by which men substitute a settled government for
the state of nature, is to secure the common good, which
is taken to be identical with the protection of property.
The source of property itself, and this is a point of extreme importance to which I shall need to return later,
is manual labor. The will of the people, conceived as the
will of the majority, is to be supreme. This will, however, is to be expressed not directly but through the
legislative, which as the organ of the popular will is to
dominate both the executive and the judiciary. Practically, Locke's treatise reflects the upshot of the Revolution of 1688, the transfer, namely, of the final power
of the state from the king to Parliament. The legislative is especially vigilant in its control over the executive
in all that relates to the common interest, that is, the
safety of property. (Taxation without representation is
tyranny.)

Even a theorist of divine right like Bossuet admits the
danger of an uncontrolled executive. "Let us candidly
confess," he says, "that there is no temptation equal to
that of power, nor aught more difficult than to refuse

yourself anything when men grant you everything, and think only of forestalling or even of stimulating your desires." As for Locke, he does not even deem it worth while to reply to those who maintain that a ruler, though not limited by men, may be limited by his responsibility to what is above him. For him, a king is in a state of nature not only with reference to other kings, but with reference to his own subjects; and being thus unrestrained he is at the same time corrupted with flattery and armed with power. Though Locke is thus on his guard against an uncontrolled royal will, it is hard to see that he has taken any precautions against the opposite danger. However moderately he himself may interpret the sovereignty of the people, it is not easy to discover in his theory anything that will prevent this sovereignty from developing into a new absolutism. The people exercises not only legal control over its legislators, but has the right, if they seem to be acting contrary to the people's interest, to rise up against them in insurrection. In the final analysis, the only check to the evils of an unlimited democracy will be found to be the recognition in some form of the aristocratic principle. Such a recognition is entirely lacking in Locke. The very logic of natural rights runs counter to the idea of deference and subordination, at least on any other basis than that of force. In the state of nature, says Locke, all men are equally kings, and subject to nobody; and this equality does not suffer serious diminution as the result of the social contract. Locke simply dodges the political problem that seems so important to an Aristotle and a Confucius, namely, the problem of leadership. It is characteristic of the English that the radical and egalitarian side of Locke should be slow to develop. The Revolution of 1688, of which he is the theorist, gave the control of government to an oligarchy that owed its power and prestige to the survival of the traditional subordinations. The difficulties of the Whig position, that of carrying on government by an aristocracy that lacks doctrinal justification, became manifest in time. This aristocracy virtually abdicated at the time of the Reform Bill (1832). The full results of the movement that was getting under way in the time of Locke are becoming apparent in our own day. The people, especially the people of the great urban centers, no longer look up with respect to representatives who are themselves so imbued with the utilitarian temper encouraged by Locke that they have perhaps ceased to be worthy of respect. If the aristocratic principle continues to give way to the egalitarian denial of the need of leadership, parliamentary government may ultimately become impossible.

It is Locke's aim to deal with human nature in a more empirical or experimental way than his philosophical predecessors. At the same time he has a strongly rationalistic side that reveals the Cartesian influence. By their assertion of a "reason" in man that can prevail unaided over the imagination and expansive desires, both Locke and Descartes renew the Stoical position. The counterassertion of Pascal that unaided reason cannot win any such easy victory, that on the contrary "imagination rules everything," seems nearer to the observed facts, and, therefore, more truly experimental. According to Locke, imagination becomes embodied in customs and traditions that may from the point of view of reason be dismissed as mere prejudice. By the opposition that he thus establishes between reason and prejudice, Locke becomes, along with Descartes, a main influence on the period of European culture known as the Enlightenment. Although no one perhaps did more for Locke's French and European influence in general than Voltaire, in the field of political theory, on the other hand, this influence is perhaps best studied in Montesquieu.[10] Like Locke, he stands for parliamentary control of the executive, especially in all that relates to taxation and the initiation of money bills. He tends, however, to separate more sharply than Locke the legislative, the judiciary, and the executive, and to make the judiciary and the executive more independent of the legislative, in such wise that the different functions of government may serve as a system of checks and balances upon one another. As is well known, it was this side of Montesquieu that was most influential on early American political theory. At the same time, only an unfriendly critic will see in the framers of the American Constitution pure disciples of Montesquieu. They possessed in a marked degree something that can scarcely be claimed for Montesquieu—practical sagacity. Compared with the political views of a Machiavelli, those of Montesquieu have about them an atmosphere of unreality; so much so that even the angelic Joubert said that one might learn more of the art of government from a page of Machiavelli than from a volume of Montesquieu. Moreover, our own constitutional statesmen did not for the

---

[10]See J. Dedieu, *Montesquieu et la tradition politique anglaise en France.*

most part share Montesquieu's general philosophy. This philosophy as it appears in *L'Esprit des Lois* (1748) suffers from certain inconsistencies, but on the whole it shows, even when compared with that of Locke, a noteworthy advance in the direction of a pure naturalism. The theological has given way still further to the sociological point of view, so much so that Montesquieu has been regarded by some as the founder of sociology. "He is the least religious spirit that ever was," says Faguet; and in truth he reveals an almost total lack of sense of the values of the inner life. To be genuinely religious or humanistic, one must assert whether in the form of divine grace or of free moral choice, a power in the heart of the individual that may lift him above physical nature. In the three main forms of government that he recognizes—monarchical, republican, and despotic—Montesquieu gives little weight to any such specifically human factor. Though he does lipservice to Christianity, he leans toward determinism and the empire of physical causes, putting special stress, as is well known, on the relation between climate and national character. His insistence, therefore, that laws must not be regarded as anything absolute, but must coincide in their general spirit with national character, is very different from the Aristotelian emphasis on ethos. For though Aristotle recognizes the influence of climate, he is on the whole less concerned with what nature makes of man than with what man makes of himself. In Montesquieu's view, even religion is largely a matter of climate. Climate determines the parts of the world that are to be Muhammadan or Christian,[11] and within Christianity it-

---

[11] *Esprit des Lois*, liv. 24, chap. 26.

self those that are to be Protestant or Catholic.[12] "Good
sense" is likewise, it would seem, a matter of climate.[13]
This naturalistic relativism implies a revolution in the
very basis of ethics. As a matter of fact, Montesquieu has
the grace to warn us that he is not using a word like
"virtue" in the traditional meaning. "What I call virtue
in a republic," he says, "is not a moral or Christian virtue,
it is the love of country, that is to say, the love of
equality." He develops admirably the thesis that this republican love of equality must not be pushed to a point
where it becomes incompatible with the necessary subordinations. The obvious reply of a Bossuet would be
that if subordination is to rest on any other principle
than force, it must imply the submission of man's ordinary will to some higher will, it must in other words be
ultimately rooted in humility. To be sure, Montesquieu
seems at times to recognize the relation between republican virtue and religious control. He says in a celebrated
sentence: "Rome était un vaisseau tenu par deux ancres
dans la tempête—la religion et les moeurs." With the
decay of this traditional ethos, luxury increased and liberty declined.[14]

Montesquieu conceives in an external and formalistic
fashion the honor that is the informing principle of mon-
archy. It has little to do with virtue either as he defines it
or as it has been traditionally understood. His treatment
of this form of the aristocratic principle, however faith-

---

[12] *Ibid.*, chap. 5.

[13] *Ibid.*, liv. 14, chap. 3.

[14] Yet in another chapter—and this is a good sample of his inconsistency
—he adopts Mandeville's arguments in favor of luxury (*ibid.*, liv. 19,
chap. 9).

fully it may reflect what aristocracy had actually become in the age of Louis XV, can scarcely be said to do justice to the implications of the maxim *noblesse oblige*. In the humanistic poise that the gentleman (*honnête homme*) sought to combine with the cult of honor, he discovers little more than a veneer of politeness that dissimulates the scramble of courtiers for the royal favor.

Since laws and governments, according to Montesquieu, are relative, and relative chiefly to physical causes, one might suppose that not much is to be gained from human interference with the working of these causes. As a matter of fact, there is another side of Montesquieu that suggests that though man cannot modify himself from within along humanistic or religious lines, he may be modified from without not merely by climate but by institutions; and that these institutions may be of a more or less progressive character. He displays, in short, the usual confidence of the man of the Enlightenment in the final triumph of reason over prejudice. His influence can be traced on those persons, especially numerous toward the end of the eighteenth century, who hoped to renovate society by an ingenious manipulation of political machinery, and who had an almost unlimited faith in the efficacy of paper constitutions.

I have just used the word "progressive." As a matter of fact, the idea of progress, which was to give its distinctive note to modern naturalism, was just taking definite shape in the time of Montesquieu. Only the barest beginnings of this idea can be found in the naturalism, whether Stoic or Epicurean, of ancient Greece and Rome. The idea of progress has its ultimate source in the first triumphs of scientific method in the Renaissance. In its

early English form, it is associated with the Baconian influence and the founding of the Royal Society (1662),
and tends to be practical and empirical. In its early French
form, it is associated with the Cartesian influence, and
tends to be more abstract and logical. The Baconian and
Cartesian currents come together in the eighteenth century, especially in France. The result is an ever-growing
confidence in human perfectibility. The Abbé de Saint-
Pierre is already a fairly complete specimen of what one
may term the professional philanthropist. Diderot and
other Encyclopedists set out deliberately to substitute the
Baconian kingdom of man for the traditional kingdom
of God. At the same time, the new doctrine did not have
all that it needed if it was to develop into what has been,
for several generations past, the true religion of the Occident—the religion of humanity. The movement thus far
had been predominantly rationalistic. Its main achievement had been to develop, largely on Cartesian lines, the
idea of universal mechanism, and to oppose nature, conceived as a system of constant and inflexible laws, to the
providential interference with natural law that had been
asserted, in some form or other, by the older dualists. A
Christian supernaturalist like Bossuet was, therefore,
justified from his own point of view in putting at the
very center of his defense of religion against naturalistic
tendency the idea of Providence. The substitution of the
idea of law for Providence is not in itself, from the point
of view of the strict positivist, a chimerical undertaking.[15]

---

[15]Buddha, for example, bestowed his final homage not upon Providence
in the Christian sense, but upon the Law ("Dhamma"); a law, one
scarcely need add, quite distinct from that of physical nature.

But in that case one would have needed, if the truths of the inner life were to be retained, to assert two laws—a law for man as well as a law for thing. The whole point of the new movement, however, was that it did nothing of the kind. It sought to bring both the natural and the human order under one law, and then, following the lead of Descartes, to reduce this one law to mathematical and mechanical formulae. To be sure, in the deistic movement, an important intermediary stage in the passage from the older dualism to modern monistic conceptions, the idea of Providence is still retained after a fashion. This deistic Providence, however, acts not immediately, as in true Christianity, but mediately through the laws of nature, which Providence was deemed, therefore, to have contrived with a special view to man's benefit. Hence the emphasis that most deists put on the doctrine of final causes, and their consternation at an event like the Lisbon earthquake which scarcely seemed to square with their theory of a Providence that worked for man's good through the natural order.

The deistic movement, and indeed, as I have already said, the whole naturalistic movement from the Renaissance down, had been thus far predominantly rationalistic. Now it has been a constant experience of man in all ages that mere rationalism leaves him unsatisfied. Man craves in some sense or other of the word an enthusiasm that will lift him out of his merely rational self. Even Voltaire, perhaps the outstanding figure of the Enlightenment, declared that illusion is the queen of the human heart. In the field of political thought, the conception of the rights of man remained comparatively inert as long as these rights were derived from a hypothetical state of nature merely by a process of abstract reasoning. "Cold reason," as Rousseau declared, "has never done anything illustrious." Rousseau had many precursors, as appears from what I have already said about the English background, yet it was he who more than any other one person put behind the doctrine of the rights of man the imaginative and emotional driving power it still lacked, and at the same time supplied the missing elements to the religion of humanity. Among those who took up the defense of the traditional order against Rousseau, Burke is easily first, because he too perceived in his own way the truth that cold reason has never done anything illustrious. He saw that the only conservatism that counts is an imaginative conservatism. One may, therefore, without being fanciful, regard the battle that has been in progress in the field of political thought since the end of the eighteenth century as being in its most significant phase a battle between the spirit of Burke and that of Rousseau. And this opposition between Burke and Rousseau will itself be found to turn, in the last analysis, on the opposition between two different types of imagination.

CHAPTER 2

Rousseau and the Idyllic Imagination

The period that extends from the Renaissance to the eighteenth century was, as I have indicated in my first chapter, marked by the progressive emancipation of the individual from outer authority and the supernatural beliefs that this authority sought to impose. The individual did not use his new liberty to work out some critical equivalent of traditional religion; on the contrary, he became increasingly naturalistic. At the same time he often indulged in theories of government that were at the opposite pole from those of Machiavelli, the typical political naturalist. This is because certain virtues were associated more and more with "nature," virtues that the past had deemed the hard-won fruit not merely of humanistic but of religious discipline. If the legitimacy of this association could be established, the Aristotelian generalization with which I started as to the necessary relation between ethos and government would evidently

have to be abandoned. Before deserting Aristotle, however, we may do well to consider whether some sophistry
does not lurk in what came to be the popular interpretation of the "state of nature."

The notion of a state of nature and of a law of nature
antecedent to positive law and organized society is, as we
have seen, nothing new. It emerges in classical antiquity,
especially among the Stoics, and survives throughout the
Middle Ages, largely as a result of the infiltration of the
Stoical influence into Roman law. It is reinforced again, as
I have said, by the direct return of the Renaissance to the
Stoical[1] and other ancient sources. Moreover, one may
find as early as the church fathers a tendency to identify
the supposed state of nature with the state of man before
the Fall and then to give to this state a communistic coloring, and at the same time to associate with man's lapse
from innocence the rise of private property.[2] Though the
law of nature was conceived to be in its own way divine,
its authority was after all not to be compared with that of
the divine law of which one secured knowledge through
revelation. As long as one held to this positive form of
God's law, one's assertion of a state of nature was sure to
be tempered by a lively conviction of the survival in man
of the "old Adam." Hooker, for example, whose *Ecclesiastical Policy* appeared in 1592, looks forward in many
of his ideas about natural law to Locke. But though asserting this law he declares: "Laws politic, ordained for ex-

---

[1] See L. Zanta, *La Renaissance du stoïcisme au xvie siècle.*

[2] The Stoical influence can be traced here also. See Seneca, *Epistles*, xiv, 2.
Cf. also *The Social and Political Ideas of Some Great Medieval Thinkers* (ed. F. J. C. Hearnshaw), pp. 43 ff.

ternal order and regimen among men, are never framed as they should be, unless presuming the will of man to be obstinate, rebellious, and averse from all obedience to the sacred laws of his nature; in a word, unless presuming man to be in regard of his depraved mind, little better than a wild beast." In the period between Hooker and Locke, the conviction of man's depravity undergoes a notable diminution. Grotius already affirms that, even if there were no God and no positive revelation, man might be guided aright in matters political by the law of nature conceived as a law of right reason. Along with this glorification of reason, one should note as far back as the sixteenth century an incipient glorification of instinct that was later to culminate, in one of its most characteristic expressions, in the cult of the noble savage. It is only, however, with the early eighteenth century that the glorification of instinct takes on so distinctly emotional a cast as to affect the very basis of ethics. Shaftesbury's doctrine of the "moral sense" and the instinctive goodness it implies had wide and immediate popularity. For example, Sir John Hawkins says in his *Life of Johnson:* "His [Fielding's] morality, in respect that it resolves virtue into good affections, in contradiction to moral obligation and a sense of duty, is that of Lord Shaftesbury vulgarized. He was the inventor of that cant-phrase, 'goodness of heart,' which is every day used as a substitute for probity, and means little more than the virtue of a horse or a dog."

Not only Shaftesbury, the optimistic naturalist, but the naturalistic cynic Mandeville prepared the way, as I have already said, for the emotional ethics of Rousseau. According to Rousseau, the state of nature is not a state of reason. On the contrary, the man who thinks is already highly sophisticated, or, in Rousseau's phrase, "a depraved animal." According to him, man in the state of nature is isolated and at the same time dominated by instinct. These isolated units will not, however, as Hobbes averred, be so dominated by the instinct of self-love as to make war on one another. Natural man has another instinct, namely, an instinctive dislike of seeing his fellow creatures suffer, which is alone a sufficient counterpoise to the love of self. From the concourse and combination of these two principles—love of self and instinctive pity— Rousseau seeks to derive all the rules of natural right. "Even the most outrageous detractor of human virtue" (that is, Mandeville), says Rousseau, "was forced to admit natural pity, though he did not see that from this quality alone derive all the social virtues—generosity, clemency, humanity, benevolence, and friendship itself—that he seeks to deny men." Indeed, if one considers unsophisticated man, man subject, that is, only to the primordial instincts of pity and love of self, one must conclude that he is "the most virtuous who offers the least resistance to the simple impulses of nature." According to Schopenhauer,[3] it was the glorious achievement of Rousseau to transform morality by thus basing it upon pity. A result of this achievement that should be noted is the modification, apparent in the sentence I have just quoted, in the meaning of such words as virtue. The more, indeed, one

---

[3] *Grundlage der Moral*, sec. 19, 9.

studies the eighteenth century, the plainer it becomes that all other modern revolutions were preceded at about that time by a revolution in the dictionary. For a fuller understanding of Rousseau's recoining of the word virtue, one needs to turn back for a moment to the *First Discourse* (1750). He there asserts the incompatibility between virtue and the refinement and luxury that seem to him to result necessarily from a cultivation of the arts and sciences. In his account of the undermining of Rome and other great states by the invasion of luxury, he uses by actual count the word virtue forty-three times. But one is not to suppose that in his solution of the problem of luxury that so preoccupied his age he is really seeking to recover the virtue of a Fabricius or a Lycurgus or a Calvin. What he opposes to luxury is rather a return to nature and the simple life—and the simple life, as he conceives it, is to be very simple indeed.[4] His virtue is a glorification of the instinctive and the subrational. So that Joubert was justified from his own point of view in saying that Rousseau had destroyed wisdom in men's souls by talking to them about virtue.

Though the virtue of the *First Discourse* is distinctly primitivistic, it received an essential addition in the *Second Discourse* by being associated with the idea of pity. The state of nature for Hobbes, as we have seen,

---

[4] See, for example, *Dernière Réponse à M. Bordes:* "Qu'ils paissent même, s'il le faut: j'aime encore mieux voir les hommes brouter l'herbe dans les champs que s'entre-dévorer dans les villes . . . Osera-t-on prendre le parti de l'instinct contre la raison? C'est précisément ce que je demande."

meant liberty, equality, and war; for Locke, liberty, equality, and reason. On the contrary, says Rousseau, both war and reason are the result of social sophistication. The true state of nature is liberty, equality, and fraternal pity. By his refutation of Hobbes, and his substitution of fraternity for reason, Rousseau gave to naturalism the driving power it still lacked. It thus became possible to develop it into a new evangel that seemed to culminate, like the old Evangel, in love. This conception of love in terms of expansive emotion is, as I have already said, a sort of parody of Christian charity.

In the state of nature all men are, it would seem, equally capable of pity. But in actual society the emphasis on pity leads to the setting up of a sort of inverted hierarchy. Just as in Christianity a man's spiritual rank is determined by his nearness to God, which is revealed in turn by the ardor of his charity, so in the new evangel man is to be rated by his nearness to nature, which is revealed in turn by the warmth of his commiseration. Now it is in the man of the plain people that the lively native impulse is least sicklied o'er by the pale cast of thought. "Love had he found in huts where poor men lie." As one ascends in the social scale, love diminishes, and as one approaches the top, it gives way to its opposite. As for the rich, Rousseau compares them to "ravening wolves, who having once tasted human flesh, refuse every other food, and henceforth desire to devour only men."

Rousseau is, as a matter of fact, busy in creating a new set of myths that have, in their control of the human imagination, succeeded in no small measure to the old theology. Just as in the old theology everything hinged on man's fall from God, so in Rousseau everything hinges on man's fall from nature. The first and decisive step in this fall and the source of social evils was, according to Rousseau's familiar account, the invention of private property in the form of property in land. With the invention of property, "equality disappeared." "Work became necessary, and the vast forests were changed to smiling fields that had to be watered with the sweat of men, in which slavery and wretchedness were soon seen to spring up and grow with the crops." Misery, in short, is the result of industry.

What evidently underlies the mythology that Rousseau is thus creating is a new dualism. The old dualism put the conflict between good and evil in the breast of the individual, with evil so predominant since the Fall that it behooves man to be humble; with Rousseau this conflict is transferred from the individual to society. That there is some survival of the older dualism in Rousseau is beyond question; but it is equally beyond question that the actual influence of his work has been almost entirely associated with the new dualism. He himself saw in this new dualism the essence of the apocalyptic vision that came to him under the tree by the roadside on his walk to Vincennes. The guiding principle of his writings, he says, is to show that vice and error, strangers to man's constitution, are introduced from without, that they are due in short to his institutions. Now institutions mean in practice those who administer them. A small group at the top of the artificial hierarchy, kings and priests and capitalists, sit on the lid, as it were, and keep man's native goodness (as in Shelley's "Prometheus Unbound") from gushing forth torrentially. The fault in any case is not "Nature's";

> Nature! No!
> Kings, priests, and statesmen blast the human flower
> Even in its tender bud; their influence darts
> Like subtle poison through the bloodless veins
> Of desolate society.

Whence this strange dualism arose, "how George III and Paley and Lord Eldon came to possess an existence independent of Nature, and acquired the power of turning all her good purposes to nought," is, as Leslie Stephen remarks of Shelley, "one of those questions which we can hardly refrain from asking." A similar question arises regarding the dualism of Rousseau. Most people, however, have not been inclined to subject the myth of natural goodness to any such indiscreet scrutiny. It is not only very flattering in itself; it seems to offer a convenient avenue of escape from the theological nightmare. Above all it flattered those at the bottom of the social hierarchy. Christianity at its best has sought to make the rich man humble, whereas the inevitable effect of the Rousseauistic evangel is to make the poor man proud, and at the same time to make him feel that he is the victim of a conspiracy. The establishment of society and laws made it possible to change "an adroit usurpation into an irrevocable right, and for the profit of a few ambitious persons subjected henceforth the whole of human kind to toil, servitude, and wretchedness." One need scarcely be surprised that this and similar passages of the *Second Discourse* should still be a direct source of inspiration to the bomb-throwing anarchist.[5] What one hears throughout this treatise, as elsewhere in Rousseau, is the voice of the angry and envious plebeian, who in the name of love is actually fomenting hatred and class warfare. "What was hardest to destroy in me," we read in *Emile*, "was a proud misanthropy, a certain acrimony against the rich and happy of the world as though they were so at my expense, as though their alleged happiness had been usurped from mine."

The crusader against social inequalities on Rousseauistic lines may easily become not merely an enthusiast but a fanatic. This emancipation of feeling seems at first sight the essential aspect of Rousseau's interpretation of nature. Instead of the rationalistic and mechanical nature of the Cartesian, nature is spontaneity, in the sense of an expansive and even an explosive emotionalism. "I threw reason overboard," says Rousseau himself, "and consulted nature, that is to say the inner sentiment which directs my belief independently of my reason." But on closer examination one discovers that there is in Rousseau something even more fundamental than his emotionalism, and that is his special quality of imagination. In order to make this point clear, we need to consider with some care the contrast between the natural and the artificial that he establishes in his *Second Discourse*. His method in reaching this contrast is similar in some respects to that of the

---

[5] For the testimony of a French magistrate on this point, see L. Proal: "L'Anarchisme au xviii° siècle," *Revue philosophique*, vol. 82, pp. 135–60, 202–42.

modern evolutionist. Instead of having us look forward
to ends, as Aristotle urges, if we are to understand man's
nature, he would, like the evolutionist, have us grope our
way back to beginnings. The change from primitive to
civilized man is presented as a slow development with
certain intermediary stages, each one of which Rousseau
supposes to have consumed "thousands of centuries."
This portrayal of the evolution of mankind as a whole
through various stages aided, one may note in passing,
the efflorescence in Germany of numerous philosophies of
history.[6] Rousseau's nature, however, is in one particular
violently at variance with the nature of most of the
philosophers of history and with that of all the evolutionists. Though the evolutionist is only too prone to whisk
us off into some prehistoric period where he is free to
indulge in airy hypothesis, he does not see in nature at
any stage of the evolutionary process a source of pity.
By his attribution of pity to the state of nature, Rousseau has indeed gone far to justify the sentence with
which he opens his discussion of this state in the *Second
Discourse:* "Let us begin by setting aside all the facts."
The key to Rousseau's nature, and also to what has passed
for the ideal with innumerable Rousseauists, is found in
his declaration that, not being able to discover men to his
liking in the real world, he built up for himself a "golden
age of phantasy."[7] His nature is in short what I have described elsewhere as a projection of the idyllic imagination.

---

[6] See Richard Fester: *Rousseau und die deutsche Geschichtsphilosophie.*
[7] *Lettre à M. de Malesherbes,* January 26, 1762.

Faguet complains that the image Rousseau has left on the mind of the public is that of a gentleman up in a cherry tree tossing down cherries to two maidens below (incident of Mesdemoiselles Galley and Graffenried in the *Confessions*). Perhaps the public is not so far wrong after all as to Rousseau's essential attitude. One can scarcely go through Rousseau's writings without being struck by the number of variants he has given of the pastoral theme. Let no one suppose that it is a small matter to be, like Rousseau, richly and spontaneously imaginative in this idyllic fashion. Perhaps no human trait is more universal than the longing for some golden age or land of heart's desire. This longing has not only inspired a large proportion of the art and literature of the world, but has found its way into philosophy and religion. The idyllic element is unmistakably present in the story of the Garden of Eden; the Song of Solomon is described by Milton as a "divine pastoral"; the millennial yearnings of the early Christians are not unrelated to the same type of imagination. The Krishna of the Bhagavadgîtâ is not in the least pastoral, but in the picture that often serves as frontispiece to Indian editions of this poem, Krishna appears with the pastoral flute and kine, surrounded by the *gopis* or shepherdesses.

What concerns us here is the relation of this type of imagination to modern political idealism. The agitator makes his chief appeal to it when he stirs the multitude by his pictures of the felicity that is to supervene upon the destruction of the existing social order. The English painter Edward Lear relates that in the year of revolution, 1848, he was staying in a Sicilian town. He left the town for some weeks and locked up his pictures and other things in a room, leaving the key with the hotel keeper. A revolution had just broken out when he returned, and he found the waiters full of Chianti and patriotic fervor. He ventured to ask one of them for the key of his room that he might get his clothes. The waiter utterly refused to be led from his dreams of a golden age to such details of daily life. "There isn't any longer any key or room or clothes," he exclaimed indignantly. "Everything is love and liberty. *O che bella rivoluzione!*"[8] Unfortunately when the real refuses to vanish in favor of the ideal, it is easy to persuade the simpleminded that the failure is due not to the ideal itself, but to some conspiracy. In speaking of one of these childlike disciples of Rousseau, Anatole France says that it was his misfortune to have carried into the profession of cook to which fate had condemned him an Elysian soul intended for the golden age. He had been led to the most savage ferocity by the tenderest optimism. As Anatole France adds, when one starts with the supposition that men are naturally good and virtuous, one inevitably ends by wishing to kill them all. What is remarkable about the period since the eighteenth century is the extent to which not merely the rank and file, but the leaders have followed the lure of the idyllic imagination. Thus Schiller exalts the idyll to the first places in literature, and associates it with the ideal. Elsewhere I have tried to show that the idyll does not deserve any such rank in literature. It would

---

[8] This story was a favorite of Tennyson's. I abridge it from Wilfrid Ward, *Problems and Persons*, pp. 204–5.

seem even more open to suspicion as a basis for political action. Lincoln writes to his friend Speed: "I have no doubt it is the peculiar misfortune of both you and me to dream dreams of Elysium far exceeding all that anything earthly can realize." Lincoln was in these Elysian yearnings, as in other respects, very human. He was not, however, Elysian in his actual statesmanship.

Later in this book we shall study more in detail various persons who, unlike Lincoln, have carried over the idyllic type of "vision" into the field of politics and economics. All that I wish to show now is that, in the case of Rousseau himself, even his sensibility is subject to his imagination, inasmuch as this imagination conjures up the Arcadian state that he terms "nature," towards which his emotions expand so freely. But to present Rousseau merely as an idyllic and emotional dreamer, it may be urged, is to forget that part of his writings, the *Social Contract*, for instance, in which he shows himself severely and coldly logical. The occasional severity of Rousseau's logic one may grant, but its coldness is another matter. Starting from the premise of a fictitious state of nature, it leads to conclusions that justify emotional revolt against everything established, that are indeed enough to make "the very stones of Rome to rise and mutiny." If the subjects of a despot, for example (every king in Europe was a despot according to the logic of the *Social Contract*), seem to enjoy domestic tranquillity, it is merely, says Rousseau, the tranquillity of the companions of Ulysses in the den of the Cyclops, waiting their turn to be devoured. Rousseau's logic has been compared in its relation to his emotions to a henpecked husband, who keeps

up a brave outer show of independence while actually
doing his wife's bidding. Moreover, another end is
accomplished by Rousseau's display of logical rigor. The
man at the bottom of the existing social order is flattered
by being told that he is more virtuous, more fully possessed, in other words, of the spontaneous goodness of
the state of nature than the man at the top. But, however
ready he may be to believe that he is superior in feeling,
he does not after all like to look upon himself as incapable
of thought. The multitude, says Aristotle, cannot make
distinctions. Rousseau's logic is so contrived as to give to
the multitude at least the illusion that it *can* make distinctions. He owes no small part of his amazing influence
to his flattery of the popular head as well as of the popular
heart. As Taine writes in a letter to W. S. Lilly: "What
gives extraordinary power to the ideas of Rousseau is
above all the simplicity of the conception. As a matter of
fact, the political reasoning that it produces is as easy as
the rule of three. How are you to prove to this man that
he does not understand, that the notion of the state is
one of the most difficult to form, that political reasoning
is beyond his grasp? You would insult him. He cannot
admit even as possible a thing so preposterous: and his
self-love is sufficient to blind his good sense."

Thus far I have been dealing with the Rousseau who
has actually moved the world—the Rousseau whose feelings fly out towards the vision conjured up by his imagination, and whose logic is in turn pressed into the service
of his feelings. One must, however, grant that there is
alongside of this Rousseau a very different Rousseau. It
is related that when he was in Strassburg a father told

him that he was educating his son strictly on the principles of *Emile*. He replied: "So much the worse for him." Even if not strictly true, this anecdote has a certain symbolical value. It is to be associated with his saying that his heart and his head did not seem to belong to the same individual. If his heart (to which, as I have tried to show, his logic is subservient) is revolutionary, his head is cautious. His replies to those who sought counsel of him, as any one who has been through his correspondence will testify, were frequently very shrewd and sensible. As M. Lanson says, he applies his boldest doctrines in a way to reassure conservatives and satisfy opportunists.

The contrast between the two Rousseaus is indeed so marked as to raise the question of his sincerity. As a preliminary to a discussion of this point, one needs to note that a special type of sincerity which seems to be much in request these days is itself an outcome of the Rousseauistic movement. It seems to be assumed in certain quarters that almost any opinion is justified provided it be held with sufficient emotional vehemence. One cannot help reflecting that perhaps the best examples of sincerity in this sense are to be found in insane asylums; and that much of Rousseau's sincerity, his conviction for instance during his later years that he was the victim of a universal conspiracy, was of this order. Sincerity is indeed only one of a whole class of virtues that are often taken to be primary when they are in fact only virtues with reference to something more fundamental. Thus many of our "liberals" conceive that it is in itself a virtue to be forward-looking, whereas it may be a vice, if what one is looking forward to should turn out to be pernicious or chimerical.

A similar remark applies to those who pique themselves on their open-mindedness. It is well to open one's mind, but only as a preliminary to closing it, only as a preparation in short, for the supreme act of judgment and selection. In much the same way, the value of sincerity can be estimated only with reference to the previous question of truth or error. What makes the Socratic group at Athens and the scientific investigator today seem so respectable, when compared with the emotionalist, is that they ask, first of all, not whether a man is sincere, but whether he is right or wrong. If one is right, it is of course important, at least in the domain of moral values, that he should be sincerely right.

It is hard to deny Rousseau the type of emotional sincerity that I have just been discussing—a type that in its milder form reminds one of what would be known nowadays as the will to believe, and in its extreme form, is not far removed from madness. At the same time, Rousseau's head could on occasion stand aloof and deal rather Socratically with his heart. For example, he said to Hume who had complimented him on the style and eloquence of his books: "To tell the truth, I am not displeased with myself in that particular: at the same time I dread lest my writings are good for nothing at bottom, and that all my theories are full of extravagance."[9]

It is not, however, the self-critical Rousseau of this passage that need concern us, for the simple reason that it is not this Rousseau who has moved the world. The

[9] Letter of Hume to Dr. Blair, March 25, 1766. This letter was written, it will be noticed, while Hume was still on friendly terms with Rousseau.

side of Rousseau that has moved the world, as M. Lanson continues, is the side that "exasperates and inspires revolt . . .; it is the mother of violence, the source of all that is uncompromising. It launches the simple souls who give themselves up to its strange virtue upon the desperate quest of the absolute, an absolute to be realized today by anarchy and tomorrow by social despotism."[10]

Though the Rousseau who has been influential is always Rousseau the extremist, he oscillates, as M. Lanson says, between opposite extremes. From the unflinching individualism of the *Second Discourse*, where man is conceived as a sort of isolated and unrelated particle, he passes to the no less unflinching collectivism of the *Social Contract*. He fluctuates between extremes even in his collectivistic ideal. Thus he writes to the Marquis de Mirabeau that he does not see "any endurable mean between the most austere democracy and the most perfect Hobbism." You must choose, he says, between making a man and making a citizen. You cannot hope to make both. Hitherto, I have been speaking for the most part of the virtue of man in the state of nature as depicted in the *Second Discourse*. It remains to speak of the *Social Contract*, and of the method there outlined for divesting man as completely as possible of his natural virtue in order that he may acquire the virtue of the citizen. In what I have to say about the *Social Contract*, I shall confine myself to the uncompromising main argument. That there are other elements in the *Social Contract* is beyond question. Rousseau affirms at times that the prin-

[10] *Annales de la Société Jean-Jacques Rousseau*, VIII, p. 31.

ciples of government are not absolute but relative; that
they are subject in their application to historical circumstances and physical environment, notably climate. But
this relativistic Rousseau who reveals at times the influence of Montesquieu is, as I have said, unimportant compared to the Rousseau who is straining out toward the
absolute and the unlimited. This absolutism of Rousseau
appears, as is well known, most strikingly in his doctrine
of popular sovereignty. This doctrine he reasons out from
first principles with almost geometrical rigor. The first
effect of this reasoning is to make all existing governments seem illegitimate. "Man is born free, and everywhere he is in chains." The only free and legitimate
government is that founded upon a true social compact.
On this basis, it is possible to combine the advantages of
organized government with the liberty, equality, and
fraternity that man enjoys, not as the result of moral
effort, but as a free gift, in the state of nature. Only, under the social contract, these virtues no longer reside in
the individual, but in the general will. All the clauses of
the social contract "reduce themselves to one: the total
alienation of every associate with all his rights" (including his rights to property) "to the whole community."
What guarantee is the individual to have that the community will not abuse this unlimited control that he has
granted it over his person and property? Though the state
is for Rousseau as for Hobbes not natural but artificial,
he proceeds to develop the analogy between this artificial
body and the body of an actual person. One of the most
important sources of this tendency to set up an elaborate
parallel between the individual and the state is Plato's

Republic. In Plato, however, the parallel is used to establish a severe hierarchy in the state, in much the same way that the powers and faculties of the individual must work in due order and subordination; whereas the informing spirit of the Rousseauistic conception is the idea of equality. The use that Rousseau makes of the parallel is to argue that the community cannot will the harm of any of the individuals that compose it any more than the single person can will the harm of one of his own members. On the side of theory, however, Rousseau's chief argument in favor of the disinterestedness of the general will is that it has had transferred to it by the social contract the spontaneous goodness that belongs to the will of the individual in the state of nature. At this point, however, Rousseau's good sense intervenes. Granted that the multitude from whom the general will emanates wishes the right thing, it does not always see it. The people, after all, needs guidance. Hence arises the necessity of the Lawgiver; and Rousseau goes on to imagine some person of almost superhuman sagacity, set apart from other men, and under no suspicion of self-seeking, who draws up an ideal code that is to direct the general will, a code which actually enjoys credit with the people because it seems to have religious sanction, in other words, because the Lawgiver seems to speak not for himself, but only as a channel of divine wisdom. One might suppose that the general will would be limited by the law thus imposed; that the law would become a permanent principle of control in the state, its higher self, as it were, in opposition to its mere passing desires. But at bottom, Rousseau does not want any effective check on

the reaching out of his logic and emotions toward the
unlimited; and so he finally transfers to the general will
the anarchical impressionism he has asserted for the individual. The only clear result of his speculations about
the need of a law and a Lawgiver was to encourage the
conceit of followers like Robespierre, who felt that they
had within them the making of a modern Lycurgus.
Practically the general will is lawless; it cannot bind
itself to obey its rulers, whom it regards as mere executive officers, the people's hired men as it were, revocable
at pleasure. It cannot bind itself to anything it has
willed in the past, or obligate itself in any way for the
future. An assembly of the sovereign people should invariably begin by voting separately on the two following questions: "first, whether it pleases the sovereign
to preserve the present form of government; second,
whether it pleases the people to leave the administration
of it to those who are now in charge." The sovereign
people cannot be represented by a parliament, as in
England. "At the moment a state gives itself representatives it no longer exists." Sovereignty is absolute
and indivisible. "To limit it is to destroy it." "The sovereign people, by the very fact that it is, is always all
that it should be." It has often been pointed out that
Rousseau transfers to the people the doctrine that the
king can do no wrong. But he does more than that. The
king, if not responsible to what is below him, is at least
responsible to what is above him—to God. But the sovereign people is responsible to no one. It *is* God. The
contract that it makes is with itself, like that which, according to the old theologians, was made in the council

chamber of the Trinity. "By the mere pleasure of God," says Jonathan Edwards, "I mean his sovereign pleasure, his arbitrary will, restrained by no obligation," etc. The popular will is the successor of the divine will, from which everything finally derived in the medieval theocracy.

Rousseau's idea of sovereignty, being as it is naturalistic, is of course in its ultimate essence neither medieval nor theocratic. His idea of a contract that the people makes with itself, by which it arrogates to itself full power, without any reciprocal obligation, is in important respects original with Rousseau. "We are entering," he wrote in *Emile*, "on the era of crises and the age of revolutions." He not only made the prophecy, but did more than any other one man to bring about its fulfillment. By asserting a general will that is at once absolute and shifting, he achieved the paradox of basing government on permanent revolution. Perhaps he is more closely related to Hobbes than to any previous political thinker, especially if it be true, as Sainte-Beuve says, that nothing resembles a hollow so much as a swelling. His state of nature and his sovereignty are merely the state of nature and the sovereignty of Hobbes reversed. In Rousseau the people can do anything it pleases with its ruler, in Hobbes the ruler can do anything he pleases with the people. But though the state of Hobbes has no higher self—the very idea of a higher self is foreign to his materialistic philosophy—it has at least a permanent self. The contract by which the people divests itself of its power in favor of its ruler is definitive. But Rousseau, as we have seen, will have no such element of permanency. If he had conceived of the general will as the permanent will of the people that might on occasion be in conflict with its ordinary will, his distinction[11] between a disinterested *volonté générale* and a *volonté de tous*, which may stand for nothing more than the egoistic wills of individuals or groups, might have a serious meaning. As it is, this distinction melts away under close scrutiny. It is mystical in the bad sense.

On all ordinary occasions the general will means a numerical majority at any particular moment. An individual or a minority of individuals has no appeal from the decision of this majority in its interpretation of the general will. This is logical, inasmuch as the individual has transferred to the general will the unlimited liberty that he enjoyed in the state of nature. If any one is outvoted, he can console himself by the reflection that he was mistaken, that what he took to be the general will was not this will. If his private opinion had won, he would have been doing something contrary to his true will and his true liberty. In exercising constraint upon him, therefore, the majority is simply "forcing him to be free." By this device Rousseau gets rid of the problem that has chiefly preoccupied political thinkers in the English tradition—how, namely, to safeguard the freedom of the individual or of minorities against a triumphant and despotic majority.

This solution of the problem involves the setting up

---

[11] Strictly enforced this distinction makes party government impossible. It also points the way to the decision reached by the States General in 1789 that the deputies should vote individually and not as members of an order, a decision that meant practically the triumph of the Third Estate over the clergy and nobility.

of a new dualism—that between the individual in his ordinary self and the individual as a citizen and member of the sovereign people conceived as his true self. But though the first term of this dualism, the individual in his ordinary self, may be subject to rigid control, the second term of the dualism, the state as embodied in the general will, is, let me repeat, subject to no control at all. The liberty of the general will, like that of the individual in the state of nature, can be limited, if at all, as Rousseau says significantly, only by force.

Anyone who traces the subject historically will acquire the conviction, as I have already said, that the Christian religion founded something of which not even a Plato or an Aristotle had any adequate notion—personal liberty. By its separation of the things of God and the things of Caesar, it established a domain of free conscience, in which the individual might take refuge from the encroachments of the omnipotent state. It is plain that Rousseau does not propose to leave the individual any such refuge. The last chapter of the *Social Contract* is devoted to "Civil Religion." This chapter abounds in remarks of extraordinary shrewdness and penetration (as, for instance, where he observes that the Crusades were not truly Christian in spirit) and at the same time, so far as its general conclusions are concerned, may be described in Rousseau's own phrase as a "sea of sophisms." Rousseau distinguishes three types of religion: first, organized and traditional Christianity, especially the Christianity of the Catholic church. This type of religion is so evidently bad as scarcely to merit serious refutation. "All institutions that put man in contradiction with him-

self are worthless." The obvious reply of the older type
of dualist would be that man *is* in contradiction with himself, and that the church merely reflects a primordial fact
of human nature. One can no more grant that institutions
per se are capable of any such effect than one can admit
Rousseau's counterassertion that, merely as a result of
institutions, all the members of a community may possess
good sense, justice, and integrity.[12]

The second religion that Rousseau recognizes is true
Christianity, a religion entirely of the heart, without
rites and ceremonies, and having much in common, as
he conceives it, with the fluid emotionalism of the sentimental deist. True Christians are like those great cosmopolitan spirits of whom Rousseau speaks in the *Second
Discourse*, who "transcend the imaginary barriers that
separate peoples, and like the sovereign being who has
created them, embrace the whole human race in their
benevolence." The person, however, in whom natural
pity has thus blossomed into universal benevolence is not
necessarily either otherworldly or humble, and Rousseau
is shrewd enough to see that the true Christian is both.
He, therefore, proceeds to attack not merely institutional
Christianity but true Christianity. It also divides man
against himself, and by giving him a celestial fatherland
weakens his allegiance to the *civitas terrena*. Rousseau
brings up questions of extraordinary complexity regarding the distinction between a spiritual and a secular order,
and the actual political results of this distinction as
worked out in Christianity, questions that for their proper

---

[12] *Contrat Social*, liv. 4, chap. 3.

elucidation would require a volume. The main point that concerns us here is his attack on humility, the underlying Christian virtue, on the ground that it is incompatible with the full virtue of the citizen. To be humble is to be submissive; so that "true Christians are meant to be slaves." One should, therefore, discard humility in favor of patriotic pride, of the kind that flourished in the great days of Rome and Sparta.

Here again in his dealings with the relations of church and state, Rousseau reminds us of Hobbes. "Of all Christian authors," he himself says, "the philosopher Hobbes is the only one who saw clearly the evil and the remedy and ventured to propose bringing together the two heads of the eagle," thus subordinating everything to political unity. But before Hobbes, Machiavelli, as I have already remarked, had sought to discredit the idea of a separate spiritual order, and also of Christian humility itself, so that the state might be all in all. Quite apart from Rousseau's admiration of Machiavelli and from any conscious discipleship, his view of the state has more in common with the Machiavellian view than one might at first suppose. Machiavelli is not, of course, like Rousseau, an emotionalist, but is, in his main trend, utilitarian. It is no accident that Francis Bacon, the prophet of utilitarianism, should be, as Lord Acton points out, his most distinguished English disciple. But Rousseau too has a strongly utilitarian side. Indeed one finds in him, as in the whole of our modern age, an endless interplay of sentimental and utilitarian elements.

This utilitarian side of Rousseau appears in the third form of religion he discusses in the *Social Contract*.

After rejecting both institutional Christianity and true Christianity, on the ground that they are antinational, he proposes as worthy of approval a religion which, properly speaking, is not a religion at all, but a social utility. The articles of its creed, which are determined by the sovereign, are to be imposed not precisely as dogmas, but as promoting sentiments of sociability. The positive dogmas of this civil creed are, as Rousseau states them, fairly substantial (e.g., the existence of God, the future life, the happiness of the just, and the punishment of the wicked). If any one does not believe them he may be banished from the state, not as impious but as unsocial. "If anyone, after having recognized publicly these same dogmas, conducts himself as though he did not believe them, let him be punished with death." The civil religion is to have only one negative dogma—the condemnation of intolerance. This is directed especially against institutional Christians, but it is hard to see how anyone can escape this condemnation who holds in matters religious to a definite standard of right and wrong, quite apart from the omnipotent state and its supposed utility.

Rousseau's "civil religion" evidently looks forward to such an event as Robespierre's Festival of the Supreme Being. Unfortunately, it also looks forward to the Civil Constitution of the Clergy and to the guillotining as "fanatics" of many of the priests who refused to forswear their allegiance to Rome. It is fair to add that the *Social Contract* is only one source[13] of the strife between

---

[13] Cf. P.-M. Masson, *La Religion de J.-J. Rousseau*, III, chap. 5.

clericals and anticlericals that has been so prominent in France since the Revolution as to amount at times almost to civil war. In general we should recollect that Rousseau was less an originator of the ideas we have been discussing than the most important single figure in a vast movement that had been gaining head for generations. In the words of Madame de Staël he invented nothing, but set everything on fire. Burke, the chief antagonist of Rousseau, took serious cognizance of this movement and of the enthusiasm it inspired only when they had begun to translate themselves into great historical events. It was Rousseau and all he typified that he attacked in the French Revolution.

CHAPTER 3

Burke and the Moral Imagination

"Everybody knows," Burke writes of the members of the French National Assembly, "that there is a great dispute amongst their leaders, which of them is the best resemblance of Rousseau. In truth, they all resemble him. His blood they transfuse into their minds and into their manners. Him they study; him they meditate; him they turn over in all the time they can spare from the laborious mischief of the day, or the debauches of the night. Rousseau is their canon of holy writ; in his life he is their canon of *Polycletus*; he is their standard figure of perfection. To this man and this writer, as a pattern to authors and to Frenchmen, the founderies of Paris are now running for statues, with the kettles of their poor and the bells of their churches."

I have presented Rousseau in his essential influence as the extremist and foe of compromise. In contrast to Rousseau, Burke is usually and rightly supposed to embody the spirit of moderation. Many of his utterances on the French Revolution, however (the passage I have just quoted may serve as a sample), are scarcely suggestive of moderation, and toward the end he becomes positively violent. There is at least this much to be said in justification of Burke, that in his writings on the Revolution, he is for the most part debating first principles, and when it comes to first principles, the issue raised is one not of moderation, but of truth or error. Burke was no mere partisan of the *status quo*. He was not opposed on principle to revolutions. He is perhaps open to the charge of pushing too far his admiration for the Revolution of 1688. His attitude toward the American Revolution was consistently one of compromise and in many respects of sympathy. He did not stand in any undue awe of those in authority. No one could on occasion call them to a stricter accounting or show himself a more disinterested champion of the victims of unjust power. He recognized specifically the abuses of the Old Regime in France, and was ready to admit the application to these abuses of fairly drastic remedies. If he refused, therefore, to compromise with the French Revolution, the reason is to be sought less in the field of politics than in that of general philosophy, and even of religion. He saw that the Revolution did not, like other revolutions, seek to redress certain specific grievances, but had universal pretensions. France was to become the "Christ of nations" and conduct a crusade for the political regeneration of mankind. This particular mixture of the things of God and the things of Caesar seemed to him psychologically unsound, and in any case subversive of the existing social order of Europe. The new revolutionary evangel was the final outcome of the speculations that had been going on for generations about a state of nature, natural rights, the social contract, and abstract and unlimited sovereignty. Burke is the chief opponent of this tendency toward what one may term metaphysical politics, especially as embodied in the doctrine of the rights of man. "They are so taken up with the rights of man," he says of the members of this school, "that they have totally forgotten his nature." Under cover of getting rid of prejudice they would strip man of all the habits and concrete relationships and network of historical circumstance in which he is actually implicated and finally leave him shivering "in all the nakedness and solitude of metaphysical abstraction." They leave no limit to logic save despotism. In his attack on the enemies of prejudice, by which was meant practically everything that is traditional and prescriptive, Burke has perhaps neglected unduly certain minor though still important distinctions, especially the distinction between those who were for getting rid of prejudice in the name of reason, and those who, like Rousseau, were for getting rid of it in the name of feeling. The rationalists and the Rousseauists were actually ready to guillotine one another in the Revolution, an opposition prefigured in the feud between Rousseau and various "philosophers," notably Voltaire. Rousseau was as ready as Burke, though on different grounds, as I shall try to show presently, to protest against the "solid darkness of this enlightened age."

By the dismissal as mere prejudice of the traditional forms that are in no small measure the funded experience of any particular community, the state loses its historical continuity, its permanent self, as it were, that unites its present with its past and future. By an unprincipled facility in changing the state such as is encouraged by Rousseau's impressionistic notion of the general will, the generations of men can no more link with one another than the flies of a summer. They are disconnected into the dust and powder of individuality. In point of fact, any political philosophy, whether that of Hobbes or of Rousseau, which starts from the supposition that men are naturally isolated units, and achieve society only as the result of an artifice, is in its essence violently individualistic. For this atomistic, mechanical view of the state, Burke is usually supposed to have substituted an organic, historical conception. Much of his actual influence, in Germany[1] and elsewhere, has certainly been along these lines. Yet this is far from being the whole truth about Burke. A one-sided devotion to the organic, historical conception is itself an outcome of the naturalistic movement. It may lead to fatalistic acquiescence in traditional forms, and discourage, not merely abstract rationalism, but a reasonable adjustment of these forms to shifting circumstances. It relates itself very readily to that side of the romantic movement that exalts the unconscious at the expense of moral choice and conscious deliberation. Once obscure this capacity in the individual, which alone raises him above phenomenal nature, and it will not be easy in the long run to preserve his autonomy; he will tend, as so often in German theory,

---

[1] On Rehberg, Savigny, etc.

to lose his independent will and become a mere organ of the all-powerful state. Though Taine, again, often professes to speak as a disciple of Burke in his attacks on the French Revolution, it is not easy to see a true follower in a philosopher who proclaimed that "vice and virtue are products like sugar and vitriol."

The truth is that Burke is in no sense a collectivist, and still less, if possible, a determinist. If he had been either, he would not have attained to that profound perception of true liberty in which he surpasses perhaps any other political thinker, ancient or modern. For one who believes in personal liberty in Burke's sense, the final emphasis is necessarily not on the state but on the individual. His individualism, however, is not, like that of Rousseau, naturalistic, but humanistic and religious. Only, in getting the standards by which the individual may hope to surpass his ordinary self, and achieve humanism or religion, he would have him lean heavily on prescription. Burke is antiindividualistic in that he would not set the individual to trading on his own private stock of wit. He would have him respect the general sense, the accumulated experience of the past that has become embodied in the habits and usages that the superficial rationalist would dismiss as prejudice. If the individual condemns the general sense, and trusts unduly his private self, he will have no model; and a man's first need is to look up to a sound model and imitate it. He may thus become exemplary in his turn. The principle of homage and service to what is above one has its culmination and final justification in fealty to God, the true sovereign and supreme exemplar. Burke's conception of the state may be described as a free and flexible adaptation of genuinely Platonic and Christian elements. "We know, and what is better, we feel inwardly, that religion is the basis of civil society, and the source of all good and all comfort." "God willed the state." (Thus to conceive the highest in terms of will is Christian.) "He willed its connection with the source and original archetype of all perfection." (The language is here Platonic.) Not merely religion but the actual church establishment is held by Englishmen to be essential to their state, as being indeed the very foundation of their constitution.

"Society is indeed a contract," though the basis of the contract is not mere utility. The state is not to be regarded as a partnership agreement in a trade of pepper and coffee. It is not, as a contemporary pacifist has maintained, the "pooled self-esteem" of the community, but rather its permanent ethical self. It is, therefore, a partnership in all science and art and in every virtue and perfection. "As the ends of such a partnership cannot be obtained in many generations, it becomes a partnership not only between those who are living, but between those who are living, those who are dead, and those who are to be born."

Though Burke thus uses the language of contract, it is plain that he moves in a different world from all those, including Locke, for whom the idea of contract meant that man has certain rights as a free gift of nature and anterior to the performance of his duties. Talk to the child, says Rousseau, of something that will interest him—talk to him of his rights, and not of his duties.[2] To

---

[2] *Emile*, liv. 2.

assert, as Burke does in the main, that one has only concrete historical rights, acquired as the result of the fulfillment of definite obligations, is evidently remote from Rousseau's assertion that a man enjoys certain abstract rights simply because he has taken the trouble to be born. The difference here is not merely between Burke and Rousseau, but also between Burke and Locke. The final superficiality of Locke is that he granted man abstract natural rights anterior to his duties, and then hoped that it would be possible to apply this doctrine moderately. But it has been justly said that doctrines of this kind are most effective in their extreme logical form because it is in this form that they capture the imagination. Now if the out-and-out radical is often highly imaginative in the fashion that I have attributed to Rousseau, the Whigs and the liberals who follow the Whig tradition are rather open to the suspicion of being deficient on the side of imagination. One cannot help feeling, for instance, that if Macaulay had been more imaginative, he would have shown less humanitarian complacency in his essay on Bacon. Disraeli again is said to have looked with disdain on J. S. Mill because of his failure to perceive the role of the imagination in human affairs, a lack that can scarcely be charged against Disraeli himself, whatever one may think of the quality of his imagination.

Now Burke is the exceptional Whig, in that he is not only splendidly imaginative, but admits the supreme role of the imagination rather more explicitly than is common among either Christians or Platonists with whom I have associated him. He saw how much of the wisdom of life consists in an imaginative assumption of the experience of the past in such fashion as to bring it to bear as a living force upon the present. The very model that one looks up to and imitates is an imaginative creation. A man's imagination may realize in his ancestors a standard of virtue and wisdom beyond the vulgar practice of the hour; so that he may be enabled to rise with the example to whose imitation he has aspired. The forms of the past and the persons who administer them count in Burke's eyes chiefly as imaginative symbols. In the famous passage on Marie Antoinette one almost forgets the living and suffering woman to see in her with Burke a gorgeous symbol of the age of chivalry yielding to the age of "sophisters, economists, and calculators." There is in this sense truth in the taunt of Tom Paine that Burke pities the plumage and forgets the dying bird. All the decent drapery of life, Burke complains of the new philosophy, is to be rudely torn off. "All the superadded ideas, furnished from the wardrobe of a moral imagination, . . . are to be exploded as a ridiculous, absurd, and antiquated fashion."

The apostles of the rights of man were, according to Burke, undermining the two principles on which everything that was truly civilized in the European order had for ages depended: the spirit of religion and the spirit of a gentleman. The nobility and the clergy, who were the custodians of these principles and of the symbols that embodied them and ministered to the moral imagination, had received in turn the support of the learned. Burke warns the learned that in deserting their natural protectors for Demos, they run the risk of being "cast into the mire and trodden under the hoofs of a swinish multitude."

Burke is in short a frank champion of aristocracy. It is here especially, however, that he applies flexibly his Christian-Platonic, and humanistic principles. He combines a soundly individualistic element with his cult of the traditional order. He does not wish any static hierarchy. He disapproves of any tendency to deal with men in classes and groups, a tendency that the extreme radical shares with the extreme reactionary. He would have us estimate men, not by their hereditary rank, but by their personal achievement. "There is," he says, "no qualification for government but virtue or wisdom, actual or presumptive. Wherever they are actually found, they have in whatever state, condition, profession or trade, the passport of Heaven to human place and honor." He recognizes, to be sure, that it is hard for the manual worker to acquire such virtue and wisdom for the reason that he lacks the necessary leisure. The ascent of rare merit from the lower to the higher levels of society should, however, always be left open, even though this merit be required to pass through a severe probation.

In the same fashion, Burke would admit innovations in the existing social order only after a period of severe probation. He is no partisan of an inert traditionalism. His true leader or natural aristocrat, as he terms him, has, in his adjustment of the contending claims of new and old, much of the character of the "trimmer" as Halifax has described him. "By preserving the method of nature in the conduct of the state, in what we improve we are never wholly new; in what we retain, we are never wholly obsolete." "The disposition to preserve, and ability to improve, taken together, would be my standard of a statesman." In such utterances Burke is of course simply giving the theory of English liberty at its best, a theory almost too familiar for restatement. In his imaginative grasp of all that is involved in the task of mediating between the permanent and the fluctuating element in life, the Platonic art, as one may say, of seeing the One in the Many, he has had few equals in the field of political thinking.

Burke is, however, in one important respect highly un-Platonic, and that is in his attitude toward the intellect. His distrust of what we should call nowadays the intellectual may be variously explained. It is related in some respects to one side, the weak side, one is bound to add, of Christianity. "A certain intemperance of intellect," he writes, "is the disease of the time, and the source of all its other diseases." He saw so clearly the dangers of this abuse that he was led at times, as the Christian has at times been led, to look with suspicion on intellect itself. And then he was familiar, as we are all familiar, with persons who give no reasons at all, or the wrong reasons, for doing the right thing, and with other persons who give the most logical and ingenious reasons for doing the wrong thing. The basis for right conduct is not reasoning but experience, and experience much wider than that of the individual, the secure possession of which can result only from the early acquisition of right habits. Then, too, there is something specifically English in Burke's disparagement of the intellect. The Englishman, noting the results of the proneness of a certain type of Frenchman to reason rigorously from false or incomplete premises, comes to prefer his own piecemeal good sense and proclivity for "muddling through." As Disraeli told a foreign visitor, the country is governed not by logic but by Parliament. In much the same way Bagehot in the course of a comparison between the Englishman and the Frenchman in politics, reaches the semihumorous conclusion that "in real sound stupidity the English are unrivaled."

The antiintellectual side of Burke reminds one at times of the antiintellectual side of Rousseau: when, for instance, he speaks of "the happy effect of following nature, which is wisdom without reflection and above it." The resemblance is, however, only superficial. The wisdom that Rousseau proclaimed was not *above* reflection but *below* it. A distinction of this kind is rather meaningless unless supported by careful psychological analysis. Perhaps the first contrast between the superrational and the subrational is that between awe and wonder.[3] Rousseau is plainly an apostle of wonder, so much so that he is probably the chief single influence in the "renascence of wonder" that has resulted from the romantic movement. The romantic objection to intellect is that by its precise analysis and tracing of cause and effect, it diminishes wonder. Burke, on the other hand, is fearful lest an indiscreet intellectual activity may undermine awe and reverence. "We ought," he says, "to venerate where we are unable presently to understand." As the best means of securing veneration, Burke leans heavily upon habit, whereas the romantics, from Rousseau to Walter Pater, are no less clearly hostile to habit because it seems to lead to a stereotyped world, a world without vividness

---

[3] Cf. *Rousseau and Romanticism*, pp. 49 f.

and surprise. To lay stress on veneration meant for Burke, at least in the secular order, to lay stress on rank and degree; whereas the outstanding trait perhaps of the state of nature projected by Rousseau's imagination, in defiance of the actual facts of primitive life so far as we know them, is that it is equalitarian. This trait is common to his no-state and his all-state, his anarchistic and his collectivistic utopia. The world of the *Social Contract*, no less than that of the *Second Discourse*, is a world without degree and subordination; a world in which no one looks up to anyone else or expects anyone to look up to him; a world in which no one (and this seems to Rousseau very desirable) has either to command or to obey. In his predominant emphasis on equality,[4] Rousseau speaks, to some extent at least, not merely for himself but for France, especially the France of the last two centuries. "Liberty," says Mallet du Pan, "is a thing forever unintelligible to Frenchmen."[5] Perhaps liberty has not been intelligible in its true essence to many persons anywhere. "The love, and even the very idea, of genuine liberty," Burke himself admits, "is extremely rare." If this basis of this genuine liberty is, as Burke affirms, an act of subordination, it is simply incompatible with Rousseauistic equality.

---

[4] It would not be easy to find in an English author of anything like the same intellectual distinction the equivalent of the following passage from Proudhon (*Oeuvres*, 2, p. 91): "L'enthousiasme qui nous possède, l'enthousiasme de l'égalité, . . . est une ivresse plus forte que le vin, plus pénétrante que l'amour: passion ou fureur divine que le délire des Léonidas, des Saint Bernard et des Michel-Ange n'égala jamais."

[5] Cf. E. Faguet, *Politiques et moralistes*, vol. 1, p. 117: "Il est à peu près impossible à un Français d'être libéral, et le libéralisme n'est pas français." See also *ibid.*, 3, p. 95.

The act of subordination to any earthly authority is justified only in case this authority is looking up to something still higher; so that genuine liberty is rooted in the virtue that also underlies genuine Christianity. "True humility, the basis of the Christian system, is the low, but deep and firm foundation of all real virtue. But this, as very painful in the practice and little imposing in the appearance," he goes on to say of the French revolutionists, "they have totally discarded." They have preferred to follow Rousseau, the great "professor and founder of the philosophy of vanity." Rousseau himself said that he based his position on the "noblest pride," and pride is, even more than vanity, the significant opposite of humility. I have already spoken of Rousseau's depreciation of humility in favor of patriotic pride. The problem of pride versus humility is, of course, not primarily political at all. It is a problem of the inner life. Rousseau undermined humility in the individual by substituting the doctrine of natural goodness for the older doctrine of man's sinfulness and fallibility. The forms and traditions, religious and political, that Burke on the other hand defends, on the ground that they are not arbitrary but are convenient summings up of a vast body of past experience, give support to the imagination of the individual; the imagination, thus drawn back as it were to an ethical center, supplies in turn a standard with reference to which the individual may set bounds to the lawless expansion of his natural self (which includes his intellect as well as his emotions). From a purely psychological point of view, Burke's emphasis on humility and on the imaginative symbols that he deems necessary to secure it, reduces itself to an em-

phasis on what one may term the centripetal element in
liberty. Rousseau, at least the Rousseau that has influenced the world, practically denies the need for any such
centripetal element in liberty, inasmuch as what will
emerge spontaneously on the disappearance of the traditional controls is an expansive will to brotherhood.
If one rejects like Burke this gospel of "universal benevolence," it is hard not to conceive of liberty in Burke's
fashion—namely, as a nice adjustment between the taking on of inner control and the throwing off of outer
control. "Society," he says, "cannot exist unless a controlling power upon will and appetite be placed somewhere, and the less of it there is within, the more there
must be without." This adjustment between inner and
outer control, which concerns primarily the individual,
is thus seen to determine at last the degree to which any
community is capable of political liberty. True statesmanship is in this sense a humanistic mediation and not
an indolent oscillation between extremes. "To make a
government requires no great prudence. Settle the seat
of power; teach obedience; and the work is done. To
give freedom is still more easy. It is not necessary to
guide; it only requires to let go the rein. But to form a
free government—that is, to temper together these opposite elements of liberty and restraint in one consistent
work, requires much thought, deep reflection, a sagacious, powerful, and combining mind."

I have already said that Burke is very exceptional in
that he is a splendidly imaginative Whig. As a matter
of fact, most of the typical Whigs and liberals in the
Whig tradition, are, like Burke, partisans of liberty in

the sense of personal liberty and of moderation. They do not, however, give their personal liberty and moderation the same basis of religion and humanistic control. On the contrary, they incline to be either rationalists or emotionalists, which means practically that they found their ethics either on the principle of utility, or else on the new spirit of sympathy and service, or more commonly on some compound of these main ingredients of humanitarianism. The liberty of Burke, I have tried to show, is not only religiously grounded, but also involves in its political application a genuine humanistic mediation. The Whig compromise, on the other hand, is only too often an attempt to compromise between views of life, namely, the religious-humanistic and the utilitarian-sentimental, which are in their essence incompatible. Thus the liberalism of J. S. Mill is, compared with the liberalism of Burke, open to the charge of being unimaginative. Furthermore, from a strictly modern point of view, it is open to the charge of being insufficiently critical. For the liberty Mill desires is of the kind that will result only from the traditional spiritual controls, or from some adequate substitute, and his philosophy, as I shall try to show more fully later, supplies neither.

Burke can scarcely be charged with the form of superficiality that consists in an attempt to mediate between incompatible first principles. One may, however, feel that he failed to recognize the full extent and gravity of the clash between the new principles and the old; and one may also find it hard to justify the obscurantist element that enters into his defense of his own religious and humanistic position. One might gather from Burke that England was almost entirely made up of Christian gentlemen ready to rally to the support of the majestic edifice of traditional civilization, to all the decencies of life based finally on the moral imagination, whereas the "sophisters, economists, and calculators" who were destroying this edifice by their substitution for the moral imagination of an abstract metaphysical reason were almost entirely French. He does indeed refer to the English deists, but only to dismiss them as obscure eccentrics. The English intellectuals and radical thinkers of his own time he waves aside with the utmost contempt, opposing to them not those who think more keenly, but those who do not think at all. "Because half a dozen grasshoppers under a fern make the field ring with their importunate chink, while thousands of great cattle, reposed beneath the shadow of the British oak, chew the cud and are silent, pray do not imagine that those who make the noise are the only inhabitants of the field; that, of course, they are many in number; or that, after all, they are other than the little, shrivelled, meager, hopping, though loud and troublesome, insects of the hour."

In this passage we have the obscurantist Burke at his weakest. The truth is that the little, meager, hopping insects of the hour were representatives of an international movement of a vast scope, a movement destined finally to prevail over the prejudice and prescription that Burke was defending. Moreover, this movement was largely, if not indeed primarily, of English origin. "It is from England," says Joubert, "that have issued forth, like frogs, the metaphysical and political ideas which have darkened everything." It is hard to trace the main currents of European life and thought from the Renaissance, especially the rise of humanitarianism in both its utilitarian and its sentimental aspects, and not assent in large measure to the assertion of Joubert. Burke's conception of man and of the state with its strong tinge of Platonic realism (in the older sense of the word) and its final emphasis on humility, or submission to the will of God, has important points of contact with the medieval conception. Now, even before Francis Bacon, men from the British Islands played an important part in breaking down this realism. Duns Scotus discredited reason in theology in favor of an arbitrary divine will, and so released reason for use in the secular order. William of Occam asserted a nominalism that looks forward to our type of realism, a realism, that is, not of the One but of the Many, and, therefore, at the opposite pole from the medieval variety. Roger Bacon is significant for the future both by his interest in the physical order and by the experimental temper that he displays in dealing with this order.

To come to a later period, the upshot of the civil convulsions of seventeenth-century England was to diminish imaginative allegiance to the past. The main achievement of Cromwell himself was, as his admirer Marvell avowed, to "ruin the great work of time." As loyalty to the great traditions declined, England concentrated on the utilitarian effort of which Francis Bacon is the prophet, and thus did more than any other country to prepare and carry through the industrial revolution, compared with which the French Revolution is only a melodramatic incident.

If the Christian classical England that Burke took to be truly representative has survived in a place like Oxford, utilitarian England has got itself embodied in cities like Birmingham, so that the opposition between the two Englands, an opposition that is one of first principles, has come to be written on the very face of the landscape. The Englishman, however, does not proceed by logical exclusions, and is capable of maintaining in more or less friendly juxtaposition things that are ultimately incompatible. Thus a young man receives a religious-humanistic training at Oxford as a preparation for helping to administer the British Empire in India, an empire which is, in its origins, chiefly an outcome of the utilitarian and commercially expansive England. The kind of leadership that Burke desired, the leadership of the true gentleman, still plays no small part in the affairs of England and of the world. The Englishman whom he conceives to be typical, who "fears God, looks up with awe to kings, with affection to parliaments, with duty to magistrates, with reverence to priests, and with respect to nobility," is still extant, but is considerably less typical. Above all, his psychology is not that of the great urban masses that owe their existence to the industrial revolution. What Birmingham stands for has been gaining steadily on what Oxford stands for, and that even at Oxford itself. I have said that the only effective conservatism is an imaginative conservatism. Now it has not only became increasingly difficult to enter imaginatively into certain traditional symbols, but in general the imagination has been drawn away more and more from the element of unity in things to the element of diversity. As a result of the type of progress that has been proclaimed, everything good has come to be associated with novelty and change, with the piling up of discovery on discovery. Life, thus viewed, no longer involves any reverence for some center or oneness, but is conceived as an infinite and indefinite expansion of wonder and curiosity. As a result of all this intoxication with change, the world is moving, we are asked to believe, toward some "far-off divine event." It is at this point that the affinity appears between the utilitarian or Baconian, and the emotional or Rousseauistic side of the humanitarian movement. The far-off divine event is, no less than Rousseau's state of nature, a projection of the idyllic imagination. The felicity of the divine event, like that of the state of nature, is a felicity that can be shown to involve no serious moral effort or self-discipline on the part of the individual. Rousseau himself put his golden age in the past, but nothing is easier than to be a Rousseauist, and at the same time, like the Baconian, put one's golden age in the future. The differences between Baconian and Rousseauist, and they are numerous, are, compared with this underlying similarity in the quality of their "vision," unimportant. I remarked at the outset that the modern political movement may be regarded in its most significant aspect as a battle between the spirit of Rousseau and that of Burke. Whatever the explanation, it is an indubitable fact that this movement has been away from Burke and toward Rousseau. "The star of Burke is manifestly fading,"

Lecky was able to write a number of years ago, "and a great part of the teaching of the *Contrat Social* is passing into English politics." Professor Vaughan, again, the editor of the recent standard edition of Rousseau's political writings, remarked in his introduction, apparently without awakening any special contradiction or surprise, that in the essentials of political wisdom Burke is "immeasurably inferior to the man of whom he never speaks but with scorn and loathing; to the despised theorist, the metaphysical madman of Geneva."

Burke will be cherished as long as anyone survives in the world who has a perception of the nature of true liberty. It is evident, however, that if a true liberalism is to be successfully defended under present circumstances, it will not be altogether by Burke's method. The battle for prejudice and prescription and a "wisdom above reflection" has already been lost. It is no longer possible to wave aside the modernists as the mere noisy insects of an hour, or to oppose to an unsound activity of intellect mere stolidity and imperviousness to thought —the great cattle chewing their cud in the shadow of the British oak. But before coming to the question of method, we need to consider what the triumph of Rousseau has actually meant in the history of modern Europe, during and since the Great Revolution. A survey of this kind will be found to involve a consideration of the two chief political problems of the present time, the problem of democracy and the problem of imperialism, both in themselves and in their relation to one another.

CHAPTER 4

Democracy and Imperialism

In our recent crusade to make the world safe for democracy it was currently assumed that democracy is the same as liberty and the opposite of imperialism. The teachings of history are strangely different. Democracy in the sense of direct and unlimited democracy is, as was pointed out long ago by Aristotle, the death of liberty; in virtue of its tyrannical temper, it is likewise, in the broad sense in which I have been using the term, closely akin to imperialism. Now the distinction of Rousseau is, as we have seen, to have been the most uncompromising of all modern theorists of direct democracy. How far have the actual results of Rousseauism justified Aristotle rather than those who have anticipated from the diffusion of the Rousseauistic evangel, a paradise of liberty, equality, and fraternity? The commanding position of Rousseau in the democratic movement is at all events beyond question, though even here it is possible to exaggerate. "Democracy," says M. de Vogüé, "has only one father—Rousseau. . . . The great muddy stream which is submerging us flows from the writings and the life of Rousseau like the Rhine and the Po from the Alpine reservoirs which feed them perpetually."[1] It is interesting to place alongside of this and similar passages which might be multiplied indefinitely, passages[2] from German authorities, likewise very numerous, to the effect that Rousseau is more than any other person the father of their *Kultur*. Here, too, one must allow for an element of exaggeration. Much in Germany that is often ascribed to Rousseau may be traced to English influences, the same influences that acted on Rousseau himself.

Passages of the kind I have just cited seem to establish a first connection between *Kultur*, which has come to be regarded as in its essence imperialistic, and Rousseauistic democracy. *Kultur*, when closely scrutinized, breaks up into two main elements—on the one hand, scientific efficiency, and on the other, a nationalistic enthusiasm to which this efficiency is made to minister. The relationship to Rousseauism must evidently be looked for first of all in the second of these elements, that of nationalistic enthusiasm. One needs to recall here a saying of Renan's that goes back to the seventies of the last century. "The sentiment of nationalities is not a hundred years old in the world."[3] Renan might have

---

[1] *Introduction à l'Iconographie de J.-J. Rousseau*, I, pp. vii–viii.
[2] I have cited some of these passages in *Rousseau and Romanticism*, p. 194 n.
[3] *Réforme intellectuelle et morale*, p. 194.

said with about equal truth that international or cosmopolitan sentiment is likewise not a hundred years old.
Both sayings are approximately true, provided sufficient
emphasis is put on the word sentiment. One scarcely
needs to repeat that the Middle Ages were cosmopolitan,
and that a chief result of Protestantism was the development of the national idea, and that the national idea
was also promoted, though on different postulates, by
Machiavelli. But with the eighteenth century, nationalism and internationalism take on a more emotional
coloring. An underlying influence here is Rousseau's reinterpretation of "virtue," a reinterpretation that is itself,
as I have tried to show, the outgrowth of a considerable
previous movement. According to the new ethics, virtue is not restrictive but expansive, a sentiment and even
an intoxication. In its unmodified natural form, it has
its basis in pity which may finally develop into the virtue of the great cosmopolitan souls of whom he speaks
in the *Second Discourse*, who transcend national frontiers and embrace the whole of the human race in their
benevolence. We are here at the headwaters of the sentimental internationalism of the past century. But Rousseau, as I have already said, distinguishes sharply between
the virtue of man simply as man and the virtue of the
citizen. When man is "denatured" by entering the state,
his virtue is still a sentiment and even an intoxication, but
is very far from being cosmopolitan. Rousseau oscillates
between the two types of virtue, that of the man and that
of the citizen, and can scarcely be said to have attempted
a serious mediation between them. According as he wants
the one or the other type of "virtue," he devises different

systems of education. In *Emile*, for example, he sets out to make a man, in the "Considerations on the Government of Poland," a citizen. The love of country and the love of mankind are, he declares, incompatible passions.[4] What is Rousseau's own choice, one may ask, as between an emotional nationalism and an emotional internationalism? On this point no doubt is possible. The love of country he takes to be the more beautiful passion. The virtuous intoxication of the internationalist seems to him pale and ineffectual compared with the virtuous intoxication of the citizen; and herein history has certainly confirmed him. The fact that *l'ivresse patriotique* may make the citizens of one country ruthless in their dealings with the citizens of other countries seems to him a matter of small moment.[5] In his schemes for inbreeding patriotic sentiment, he seems to be looking forward to the type of nationalism that has actually emerged during the last century, especially perhaps in Germany. The question of war becomes acute if Europe, and possibly the world, is thus to be made up of states, each animated by what one is tempted to term a frenzied nationalism, without any countervailing principle of unity. That the new nationalism is more potent than the new internationalism was revealed in August 1914 when millions of socialists, in response to the call of country, marched away to the slaughter of their fellow socialists in other lands. That Protestant unity has likewise proved inadequate seems

---

[4] See *Political Writings* (Vaughan), II, p. 172.
[5] See the opening paragraphs of *Emile* ("Tout patriote est dur aux étrangers," etc.).

sufficiently clear from the fact that the men of the two chief Protestant countries, at the same time that they were blowing one another to pieces with high explosives, sought to starve one another's women and children *en masse*. The papacy again, representing the traditional unity of European civilization, has also shown itself unable to limit effectively the push of nationalism.

Furthermore, nationalities of the kind that have grown up in modern Europe will not, as Rousseau points out, be kept from fighting with one another by treaties and alliances. He warns the Poles that among the Christian nations, treaties and alliances are only scraps of paper, though the Turks, he adds, show a little more respect for their international obligations.

Rousseau had this order of problems forced upon his attention when he made his *Abridgment* (1761) of the Abbé de Saint-Pierre's *Project for Perpetual Peace* (originally published in 1712-17) and wrote his *Judgment* on the *Project* (published in 1782). The Abbé de Saint-Pierre sought to revive the plan for a United States of Europe (*le Grand Dessein*) that Sully attributes to Henry IV. Rousseau shows much shrewdness in reviewing in connection with his editing of Saint-Pierre the problem of peace and war in Europe from the Middle Ages down. One institution, he admits, had done much in the past to lessen political conflicts. It is undeniable, he says, that Europe owes to Christianity above all, even today, the species of union that has survived among its members. He goes on to say, anticipating Heine and following Hobbes, that Rome, having suffered material defeat, sent her dogmas instead of her legions into the provinces. To this spiritual Rome, medieval and modern Europe has owed what small equivalent it has enjoyed of the *Pax romana*. The ultimate binding element in the medieval order was subordination to the divine will and its earthly representatives, notably the pope. The latter Middle Ages and the Renaissance saw a weakening of this principle of union and the rise of great territorial nationalities. According to the school of Grotius, the relations of these nationalities are to be regulated primarily not by will in any sense, but by reason. The Abbé de Saint-Pierre, perhaps the earliest complete French example of the professional philanthropist, has a still more naive confidence in reason. He saw well enough, says Rousseau, how his schemes would work if they were once established, but was childish (and herein he resembled other "reformers" down to the present day) in his notions of the means for getting them established. His fundamental error, Rousseau complains, was in thinking that men are governed by their reason, when they are in reality governed by their passions.[6]

For Rousseau the state of nature is not in any case a state of reason. In his less idyllic moods, he inclines, so far as the relation of nation to nation is concerned, to agree with Hobbes that it is a state of war. As a remedy he seems to favor some such application of the federative principle as a league of nations or a league to enforce peace. He shows, however, a much more lively sense of the perils of such schemes than some of their modern advocates. "It might do more harm at a stroke," he says

---

[6] *Political Writings* (Vaughan), I, p. 392 n.

of a league to enforce peace, "than it could prevent for centuries." Though approving of the "Grand Dessein" of Henry IV, he saw that the driving power behind this scheme was neither Christian, in the medieval sense, nor again, humanitarian, but imperialistic—the desire to abase Spain and the House of Austria, and to exalt France to the hegemony of Europe. Henry IV was preparing a war which was to end war, when his assassination took place, and "banished forever the last hope of the world." Rousseau foresees that the states of Europe are destined to ruin themselves by their military preparations. He leaves us, in short, without any adequate solution of a problem, that of the centrifugal nationality, which he himself was doing so much to intensify.

Though Rousseau can speak on occasion with positive contempt of cosmopolitans, he can be shown to have exercised his main influence on those who began by standing, both nationally and internationally, for fraternity, a fraternity that was to be ideally combined with liberty and equality. We need to trace briefly the imperialistic upshot of this evangel, especially in the French Revolution, and then, turning away from the more peripheral aspects of the relation between democracy and imperialism, to try to get at the root of the whole matter in the psychology of the individual.

Rousseau, we have seen, seeks to discredit not merely a particular aristocracy, but the aristocratic principle in general. "The people," he says, "constitute the human race": all that is not the people is parasitic and "scarcely deserves to be counted were it not for the harm it does." Perhaps no doctrine has ever been more cunningly devised to fill the poor man and the plebeian with self-righteous pride, and at the same time to inflame him with hatred and suspicion of those who enjoy any social or economic superiority. It is a curious fact, known to all students of the period, that those who perhaps did the most to promote Rousseauism, and in general the new philanthropy, were the members of the privileged classes themselves. The causes of this strange phenomenon are complex, but have been traced with sufficient accuracy by Taine in his *Ancien Regime*. The members of the French aristocracy, and that as far back as Richelieu and Louis XIV, had largely ceased to perform the work of an aristocracy. They had become drawing-room butterflies and hangers-on at court. Now the enemy of those who have ceased to work, in some sense or other of the word, has always been ennui; and in addition, the denizens of the drawing-room suffered during the first half of the eighteenth century from rationalistic dryness and an excess of artificial decorum. They finally sought relief in a return to nature and the simple life. An idyllic element had been present in the life of the drawing-room from the start, as all know who have studied the influence of d'Urfé's *Astrée* on the Marquise de Rambouillet and her group; and this perhaps made the way easier for another form of pastoralism. "The fops," as Taine phrases it, "dreamt between two madrigals of the happiness of sleeping naked in the virgin forest." Marie Antoinette milked her own cows and lived the pastoral dream at the Petit Trianon. Many of the nobles and higher clergy, won over to the new enthusiasm, took oath to divest themselves of all the privileges of rank in favor of the new equality which was itself to be only a preliminary to the golden dawn of brotherhood. The advent of this brotherhood was actually celebrated in the Federation of the Champ de Mars (1790) which was meant to symbolize the melting of all Frenchmen together in a fraternal embrace. Anacharsis Cloots, the "orator of humankind," had representatives of the different races and nations of the Earth, each appropriately garbed, parade before the National Assembly as the symbol of a still more universal fraternity. "Never," says the Comte de Ségur, "were more delightful dreams followed by a more terrible awakening." Instead of universal brotherhood there was a growing mania of suspicion. The malady of Rousseau became epidemic, until, at the height of the Terror, men were "suspect of being suspect." The very persons who had rushed into one another's arms at the Federation of the Champ de Mars began to guillotine one another. In the number of those who thus perished was the "orator of humankind." Among the earliest victims were the members of the privileged classes who had been so zealous in promoting the new philanthropy, just as the parlor socialists of our own day would be among the first to suffer if the overturn they are preaching should actually occur. As Chesterton says, if the social revolution takes place, the streets will run red with the blood of philanthropists.

If one wishes to enter into the psychology of the later stages of the Revolution, one should devote special attention to avowed disciples of Rousseau like Robespierre. He adopts in a rather uncompromising form Rousseau's view of "virtue," and so is led to set up an "ideal" France over against the real France, and this "ideal" France is largely a projection of what I have termed the idyllic imagination. The opposition that he established between the virtuous and the vicious is even less an opposition between virtuous and vicious individuals than between whole classes of individuals. The judging of men by their social grouping rather than by their personal merits and demerits, that seemed to Burke so iniquitous, has, as a matter of fact, been implicit in the logic of this movement from the French to the Russian Revolution. Danton already says: "These priests, these nobles are not guilty, but they must die, because they are out of place, interfere with the movement of things, and will stand in the way of the future." Danton, so far as he was responsible for the September Massacres, made some application of this revolutionary logic. Leaders like Robespierre and Saint-Just, however, developed it far more than Danton into a program of wholesale proscription. The actual France was too rich and populous. Robespierre and Saint-Just were ready to eliminate violently whole social strata that seemed to them to be made up of parasites and conspirators, in order that they might adjust this actual France to the Sparta of their dreams; so that the Terror was far more than is commonly realized a bucolic episode.[7] It

---

[7] Cf. Chateaubriand, *Mémoires d'Outre-Tombe*, ii, pp. 12–14: "Tandis que la tragédie rougissait les rues, la bergerie florissait au théâtre; il n'était question que d'innocents pasteurs et de virginales pastourelles: champs, ruisseaux, prairies, moutons, colombes, âge d'or sous le chaume, revivaient aux soupirs, du pipeau devant les roucoulants Tircis et les naïves tricoteuses qui sortaient du spectacle de la guillotine. Si Sanson en avait eu le temps, il aurait joué le rôle de Colin, et Mademoiselle Théroigne de Méricourt celui de Babet. Les Conventionnels se piquaient d'être les plus bénins des hommes: bons pères, bons fils, bons maris, ils menaient promener les petits enfants; ils leur servaient de nourrices; ils pleuraient de tendresse à leurs simples jeux; ils prenaient

lends color to the assertion that has been made that the last stage of sentimentalism is homicidal mania.

In theory, Robespierre is, like Rousseau, rigidly egalitarian. He is not a real leader at all—only the people's "hired man." But at critical moments, in the name of an ideal general will, of which he professes to be only the organ, he is ready to impose tyrannically *his* will on the actual people. The net result of the Rousseauistic movement is thus not to get rid of leadership, but to produce an inferior and even insane type of leadership, and in any case leadership of a highly imperialistic type. This triumph of force can be shown to be the total outcome of liberty, equality, and fraternity in the Rousseauistic sense. Rousseau himself, as we have seen, would force people to be free. The attempt to combine freedom with equality led, and, according to Lord Acton, always will lead, to terrorism. As for Jacobinical fraternity, it has been summed up in the phrase: "Be my brother or I'll kill you." Moreover, the clash of a leader like Robespierre is not only with enemies of the Revolution, but with other more or less sincere revolutionary fanatics whose imaginations are projecting different "ideals." The sole common denominator of leaders thus obstinate, each in the pursuit of a separate dream, is force. The movement had repudiated the traditional controls, and so far as any new principle of cohesion was concerned, had turned out

---

doucement dans leurs bras ces petits agneaux, afin de leur montrer le *dada* des charrettes qui conduisaient les victimes au supplice. Ils chantaient la nature, la paix, la pitié, la bienfaisance, la candeur, les vertus domestiques; ces béats de philanthropie faisaient couper le cou à leurs voisins avec une extrême sensibilité, pour le plus grand bonheur de l'espèce humaine."

to be violently centrifugal. The only brotherhood the Jacobinical leaders had succeeded in founding was, as Taine puts it, a brotherhood of Cains.

Robespierre, however, was not the type of leader finally destined to emerge from the Revolution. As early as 1790 Burke had predicted that the Revolution would turn at last to the profit of some military adventurer. The doctrine of popular sovereignty as developed from the *Social Contract* had been found to encourage a sort of chronic anarchy. Inasmuch as society cannot go on without discipline of some kind, men were constrained, in the absence of any other form of discipline, to turn to discipline of the military type. In the army it was still possible to find the orderly subordination and loyalty to acknowledged merit that the Jacobins had, on principle, been undermining in civil France. Bonaparte is therefore no accident. He is the true heir and executor of the Revolution. After his grenadiers had chased members of the Cinq-Cents through the doors and out of the windows of the Orangerie at Saint-Cloud (18 Brumaire), and when he had revealed himself more and more nakedly as the imperialistic superman, it is not to be supposed that the Jacobins as a body stood aloof. What became apparent, on the contrary, was the affinity that has always existed between an unlimited democracy and the cult of ruthless power. No one crawled more abjectly at the feet of Napoleon than some of the quondam Terrorists. "On the point of becoming barons and counts, the Jacobins spoke only of the horrors of 1793, of the necessity of punishing the proletarians and of repressing popular excesses. From day to day there was taking place the transformation of republicans into imperialists and of the tyranny of all into the despotism of a single man."[8]

Chateaubriand's disapproval of Napoleon was ineffective, one may note in passing, because his head was not in accord with his heart. He was in secret sympathy with Napoleon because of a likeness that he recognized between the Napoleonic quality of imagination and his own. The imaginations of both men were, in a sense that I have sought to define elsewhere, romantic: they were straining, though along very different lines, out toward the unlimited. Victor Hugo, again, denounced Napoleon as the author of the 18 Brumaire, and at the same time was so fascinated by him imaginatively, that he was one of the chief artificers of the Napoleonic legend.

I have been trying to make clear the relation between Rousseauistic democracy and imperialism in France itself. The same relationship appears if we study the Rousseauistic movement internationally. Perhaps no movement since the beginning of the world has led to such an inbreeding of national sentiment of the type that in the larger states runs over very readily into imperialistic ambition. I have said that the Revolution almost from the start took on the character of a universal crusade. The first principles it assumed made practically all existing governments seem illegitimate. The various peoples were invited to overthrow these governments, based upon usurpation, and, having recovered their original rights, to join with France in a glorious fraternity. What followed is almost too familiar to need repetition. Some of the

---

[8] Chateaubriand, *Mémoires d'Outre-Tombe*, II, p. 243.

governments whose legitimacy was thus called into question took alarm and, having entered into an alliance, invaded France.[9] This foreign menace moved France to the
first great burst of national enthusiasm in the modern
sense. The cry of the revolutionary army—*Vive la nation*
—heard by Goethe in a pause of the cannonading of
Valmy—was rightly taken by him to mark the dawn of
a new era.[10] The beginnings of the very type of warfare
we have recently been witnessing in Europe, that is, the
coming together of whole nations for mutual massacre
(*la levée en masse*), go back to this period. The new national enthusiasm supplied France with soldiers so numerous and so spirited that she not only repelled her
invaders, but began to invade other countries in turn,
theoretically on a mission of emancipation. In the actual
stress of events, however, the will to power turned out
to be stronger than the will to brotherhood, and what had
begun as a humanitarian crusade ended in Napoleon and
imperialistic aggression. This aggression awakened in
turn the new national sentiment in various countries, and
did more than all other agencies combined to prepare the
way for a powerful and united Germany.[11] France ceased
to be the "Christ of nations" and became the traitor to

---

[9] Both monarchists and revolutionary idealists had of course other
motives in addition to those they professed. For this whole period, see
E. Bourgeois, *Manuel historique de politique étrangère*, II, pp. 1–184.

[10] According to M. Chuquet, the remark of Goethe to which I refer dates
from 1820 and not from the evening of the battle (September 20, 1792).
See article in *Revue hebdomadaire*, December 18, 1915.

[11] "La Révolution française fut le fait générateur de l'idée de l'unité
allemande." Renan, *Réforme intellectuelle et morale*, p. 130.

humankind universally denounced by the disillusioned radicals of the time, especially after the invason of Switzerland (1798).[12]

Anyone who rejects the humanitarian theory of brotherhood runs the risk of being accused of a lack of fraternal feeling. The obvious reply of the person of critical and experimental temper is that, if he rejects the theory, it is precisely because he desires brotherhood. After an experience of the theory that has already extended over several generations, the world would seem at times to have become a vast seething mass of hatred and suspicion. What Carlyle wrote of the Revolution has not ceased to be applicable: "Beneath this rose-colored veil of universal benevolence is a dark, contentious, hell-on-earth." One is finally led to the conviction that the contrast between the ideal and the real in this movement is not the ordinary contrast between the willingness of the spirit and the weakness of the flesh; that on the contrary this particular field of union among men actually promotes the reality of strife that it is supposed to prevent. One might without being too fanciful establish a sort of synchronism between the prevalence of pacifistic schemes and the actual outbreak of war. The propaganda of the Abbé de Saint-Pierre was followed by the wars of Frederick the Great. The humanitarian movement of the end of the eighteenth century, which found expression in Kant's treatise on "Perpetual Peace," was followed and attended by twenty years of the bloodiest fighting the

---

[12] See Coleridge's *France: An Ode.* For corresponding German developments, see G. P. Gooch, *Germany and the French Revolution, passim.*

world has ever known. The pacifist agitation of the early twentieth century, that found outer expression in the Peace Palace at The Hague, was succeeded by battle lines hundreds of miles long. The late M. Boutroux, whom no one will accuse of being a cynic, said to a reporter of the *Temps* in 1912 that from the amount of peace talk abroad, he inferred that the future was likely to be "supremely warlike and bloody." In the matter of war and peace, as elsewhere, the humanitarian, to be sure, has an ever-ready explanation for all the failures of his theory to work: it would, he insists, have worked beautifully if it had not been for this or that conspiracy. Nothing short of the suicide of the planet would avail to convince certain humanitarians that anything is wrong with their theory—and even then, the last surviving humanitarian would no doubt continue to moan "conspiracy."

From a strictly psychological point of view, the movement we are studying had not only produced all its characteristic fruits over a hundred years ago, but also its two outstanding and truly significant personalities—Rousseau and Napoleon. If there had been no Rousseau, Napoleon is reported to have said, there would have been no Revolution, and without the Revolution, *I* should have been impossible. Now Rousseau may be regarded as being more than any other one person the humanitarian Messiah. Napoleon, for his part, may be defined, in Hardy's phrase, as the Christ of War. So that the humanitarian Messiah set in motion forces that led by a process that I have attempted to sketch in rough general outline to the rise of a Christ of War.

A remarkable feature of the humanitarian movement, on both its sentimental and utilitarian sides, has been

its preoccupation with the lot of the masses. "All institutions," says Condorcet, for example, "ought to have for
their aim the physical, intellectual, and moral ameliora-
tion of the poorest and most numerous class." But on the
utilitarian no less than on the sentimental side of the
movement, the contrast between the ideal and the real
is so flagrant as to suggest some central omission in humanitarian psychology. If the Rousseauist set up an ideal
of universal brotherhood that led actually to universal
conscription, the utilitarian for his part has put prime
emphasis on material organization and efficiency and so,
with the aid of physical science, has gradually built up
an enormous mass of interlocking machinery which was,
in theory, to serve humanity and promote the greatest
good of the greatest number, but has in practice been
pressed into the service of the will to power of individuals
and social groups and nationalities. As a result of the
coming together of the various factors I have enumerated,
war has become almost inconceivably maleficent. The
chief victims have been the very masses whom both Rousseauist and Baconian have professed themselves so eager
to benefit. The clashes between states and coalitions of
states have, under existing conditions, become clashes between Frankenstein monsters. One should recollect that
the Frankenstein monster was not, as is commonly supposed, a soulless monster. On the contrary, as depicted
by Mrs. Shelley, he is, in the Rousseauistic sense, a beautiful soul—possibly as a result of having learned to read
from works like the *Sorrows of Werther*.[13] He becomes
ruthless only when the beauty of his soul and his yearn-

---

[13] See *Frankenstein, or The Modern Prometheus*, chap. 15.

ings for sympathy are unappreciated by others and he is forced back into psychic solitude. Here again the last stage of sentimentalism is homicidal mania.

The whole Occident, and increasingly, indeed, the whole world, is now faced with a similar problem as to the quality of the "soul" that animates the vast mechanism of material efficiency, to the building up of which the Occident has for several generations past been devoting its main effort. Is this "soul" a Rousseauistic or a genuinely ethical "soul"? One is tempted to define the civilization (or what we are pleased to term such) that has been emerging with the decline of the traditional controls as a mixture of altruism and high explosives. If anything is amiss with the altruism, the results may prove to be rather serious. The idealists affirm either that man is so lovely in his natural self that he needs no control at all, or else that he can be induced to exercise the necessary control with reference to the good of his fellows. Everything hinges, in either case, on the presence in the natural man of an element of love or will to service that is of itself a sufficient counterpoise to the natural man's will to power. Here is the dividing line between egoists and altruists, and not merely in the appeal to utility. The principle of the greatest good of the greatest number is, as has been pointed out, asserted by Machiavelli himself.[14]

Now the facts in this debate as to the relative strength in the natural man of the will to brotherhood and the will to power seem, on an impartial survey, to favor the Machiavellians rather than the "idealists." Those who

---

[14] See *Mandragola*, act 3, scene 4. The application of the principle in this particular passage is, however, ironical.

so pride themselves on being forward-looking should have a special cult for Machiavelli. He has claims to be regarded as the most successful of all the forward-lookers. In the phrase of Gervinus, "he guessed the spirit of modern history." The last war has been correctly described as a "return of Machiavelli." But with the progress that science has made, and is constantly making in "improving the mystery of murder," so that it is already possible apparently to destroy great cities in a few minutes from the air, it should be evident even to the most obtuse that we cannot afford to allow Machiavelli to return. One or two more such returns on a large scale will, under existing conditions, mean the end of white civilization, and possibly of the white race itself. A gross and palpable error of the era that is just closing has been its confusion of mechanical and material progress with moral progress. Physical science is excellent in its own place, but when supreme moral issues are involved, it is, as has been rightly remarked, only a multiplying device.[15] If there is rightness at the center, it will no doubt multiply the rightness. If, on the other hand, there is any central error, the peripheral repercussion, with men bound together as they are at present, will be terrific. With the development of inventions like the radio and the wireless telephone, the whole world is becoming, in a very literal sense, a whispering-gallery. It is hardly necessary to dilate on what is likely to follow if the words that are whispered are words of hatred and suspicion. An increasing material union among men who remain spiritually centrifugal

---

[15] This point has been well made by Mr. J. Middleton Murry in his essay "The Nature of Civilization" (*The Evolution of an Intellectual*, p. 168).

means a return of Machiavelli, a triumph in other words of the law of cunning and the law of force, on a scale to which the past has seen no parallel. Superlatives are dangerous things, but one is perhaps justified in describing the present situation as one of unexampled gravity.

In dealing with democracy and the special type of fraternity it has preached, as related to imperialism, I have thus far been confining myself for the most part to the national and international phases of this relationship. It is time to fulfill my promise, and, working in from the periphery toward the center, seek to get at the root of the whole matter in the psychology of the individual. For behind all imperialism is ultimately the imperialistic individual, just as behind all peace is ultimately the peaceful individual.

I have already made a distinction of the first importance for the study of the question of war or peace in terms of the individual, and that is the distinction between the traditional Christian conception of liberty, which implies spiritual subordination, and the Rousseauistic conception which, whether we take it in the no-state of the *Second Discourse* or the all-state of the *Social Contract*, is resolutely egalitarian. At the end of his "Prometheus Unbound" Shelley has portrayed in the very spirit of the *Second Discourse* the paradise that is to result from the abolition of the traditional subordinations and inequalities:

> The loathsome mask has fallen, the man remains
> Scepterless, free, uncircumscribed, but man
> Equal, unclassed, tribeless and nationless,
> Exempt from awe, worship, degree.

But on any attempt to carry out this program, the enormous irony and contradiction at the very heart of this movement becomes manifest. It leads one to break down standards in the real world in favor of purely chimerical ideals. For what actually follows the attempt to establish egalitarian liberty, we need to turn from Shelley to Shakespeare:

> Take but degree away, untune that string,
> And, hark, what discord follows! each thing meets
> In mere oppugnancy: . . . .
> . . . .
> Then every thing includes itself in power,
> Power into will, will into appetite.

This last line reminds one of a remark of Jeremy Taylor that, in the absence of ethical control, "men know no good but to please a wild, indetermined, infinite appetite." The word infinite adds an essential idea. Other animals have appetite, but within certain definite bounds, whereas man is, either in good or bad sense, the infinite animal. Machiavelli is very metaphorical when he speaks of his prince as combining the virtues of the lion and the fox. The lion and the fox do not put forth their power or cunning beyond what is needed for the satisfaction of their actual physical wants. They do not strive to set up a vulpine or leonine empire over other animals. One cannot truthfully say of them, as Carlyle says of his boot-black, that, if given half the universe, they will soon be quarreling with the owner of the other half. To be sure, as Swift remarks,

> Now and then
> Beasts may degen'rate into men.

But, as a rule, the man who is infinite after the fashion of Carlyle's boot-black is in a fair way to become not beastly, but fiendish. As a result of his infinitude, man is almost necessarily either better or worse than other animals. His prime need is not, as in the case of other animals, to satisfy certain limited physical wants, but to keep in good conceit with himself. Now it is of the essence of conceit, a word which, as once used, was synonymous with imagination in general, and as now used is nearly related to the egocentric type of imagination, to strain out toward the unlimited. This conceit is, it is to be feared, closely associated in unregenerate man with envy and jealousy of anyone whose conceit seems to set up rival pretensions to his own. Conceit also determines largely man's attitude toward the truth. Truth according to the natural law he welcomes because it ministers to his power or comfort and in any case piques his wonder and curiosity. Spiritual truth is less welcome because it diminishes his conceit. Truth in this sense, as Goethe says, is less congenial to human nature than error, because it imposes limitations, whereas error does not. Tell the average person that some one is planning to get into wireless communication with Mars, or to shoot a rocket at the moon, and he is all respectful interest and attention at once. Tell him, on the contrary, that he needs, in the interest of his own happiness, to walk in the path of humility and self-control, and he will be indifferent, or even actively resentful.

Man's conceit, and the tendency toward unlimited expansion that it gives to the impulses of the natural man, is of various types. Perhaps as good a classification as any of the main types is that of the three lusts distinguished by traditional Christianity—the lust of knowledge, the lust of sensation, and the lust of power. It is interesting to study the lust of power as it has appeared in the conquerors and great military adventurers of history. Saint-Evremond has made some penetrating observations on this form of imperialistic psychology in his "Dissertation on the Word Vast." The vastness that the great dominators have displayed in their projects and ambitions is due, as he points out, to the quality of their imaginations. The outward straining of the imagination toward the unlimited Saint-Evremond takes to be the weakness and not the strength of a Pyrrhus, an Alexander and a Richelieu. It is a pity that Saint-Evremond was not able to extend his scrutiny to a Napoleon. Napoleon plainly displayed two entirely different types of "vision": in dealing with the natural order, in planning a battle, for instance, he showed himself capable of a tremendous concentration upon the facts; but in his political ambitions, where factors of a more purely human order came into play, he revealed an inability to limit his imagination that was destined sooner or later to result in disaster. The coming together of the two kinds of vision I have just defined gives a type with which we have become very familiar, not only in our political and military, but in our commercial leaders—that of the efficient megalomaniac. A surprising number of these leaders have been, in intention at least, supermen, and little Napoleons.

Assuming that Napoleon's imagination is of the general type that Saint-Evremond ascribes to various great dominators of the past, we still have to explain, if we are to understand the triumph of the imperialistic push for power over Rousseauistic idealism, why a Napoleon so captivates the imagination of other men; for this sort of leader would evidently be helpless unless he had many accomplices. The Rousseauist, I have said, breaks down traditional controls without setting up new ones. What emerges in the many men who have as a result lapsed to the naturalistic level is not the will to brotherhood, but the will to power; so that in this sense the Rousseauist is actually promoting what he is in theory seeking to prevent. For what follows we need to make an application of Freudian psychology to a *libido* even more fundamental perhaps than the *libido* with which the Freudians themselves have thus far been chiefly concerned— namely, the *libido dominandi*. In a naturalistic era, the average man finds himself more or less in the state of Carlyle's boot-black, but is at the same time hampered on every side and kept from expanding freely along the lines of power, and is thus diminished in his conceit of himself. He suffers from repressed and thwarted desire. But what he is unable to get directly, he may secure vicariously. At this point one begins to perceive the meaning of Hardy's description of Napoleon as the Christ of War. The spell that Napoleon exercised was not merely over the former Jacobins of whom Chateaubriand speaks, but over the French masses. Let one reflect on the way these masses rallied to him on the return from Elba, and that, too, after he had wrought them almost incalculable evil:

> Bien, dit-on, qu'il nous ait nui,
> Le peuple encore le révère, etc.

I have said that to look on the state of Burke with its
ethical leadership as merely "pooled self-esteem" is misleading. The phrase has a certain relevancy, however,
when applied to the state that is under Napoleonic leadership. The intrusion of this imperialistic element is
strong not only in all secular establishments, but also in
the churches of the world, if only because these churches,
however immaculate they may be in theory, are administered by human beings. It is not easy to overlook
this element in the papacy, even though one does not
go so far as to say roundly with Tyrrell: "Rome cares
nothing for religion—only for power." The very divin-
ities that men have set up often impress one as being in
a considerable measure their pooled self-esteem. "We are
glad," as Dryden says, "to have God on our side to maul
our enemies, when we cannot do the work ourselves."
Jonathan Edwards has genuine religious elevation; but the
Jehovah in whose "fierceness" he plainly rejoices, and
who tramples sinners under his feet until their blood is
"sprinkled on his garments," might lead some to dismiss
Edwards as a theological imperialist. A more unmistak-
able example is that of certain members of the group of
Fundamentalists that has recently been dividing the Bap-
tist denomination, who have depicted Christ in his second
coming in colors that make Nero and Caligula seem respectable. One scarcely need dilate on the fact that
Christ was in his first coming a deep disappointment to
the Jewish populace; the Messiah they had hoped for was
far nearer to Napoleon than to the Messiah they actually
received.

It goes without saying that the imperialistic element

I have noted in religious beliefs, as well as in those who administer them, is not the whole story. Above all, it is not the whole story in the case of Christianity. Christianity has actually done more to curb the expansive lusts of the human heart, and among its other lusts, the lust for power. As Dante puts it, "men wandering wild in their bestiality," have a need of a twofold control: "that of the highest pontiff to lead them according to revelation to eternal life, and that of the emperor to lead them according to the traditions of philosophy to temporal felicity."[16] Of course the reality never coincided exactly with Dante's ideal. From his tremendous diatribes against the self-seeking rulers of his time, one might infer that Europe then was almost as mad as it certainly is today. At the same time Christianity in its medieval form actually did secure for Europe no small degree of spiritual unity and cohesion, and even when there was disunion, it was not rendered infinitely maleficent, as it is now, by the concomitant circumstance that those who were spiritually at variance were bound up together materially.

Now I scarcely need repeat what I have said here and elsewhere that the loss of this older European unity was due to the rise of what one may describe, in the most general sense, as the critical spirit, which has in turn been identical with the spirit of individualism. To be modern has meant practically to be increasingly positive and critical, to refuse to receive anything on an authority "anterior, exterior, and superior" to the individual. With those who still cling to the principle of outer au-

---

[16] *De Monarchia*, III, chap. 16.

thority I have no quarrel. I am not primarily concerned with them. I am myself a thoroughgoing individualist, writing for those who are, like myself, irrevocably committed to the modern experiment. In fact, so far as I object to the moderns at all, it is because they have not been sufficently modern, or, what amounts to the same thing, have not been sufficiently experimental. In the field of the natural law, those who have gone in for modernity evidently satisfy my test in no small measure. The substitution of positive observation for what seemed to a Bacon, for instance, the apriorism and verbal subtleties and servile leaning upon authority of the schoolmen has actually led to the fruits anticipated. But the apostles of modernity have not been content merely to minister to man's power and utility. They have also professed to have a substitute for the spiritual unity of the older order, and here, when tried experimentally, that is, according to their own principles, they have, as I have tried to show, failed disastrously. The results of the material success and spiritual failure of the modern movement are before us. It is becoming obvious to every one that the power of Occidental man has run very much ahead of his wisdom. The outlook might be more cheerful if there were any signs that Occidental man is seeking seriously to make up his deficiency on the side of wisdom. On the contrary, he is reaching out almost automatically for more and more power. If he succeeds in releasing the stores of energy that are locked up in the atom—and this seems to be the most recent ambition of our physicists—his final exploit may be to blow himself off the planet. We are told that our means of destruction are growing so terrible that no one will venture to use them—the same argument that was heard before the War. But at the same time that we are heaping up these means of destruction, the breakdown of the traditional controls combined with the failure thus far to supply any adequate substitute, is creating fools and madmen who will not hesitate to use them.

It would sometimes seem, indeed, that what wisdom we still have is a survival. One can at least understand the point of view of those who decide to stand in the ancient ways and to assume towards much of what is deemed progressive nowadays an attitude frankly reactionary. One may even catch the point of view of the ultramontane Catholic, as set forth by Pius IX in the eightieth article of the Syllabus (1864): "If any one says that the pope can and should be reconciled and make terms with progress, with liberalism and modernist civilization, let him be anathema."

It is, however, possible to admit that some vital element dropped out in the passage from the medieval to the modern era, or, what amounts to the same thing, from outer authority to individualism, and still remain a modern. But in that case one should make clear that to be a thoroughgoing modern is not such a simple matter as is sometimes assumed. I am myself fond of insisting that man is subject not to one, but to two laws; and that to be completely modern, one must be positive and critical, not merely according to the natural, but also according to the human law. Those who have piqued themselves on modernity have thus far been for the most part persons who have been more or less critical according to the natural law, and then have pieced out their incomplete survey of the facts by various rationalistic devices, or else by idyllic imagining. In the realm of the human law, the nineteenth century, so far as it stood for a radical break with tradition, was, on the one hand, an age of rationalism, on the other, an age of romantic dreaming. He who has broken with traditions in this fashion should, in my judgment, be called, not a modern but a modernist. The term modern should be reserved for the person who is seeking to be critical according to both the human and the natural law. Anyone who attempts such a task will find it necessary to give a much wider meaning to the word experiment than has of late been usual: it should be extended to cover not merely the kind of experimenting that goes on in a laboratory, but also the experimenting with various philosophies of life that has gone on in the remote as well as in the near past. To be sure, the man who turns nowadays to the past for instruction is likely to be regarded as more or less a reactionary. A more familiar type is that of the progressive who has repudiated the past, barely tolerates the present, and is at home imaginatively only in that vast, windy abode, the future. Yet Goethe speaks not as a reactionary, but as a person of keenly experimental temper, when he says that we should oppose to the "aberrations of the hour the masses of universal history." As a result of the toil of innumerable investigators, these masses of universal history are becoming fairly accessible to us from the era of the Fighting States in ancient China (third century B.C.) to the era of the fighting states in contemporary Europe. But one must grant that there are great, if not insurmountable difficulties in turn-

ing to account these records of the past, and in building
up from them standards with which to judge the "aberrations of the hour." The obvious difficulty is the element
of truth contained in the saying that history never repeats itself. If this were the whole truth, if history were
only a whirl of unrelated happenings that did not exhibit
the workings of any central human law, one would have
a right to dismiss any attempt to judge the present in the
light of past experience with the dictum of Henry Ford
or some more elegant equivalent: "History is bunk." But
though it is true that history never repeats itself, it is
about equally true that history is always repeating itself;
and this is a part of the paradox of life itself which does
not give up here an element of oneness, and there an element of change, but a oneness that is always changing.
This implication of unity in diversity is the scandal of
reason, and philosophers have, for the most part, ever
since the Greeks, been seeking with the aid of reason to
abstract the unity from the diversity, or else, by similar
rationalizing processes, to stress the diversity at the expense of the unity. Practically all the philosophers who
now have the "cry" belong, it is scarcely necessary to
add, to the latter class. But the complete positivist will
insist that wisdom is found in mediation between the
constant and the variable factors in human experience.
His objection to the unity that the Rousseauist proposes
to establish among men through the diffusion of love and
sympathy is that it is illusory. If it were only possible
to oppose to this unreal unity, a mere chimera of the
romantic imagination, some firm and fast unity, purged
of illusion with the aid of reason, and tucked away once

for all into formulas, our problem would be very easy. The man who faces life as it actually is, however, will not admit that it is possible thus to eliminate the element of illusion. To recognize this element is not to be oneself an illusionist, but on the contrary a keen observer. It is in the role that they attribute to illusion that the wisdom of the great poets, of a Shakespeare or a Sophocles, for example, is most manifest. I have tried to show elsewhere[17] how closely related this problem of illusion is to the problem of the imagination. The final contrast is not between reason or judgment and mere illusion, but between the imagination that is disciplined to what abides in the midst of the changeful and the illusory, and the imagination that is more or less free to wander wild in some "empire of chimeras."

The true vision of the disciplined imagination is needful if one is to profit by experience, a task that becomes increasingly difficult according as the experience involved is one's own experience or that of one's contemporaries or that of the near or remote past. Vision of this type would seem to be depressingly rare, and yet without it men run the risk, and that often when they are most filled with the conceit of their own progressiveness, of simply "committing the oldest sins the newest kind of ways." Experience, we are told, keeps a hard school, but fools will learn in no other; it is a rather wise fool, one is sometimes inclined to think, who can learn even from his own experience, not to speak of the experience of others.

But to return to our more immediate topic: evidently

---

[17] See Introduction to *Rousseau and Romanticism*.

the type of vision that can bring to bear the experience of the remoter past upon our democratic-imperialistic era is not easy to attain, but seems very necessary if one is to appeal to history at all. For one has to go rather far back to find any close parallel to our present imbroglio. Various persons have pointed out the analogy between the Great War and its psychological background and the period of the Peloponnesian War in Greece; and this analogy is helpful provided it can be used with sufficient caution. The period of the Peloponnesian War was, like our own, a period of commercial and imperialistic expansion; and this expansion was accompanied, especially at Athens, by an increasing trend toward an egalitarian democracy.[18] Like our own age, it was an age of "intellectuals" who were repudiating the traditional disciplines, largely in virtue of the opposition they had established between nature and convention. If negatively this cult of nature meant revolt against everything prescriptive and established, positively it meant, on the one hand, admiration for the superman, and on the other, sympathy for the weak, though this latter element was far less marked in ancient than in modern naturalism. It is hard to study the sophists of that time without being reminded of our own philosophers of the flux, or, in the phrase of Aristophanes, votaries of the God Whirl. Persons were not lacking in ancient Athens who saw the perils of this anarchical individualism.

---

[18] The typical democratic-imperialistic statesman of this age is Pericles. For a sense of the dangers of the policy of Athenian expansion and also of the importance of union among the Greeks, one has to turn to conservatives of the type of Cimon.

Some, like Aristophanes, were simply for getting back to the "good old times," and refused to distinguish between Socrates and an ordinary sophist. Socrates, however, it is hardly necessary to say, along with Plato and Aristotle and lesser disciples, was in reality seeking to build up, in lieu of the crumbling traditional standards, standards more in accord with the critical spirit. The Socratic effort was on the whole a failure, especially in the political field. The causes of this failure are complex. I will presently point out what seem to me serious omissions in the Socratic philosophy itself: and then, too, it may be maintained without paradox that Occidental civilization is still suffering from the failure, even from the time of the wily Odysseus, of the Greek character to measure up to the Greek mind.[19] If the Hellenes could only get together, says Aristotle, they might hold their own against the world. Unfortunately, they could never get together. Even when a political tradition that was in its essence identical with religion still bound together the citizens of the various city-states, these states were largely centrifugal as regards one another for the very reason that each state had different gods. With the breakdown of these politico-religious traditions and the failure to work out on Socratic or other lines some equivalent for the spiritual controls they supplied, the citizens of each city-state tended to become centrifugal not only with reference to the citizens of other city-

---

[19] Cicero, whom no one will accuse of being an enemy of the Greeks, has a passage on this subject that may be regarded as definitive. See his *Oratio pro L. Valerio Flacco*, IV.

states, but with reference to one another. There followed all the abominable incidents of class war. At Miletus, for example, the poor got the upper hand and forced the rich to flee from the city. But afterward, regretting that they had not been able to kill them, they took their children, gathered them together in barns, and had them trampled under the feet of oxen. The rich afterward returned to the city and became masters again. They took in their turn the children of the poor, covered them with pitch, and burned them alive.[20] This is the kind of thing of which our modern world has already had a substantial first installment from the French to the Russian Revolution. The decadent Greeks, like those who are preaching a class war in our own day, employed many fine phrases, but the law that actually tended to prevail was the law of force. This force was finally supplied, as frequently happens in such cases, from without, first by Macedon and then by Rome. On this final submission to an imperialistic autocrat, the decadent Greek consoled himself for what would have seemed to a Greek of the great period a deep degradation by the somewhat shabby fiction that he was submitting, not to a man, but to a god.

Any summary of the kind I have been attempting is necessarily very misleading. Nothing will take the place of a firsthand knowledge of the sources, above all of Plato, Aristotle, and Thucydides. Anyone can convince himself of the startling relevancy to existing conditions of Aristotle's *Politics* in particular, especially now that we have begun in this country to slip our constitutional moorings and to drift toward a direct or un-

---

[20] See Athenaeus, XII, 26.

limited democracy. There are passages that are as modern as the morning newspaper, and at least a hundred times more sensible. Rome later ran through a somewhat similar cycle: a constitutional republic resting ultimately on religious control gradually gave way with the weakening of this control to an egalitarian democracy which in turn passed over with the usual incidents of class war into a decadent imperialism. The imperialistic upshot of an unbridled individualism might also be illustrated from the crumbling of the feudal system in ancient China and the resulting era of the Fighting States to which I have already alluded. Some of the philosophy of this time, that of Mei-ti,[21] for example, exhibits a mingling of utilitarian and sentimental elements which is closer, perhaps, to our contemporary humanitarianism than anything to be found in Greece or Rome. Toward the end, when everything had been tried, including the balance of power, universal brotherhood, and a "league of nations," and after the perpetration of horrors unspeakable, no one apparently had any more illusions: the only question was which imperialistic leader should first succeed in imposing his will on all the others.

Evidently the outlook for our Western civilization, if

---

[21] A German translation of Mei-ti (with a laudatory introduction) has recently been published by Alfred Forke. It should be noted that *jên*, the virtue on which the Confucian puts his final emphasis, though usually rendered by "benevolence" or some such term, is something very different from altruism. This should be plain from the uncompromising hostility of Mencius to Mei-ti. The exaltation of *jên* is simply the Confucian way of affirming that love is the fulfillment of the law. Inasmuch as *jên* manifests itself on the humanistic rather than on the religious level, the nearest Western equivalent is probably the treatment of friendship by Aristotle in the *Nicomachean Ethics* (bks. 8–9).

it reaches this last stage of the imperialistic cycle through which it is now apparently running, is not cheerful, especially in view of the progress that physical science is constantly making in "improving the mystery of murder." North America, and to a considerable degree, South America, it is scarcely necessary to say, belong to the same cultural group as the states of western Europe. All the states of this group are now exhibiting in various forms and varying degrees the symptoms of an unduly centrifugal individualism. The outside world, that frequently has the last word under these circumstances, may, in view of the present facilities of communication, be taken to include all the rest of mankind, especially the great rival cultures of Asia. Now the more powerful states of the cultural group I have just defined are not only imperialistic in their attitude toward one another, but also supremely imperialistic in their attitude toward the outlying peoples and cultures. It is hard to see that the states that are supposed to be democratically ruled are very different in this matter from the rest. As early as 1790 Mirabeau warned the French enthusiasts that "free peoples are more eager for war, and democracies more the slaves of their passions than the most absolute autocracies." This is true in the obvious political sense not only in Europe, but in other parts of the world. Republican France, for example, has been reaching out eagerly for an African and Asiatic empire. But there is a type of imperialistic expansion even more important, perhaps, than this obvious political kind, and frequently leading up to it, and that is the imperialistic expansion of the commercialist. It has been said that trade follows the flag, but an even more significant truth is that the flag tends to follow trade: let one consider the origins of the British Empire in India. It is hardly necessary at this day to refute the notion held by so many liberals of the eighteenth and nineteenth centuries that trade is in itself a pacific agency. Commercial interests lead to clashes and dangerous rivalries between European nations, not merely in Europe itself, but in other parts of the world. Thus a chief aspect of imperialism at the present time is the international scramble for oil. One may read in a recent issue of a responsible French publication that "for the success of their projects, Lord Cowdray and Lord Curzon are capable of fomenting revolutions in Mexico, of sowing civil war in Asia, and, in order to crush a rival, of setting fire to Europe and the world! Their imperialism is a universal danger, but is not lacking in grandeur."[22] In my view the leaders of contemporary England are not quite so Machiavellian, but the view I have just cited is widely held in France, and scarcely leads to the confidence that is the necessary basis of harmonious relations between France and England. This issue of oil might even under certain circumstances lead to severe tension between England and America.

It is becoming more and more evident that the chief problem raised by all this imperialistic expansion is that of the relations between Asia and the Occident. There are possibilities in the present situation that may lead to the real world war, that between the East and West, a

---

[22] See *La Vie des peuples*, vol. 7, p. 195.

war to which the recent European struggle is likely to
seem in retrospect but a faint prelude. It does not on the
face of it appear probable that Europeans can hope in
the long run to enjoy the luxury of slaughtering one
another by the most recent and refined methods of scientific efficiency and at the same time inflict their imperialism and racial swagger on about nine hundred millions
of Asiatics; especially as Asiatics have an opportunity
of observing the imperialistic rivalries and almost in-
curable divisions of European powers, not only in Europe, but on the soil of Asia itself. The possibilities of
which I have spoken may not develop in a day. But
then, as Confucius remarks, "the man who does not take
far views will have near troubles," and it is surely time
to attempt this long-range view of our relations with the
Orient, especially perhaps with the land of Confucius
himself.

Now the Asiatic problem, when considered from the
political point of view, breaks up into various minor
problems. There is, for example, the problem of the
Near East which has been gravely mismanaged, largely,
it would seem, as the result of the inability of England
and France to come to a decent understanding. There is
again the problem of India. There is also the problem of
the United States in its relations with the Far East, with
the possibility in the offing of a gigantic struggle for the
empire of the Pacific. One encounters here the portent
of Japan, an Asiatic power that is learning to play the
imperialistic game along the most approved Occidental
lines, that is even learning to adapt to its own uses the
humanitarian-imperialistic cant of the "white man's

burden," and is beginning to speak of China as "Japan's burden."

Finally, most important of all, perhaps, there is the problem of Russia, a country geographically astride of Europe and Asia, and psychologically, so far as a great part of its population is concerned, at least as Asiatic as it is European. With the extermination of impoverishment of its upper classes, the psychic gap between Russia and western Europe is becoming more accentuated. The Bolshevist Revolution, which can be shown to derive in its underlying principles from the great French Revolution, has been even more virulently imperialistic than French Jacobinism. Russia is likely to remain for some time to come a fertile field of imperialistic intrigue, not only on the part of Russians, but also of Germans and Japanese, and perhaps of Turks, with the whole Moslem world in the background. Just as certain Greeks were ready to ally themselves with the extra-Hellenic world against other Greeks, so Germany in her desire to get even might be tempted to join with these extra-European forces, even though such action on her part would amount to a betrayal of the vital interests of the cultural group to which she herself belongs.

Considerations of this kind are, however, highly speculative at best, even though the person who indulges in them has a competency in the political field to which I make no claim. It is, as a matter of fact, no part of my method to deal directly with the political problem. This method is, in intention at least, purely psychological. When one approaches psychologically the question of Europe versus Asia, and takes a sufficiently long-range view, a striking fact forces itself on one's attention: the principle of true spiritual cohesion among men that the Greco-Roman world was unable to supply—for the Stoical attempt to achieve such a principle was on the whole a failure—came at last from a faith of Oriental origin—namely, Christianity. Cardinal Newman relates in his *Apologia* that what turned him as much as any one thing to Catholicism was a Latin maxim which affirms that the whole world is sound in its judgments (*Securus judicat orbis terrarum*). Now, strictly speaking, this maxim seems less favorable to the Catholic and his ultimate appeal to outer authority than to the man who seeks to deal with life experimentally. If one uses the maxim in this positive spirit, one has to insist, first of all, that the Asiatic experience that led to the rise of Christianity is only part of the total experience of Asia. To regard Europe and a small portion of Asia as together constituting the *orbis terrarum* is merely a form of our Occidental conceit and arrogance. It is to leave out of one's survey the experience of about half of the human race. In this age of universal and facile communication, it would seem especially desirable to bring together the two halves of human experience. A chief obstacle to the right interpretation of the experience of the Far East has been the fact that those who have undertaken the task have suffered not only from inadequate knowledge, but have also frequently worn theological blinders. A more serious form of narrowness today is that of the man who judges the total experience of the world, both East and West, from the point of view of a merely mechanical progress. An estimate of this total experience that is based on adequate knowledge, and is at the same time free from dogmatic preoccupations of any kind, will, I believe, flash a vivid light on the predicament into which we have been led by our one-sided naturalism. It will aid us to a purely psychological definition of the vital factor that has plainly tended to drop out in the passage from medieval to modern Europe. It will thus help us to recover and maintain this vital factor not merely in the form of "old prejudices and unreasoned habits"—the attempt to do so is, I said, the weakness of the method of Burke—but in a positive and critical form, a form, in other words, in closer accord with the modern spirit.

CHAPTER 5

Europe and Asia

Writers of books of criticism during the neo-classical period were fond of refining on the idea of decorum; at times they developed this idea on what one may term a continental scale and contrasted the decorous or typical European with the decorous or typical Asiatic. Speculations of this kind are not as fantastic as they at first sight appear. One may not only become aware of some underlying divergence in the temper of the Asiatic as compared with that of the European, but, to some extent, formulate it. In speaking, however, of Asia it is even more important than in speaking of Europe to make clear that one has in mind primarily civilized Asia, and civilized Asia at the top of its achievement. The hordes of barbaric or semibarbaric Asia have not only menaced or actually overrun Europe in the past (as they may very well do again in the future), but have also been from remote times the scourge of civilized Asia. In ancient Judaea the memory of these wild northern riders lingered in the legends of Gog and Magog. The great Wall of China is a sort of visible symbol of the separation between the two Asias. On the one hand is the Asia of Attila and Tamerlane and Genghis Khan; on the other, the Asia of Christ and Buddha and Confucius.

The mention of Christ and Buddha (of Confucius as a typical Asiatic I shall have more to say presently) is hardly necessary to remind us that it is the distinction of Asia as compared with Europe and other parts of the world to have been the mother of religions; so that if one were to work out a critical and experimental definition of religion (and my method requires nothing less), one might be put on the track of what is specifically Asiatic in the Asiatic attitude toward life. Of course, historical Christianity is far from being a purely Asiatic faith. It contains important elements drawn from Greek philosophy—Platonic, Aristotelian, Stoical, Neoplatonic; also a strong Roman element, especially what I have described as Roman imperialistic organization, not to speak of sacramental magic and elements drawn from the mystery cults, which are of mixed origin but still largely Greek. What elements in Christianity may be referred back to the Founder? We have Christ's own authorization for dealing with this question experimentally ("By their fruits ye shall know them"). Now Bacon and the utilitarians have also preached a gospel of fruits, but the fruits that Christ has in mind are plainly not of the Baconian type. They are the fruits of the spirit, and what these fruits are, Saint Paul has told us once for all: "Love, joy, peace, long-suffering, kindness, goodness, faith, mildness, self-control." The equivalent of this list in its total emphasis will not be found in any European cult or philosophy that antedates Christianity. It is possible, however, to find the equivalent in the older religious thought of Asia. About the middle of the third century before Christ, the Buddhist ruler of India, Asoka, had a very similar list of virtues carved in stone at various points throughout his vast empire: "Compassion, liberality, truth, purity, gentleness, peace, joyousness, saintliness, self-control."[1] Thus Buddhism and Christianity, which often seem to be almost hopelessly at variance when approached from the point of view of dogma, confirm one another in this striking fashion when studied experimentally and in their fruits.

If we wish to define religion adequately, we need perhaps to take a further step and inquire which of the various fruits of the spirit enumerated by Saint Paul and Asoka is most central in the truly religious life. This central virtue seems to have been overlooked by Matthew Arnold in a definition of religion that has at least the merit of being experimental: "Religion is," he says, "morality touched by emotion." Though religion normally leads through morality and, at least in its earlier stages, is very much mixed up with emotion, the final emphasis, if we are to believe the great religious leaders themselves,

---

[1] The question arises as to the influence of the older religion on Christianity. Much has been asserted on this subject and little or nothing proved. All we know positively is that Asoka sent out missionaries to Syria, Egypt, Cyrene, Macedonia, and Epirus. As to the results of this missionary effort we are not informed. A translation of the different inscriptions will be found in *Asoka* by Vincent A. Smith (2d ed., 1909).

is elsewhere. "My peace I give unto you," said Christ on his final parting with his disciples. "Come unto me, all ye that labor and are heavy-laden, and I will give you rest." Buddha conceives of the fulfillment of religion in very similar fashion: "His thought is quiet, quiet are his word and deed, when he has obtained freedom by true wisdom, when he has thus become a quiet man."[2] And what is the pathway to this peace? Dante has caught the inmost spirit of Christianity in his reply to this question: "In his will is our peace." This idea that man needs to submit his ordinary self to a higher or divine will is essential not merely to Christianity, but to all genuine religion. Muhammad is at one here with Buddha and Christ. The very word Islam means submission.

In India, though the same preoccupation with the will has prevailed, the will to which man subordinates his ordinary self is often conceived, not as a divinity that transcends him, but as his own higher self. Buddha eliminates many things that are accounted essential in other faiths, including Christianity, but this opposition between man's higher or ethical will and his natural self or expansive desires he does not eliminate. On the contrary, more than any other religious teacher, he plants himself on the naked psychological fact of this opposition; so that Buddhism, in its original form, is the most critical, or, if one prefer, the least mythological of religions.

It is important to note that much of the doctrine that has flourished in India has not been sharply dualistic

---

[2] *Dhammapada*, v. 96.

like that of Buddha or any other genuine religious teacher, but has had a more or less marked pantheistic leaning. This leaning appears in a number of the Hindus who are now professing to interpret India to the outside world. For example, Rabindranath Tagore has enjoyed no small degree of credit as an interpreter of India, not merely in the Occident, but in the Orient itself. He has the merit of seeing the importance of the whole question of East versus West, and in his criticism of the West often shows on the negative side no small degree of perspicacity. The man of the West, he says, has specialized in power and mechanical efficiency and so has been enabled to make himself the bully of the planet; but it is established in the nature of things that bullies shall come to grief. This view of the Occident has not only found adherents in China and Japan, but something very similar to it is being muttered at the present time by Muhammadan mullahs from Delhi to Tangiers. The facts, it is scarcely necessary to say, are not quite so simple. The success of the English in maintaining a hold on India is not based entirely on mechanical efficiency and still less on philanthropy or a supposed eagerness to assume the white man's burden. It has been due in part to the division among the Hindus themselves; but it is also in no small measure a triumph of character, of the sane moral realism that has made of the English the best ruling race, perhaps, that the world has yet seen.

A federation of the states of Europe, Tagore goes on to say, would, under existing circumstances, be only a federation of steam-boilers. The remedy is to get rid of the analysis that has built up this nightmare of mechanical efficiency and put in its place the principle of love.[3] It is here that the affinity of Tagore appears, not with the ancient sages of his own land, as he would have us believe, but with our Rousseauistic dreamers. One may oppose to the effeminacy of a Tagore or a Bergson and to all those, in either East or West, who seek to attain "vision" at the expense of analysis, the example of Buddha who has claims to be regarded as the ultimate Oriental. For Buddha supreme "vision" coincided with a supreme act of analysis.[4]

I have been trying to show that at the center of the great religious faiths of Asiatic origin is the idea of a higher will that is felt in its relation to man's ordinary will or expansive desires as a power of vital control. The recognition of this will, however conceived—whether one say with Christ, "Thy will be done," or with Buddha, "Self is the lord of self; who else can be the lord?"—is the source of awe and humility. The submission to this higher will is in its consummation peace.

At first sight Confucius seems very unlike other great Asiatic teachers. His interests, as I have already said, are humanistic rather than religious. The points of contact between his doctrine and that of Aristotle, the most important Occidental humanist, are numerous and striking. One is tempted to say, indeed, that, if there is such a thing as the wisdom of the ages, a central core of normal human experience, this wisdom is, on the religious level, found in Buddha and Christ and, on the humanistic level,

---

[3] See his book on *Nationalism, passim.*
[4] The tracing of the so-called chain of dependent origination.

in Confucius and Aristotle. These teachers may be regarded both in themselves and in their influence as the four outstanding figures in the spiritual history of mankind. Not only the experience of the world since their time, but much of its previous experience may be properly associated with them.[5] One may note as an interesting analogy that just as Saint Thomas Aquinas sought to combine the wisdom of Aristotle with that of Christ in his Sum of Theology, so about the same time Chu Hsi mingled Buddhist with Confucian elements in his great commentary.

Though Aristotle and Confucius come together in their doctrine of the mean, one should hasten to add that in their total attitude toward life they reveal the characteristic difference between the European and the Asiatic temper. The interests of Aristotle were far from being exclusively humanistic. He is supposed to have spent the happiest years of his life on the islands about the Aegean, observing the fish and marine life and preparing the

---

[5] Of Confucius, for example, the late Professor Chavannes of the Collège de France says: "He was, as it were, five hundred years before our era, the national conscience which gave precision and corroboration to the profound ideas of which the classic books of remote antiquity reveal to us the first outlines. . . . He went about proclaiming the necessity of conforming to the moral idea that China had slowly conceived in the course of the centuries; the men of his time refused to obey him because they found it too difficult to give up their comforts or their interests; they felt, nevertheless, that his voice had a more than human authority; they were moved and stirred to the depths of their being when they were touched by the potent spirit coming from the distant past which summoned up in them the truths glimpsed by their fathers." *Quelques Idées morales des Chinois* (lecture originally given at the Sorbonne and published in *Bulletin de la Sociéte autour du Monde,* January–May 1918, pp. 47 ff.).

material for the biological treatises that won the admiration of Darwin.[6] It is perhaps not easy to combine such a far-ranging intellectual curiosity as that of Aristotle with the humility so emphasized by Confucius and other Oriental teachers. Aristotle has had an influence great almost beyond reckoning, not merely on Christian, but on Jewish and Muhammadan religious thought; and yet one would feel something subtly incongruous in a temple to Aristotle. One does not need to be a Confucian to feel that a temple to Confucius would not be similarly incongruous. He was not, like Aristotle, a master of them that *know*, but a master of them that *will*. He was strong at the point where every man knows in the secret of his heart that he is weak. The decorum or principle of inner control that he would impose upon the expansive desires is plainly a quality of will. He is no obscurantist, yet the role of reason in its relation to will is, as he views it, secondary and instrumental. If we turn from Aristotle to Socrates, whose interests were, like those of Confucius, almost exclusively ethical, a similar contrast between the Oriental and Occidental temper appears. The Socratic conception of virtue encourages a primary emphasis on mind. Moreover, the Occident, having emancipated itself from the Oriental assertion of the primacy of will in its Christian form, has been devoting itself more and more since the Renaissance, not to the Socratic thesis that knowledge is virtue, but to the Baconian thesis that knowledge is power.

---

[6] See article on Aristotle by D. W. Thompson in *The Legacy of Greece*, p. 144.

Few would deny that humility has decreased with the decline of traditional religion. The very word humility, as M. Faguet remarks, may in a not distant future be relegated to the dictionary of archaisms. The word, so far as it survives at all, is often used incorrectly.[7] It is sometimes employed, for example, to describe the deference that the man of science should display toward the mystery and infinitude of nature, or again as a synonym for the modesty or even, it may be, meanness of spirit that a man shows in comparing himself to other men. It is well that one should not be puffed up in one's dealings with either nature or other men, but humility belongs to another and, as Pascal insists, supernatural order. The assertion of Burke that humility thus understood is the root of all the other virtues involves first principles and so is not subject to mediation or compromise. It must either be accepted as true or rejected as false. If anyone accepts the assertion as true (as I myself do), the question then arises why humility has suffered such an eclipse in the Occident. The obvious reply is that it has been associated in the past with certain doctrines, notably the doctrine of the Fall and that of divine grace, and that these doctrines have tended to be undermined by the growth of the critical spirit. The individual has refused more and more to submit to the outer authority, whether that of revelation or of the church, from which these doctrines derived their ultimate sanction; and his humility has declined, one is tempted to say, in almost exact ratio to

---

[7] Hume has a discussion of humility in animals! (*Treatise of Human Nature*, bk. 2, pt. 1, sec. 12.)

his growth in self-reliance. If anyone wishes to be a true modern, if he refuses in other words to submit to authority merely as such, he is confronted with a serious problem: it is plainly not easy to be at once humble and self-reliant. The very doctrine of self-reliance has, from the point of view of humility, a singularly clouded record in the Occident, and that from the time of the ancient Greeks to the present day. No one would ever associate humility with the Cynics who were among the first to proclaim self-reliance (*autarkeia*). The Stoics again favored self-reliance. According to Pascal, they were guilty of "diabolical pride" in their first assumptions. Even though this phrase be too strong, especially as applied to certain Stoics, e.g., Marcus Aurelius, it is hardly possible to cite the Stoics in general as examples of meekness and lowliness of spirit.

If one comes to modern apostles of self-reliance, one thinks first of all perhaps of Rousseau and his defense of the doctrine in *Emile*. As to the degree of his humility, one should be sufficiently enlightened by the first page of the *Confessions*. Nor can it be maintained that Emerson, the chief American champion of self-reliance, is conspicuously humble.[8]

If we are to grasp the problem involved in the attempt to be at once humble and self-reliant, we need to go back to the ancient individualism that Rousseau and Emerson in some respects revive and seek to get at the causes

---

[8] Mr. Brownell goes so far as to say that it would be impossible to have less humility than Emerson (*American Prose Masters*, p. 176).

of its final failure. The Stoic bases his optimism primarily, we soon discover, not, like Rousseau, on faith in his instincts, but on faith in reason. To *know* the right thing is about tantamount to doing it. Reason and will thus tend to become identical. The Stoics themselves conceived that in this matter they were simply following in the footsteps of Socrates. The whole question is, as a matter of fact, closely allied to the Platonic and Socratic identification of knowledge and virtue; and this again brings up the great point at issue between European and Asiatic as to the relation of intellect and will. The chief religious teachers of Asia have, I have already said, asserted in some form or other a higher will to which man must submit in his natural self (and in Asiatic psychology intellect belongs to the natural self), if he is to enter the pathway of peace. A comparison between Plato and Buddha might help to elucidate this contrast between East and West. Buddha like Plato sought to bring together philosophy and religion; but even so he put far less emphasis on the role of mind than Plato. The list of "unthinkables" he drew up is almost equivalent to a denial that life can in any deep sense of the word be *known* at all. It cannot be maintained that the mind (*mano*) of the Buddhist coincides exactly with the Platonic mind (*nous*). It is, nevertheless, significant that "mind" is for the Buddhist an organ of the flux, whereas Plato exalts "mind" to the first place. It is a less grievous error, according to Buddha, to look on one's body as permanent than to harbor a similar conceit about one's "mind." A Buddhist might regard as the underlying error of Occidental philosophy the tendency that goes at least as far back as Parmenides to identify thought with being.[9] Why should so chimerical a creature as man identify either thought or any other part of himself with being? As Pindar says, "What are we, what are we not? Man is but the dream of a shadow." Pindar apparently feared lest he might flatter unduly man's conceit of his own permanence if he had called him even the shadow of a dream. To suppose that one can transcend the element of impermanence, whether in oneself or the outer world, merely through reason in any sense of the word, is to forget that "illusion is an integral part of reality." The person who confides unduly in "reason" is also prone to set up some static "absolute"; while those who seek to get rid of the absolute in favor of flux and relativity tend at the same time to get rid of standards. Both absolutists and relativists are guilty of an intellectual sophistication of the facts, inasmuch as in life as it is actually experienced, unity and multiplicity are indissolubly blended.

The Buddhist (to return to our comparison of East and West) seems at first sight to belong with the apostles of the flux. As a matter of fact, comparisons have been made between Buddha and Bergson on the ground that they are both "philosophers of becoming." We are justified on other grounds than that of their distance in time and space in finding the collocation of these names startling. Bergson positively revels in change and naturalistic expansiveness and avows explicitly, as we have seen, that his philosophy of *élan vital* leads straight

---

[9] See Diels, *Fragmente der Vorsokratiker*, I, p. 117.

to imperialism. Buddha for his part is at least as much concerned as Plato with escaping from the flux and, so far from being imperialistic, is turned, to the exclusion of everything else, toward what in his own phrase makes for "tranquility, knowledge, supreme wisdom, and Nirvana." This combination of a philosophy of the flux with religious peace and humility is unlike anything we have seen in the Occident and should be a warning that in dealing with Buddha we need to proceed with extreme circumspection. One may at least form some conjecture as to the point at which Buddha diverges from philosophers in the Western tradition. As a thoroughgoing individualist, he is forced to grapple with the problem of the One and the Many; if there is no principle of unity in things with which to measure the manifoldness and change, the individual is left without standards and so falls necessarily into an anarchical impressionism. Now Buddha like a true Asiatic discovers this unifying principle, not in intellect, but in will. Though he assigns an important role to intellect, since he is himself highly analytical, this role is after all secondary and instrumental. Any attempt to deal with life directly in terms of the intellect involves in some form the attempt to put the ocean in a cup. Life reveals its secret, he seems to say, only to the man who acts; and of all forms of action the most difficult is inner action. The first step in understanding not merely Buddha but Christ is to see that they were both primarily men of action in the sense in which the Asiatic in his great moments has understood action. Buddha is for reducing theory to a minimum. The least speculative of our Western philosophers would probably have seemed to him still far too speculative. He has succeeded in compressing the wisdom of the ages into a sentence: "To refrain from all evil, to achieve the good, to purify one's own heart, this is the teaching of the Awakened."[10] The Buddhist commentary is interesting: When you repeat the words, they seem to mean nothing, but when you try to put them into practice, you find they mean everything.

Some of the difficulties inherent in any attempt to treat the problem of the One and the Many primarily as a problem of knowledge appear in the Platonic theory of ideas. It is a matter of positive perception that there is an element of oneness in all the particular objects that belong to some class. There is, for example, an element of oneness in all particular horses; and this oneness is in Platonic parlance the idea or heavenly archetype of the horse. Unfortunately, if one does not get beyond this stage, the oneness remains a mere abstraction and finally a mere word—and human nature craves the concrete. The attempt to deal intellectually with the relation of the unity to the manifoldness would seem to lead to difficulties of the kind Plato has himself set forth in the second part of his *Parmenides*. This problem as to how to escape from mere abstraction appears in the case of the chief idea of all—that of the good or of God which also coincides with what is most exalted in man. The word that stands for the idea of the good is the word par excellence, the logos. One can follow to some extent the process by which the Greek conception of the

---

[10] Eight words in the Pali original. *See Dhammapada*, v. 186.

logos was transmitted through intermediaries like Philo Judeus to the author of the Fourth Gospel. The specifically Asiatic element in the Christian solution of the problem of the logos is the subordination, either implicit or explicit, of the divine reason to the divine will. By an act of this will, the gap between a wisdom that is abstract and general and the individual and particular is bridged over at last; the Word is made flesh. The human craving for the concrete is satisfied at the essential point. The truth of the incarnation, to put the matter on purely psychological grounds, is one that we have all experienced in a less superlative form: the final reply to all the doubts that torment the human heart is not some theory of conduct, however perfect, but the man of character. Pontius Pilate spoke as a European when he inquired, "What is truth?" On another occasion Christ gave the Asiatic reply: "I am the way, the truth, and the life." In this emphasis on personality Christianity is confirmed by the most positive observation. Wherein Christianity transcends positive observation is in its tremendous projection of personality, divine and human, into the region of the infinite and the eternal.

I have of course in this whole discussion been simplifying a subject of immense difficulty and complexity at the risk of doing injustice to Plato and the other members of the Socratic group. I am not unaware of the almost inexhaustible store of wisdom in Plato. He must still be one of the chief aids of those who wish to achieve religious insight without an undue sacrifice of the critical spirit. Yet it is difficult not to have certain doubts about the Platonic and Socratic identification of knowledge and virtue. This identification is not superficial precisely—men like Plato and Socrates are never superficial. Knowledge may conceivably become so perfect that to act contrary to it would be like putting one's hand into the fire. Moreover, when one has struggled out of any maze of error, it will always seem in the retrospect that the error was due even less to a defect of will than to ignorance. Nevertheless, the Socratic thesis runs counter in certain respects to universal experience. Not only do people do what they know to be wrong, but they often take a perverse satisfaction in doing it, as Ovid,[11] anticipating the *delectatio morosa* of the theologians, was one of the first to point out. Our problem, let us remind ourselves, is to be at once self-reliant and humble. But it will not be found easy to preserve humility and at the same time to grant, after the fashion of Greek philosophy, the primacy to mind. All other forms of pride are as nothing compared with the pride of intellect; and the pride of intellect itself is most manifest in the attempt to know good and evil. So much psychological truth is, it would seem, to be found in the myth of the Fall.

Perhaps my meaning may be best elucidated by studying the Socratic movement in its fruits (and in this movement I include the Platonic and in no small degree the Aristotelian influence). Since Plato worked primarily on the religious level, one would have expected the fruits of religion to appear in the Platonic Academy. The Academy produced a number of distinguished intellectuals who inclined on the whole toward skepticism. It is, of course,

---

[11] "Video meliora proboque, deteriora sequor." "Nitimur in vetitum semper, cupimusque negata."

possible to build up faith on a skeptical basis as Socrates himself seems to have done; but it can scarcely be maintained that the successors of Plato in the Academy achieved either this or any other type of faith. In any case the contrast is striking between the Academy and the Order founded by Buddha. Anyone who studies the old records can acquire the conviction that this Order contained many men of faith, men who brought forth the very fruits of the spirit that have been so admirably defined by Saint Paul, and so deserve to be regarded as saints.

The truth is that the Greeks, on their emancipation from traditional standards, slipped rather rapidly into mere rationalism, and mere rationalism, whether in the Stoical or Epicurean form, showed its usual inability to control the expansive lusts of the human heart. Stoicism sought to achieve a principle of union among men that would have universal validity; it sought, in other words, to do the work of a religion. It saw this universal principle in reason, and proclaimed at the same time that to live according to reason was to live according to nature. Man's reason, the Stoic assumed, could prevail unaided over his outer impressions and expansive desires. That important aspects, not merely of the Socratic, but of the Platonic and Aristotelian teaching, tended to be obscured in later Greco-Roman thought is beyond question. At the same time, in assuming that right will follows upon right knowledge, the Stoic, as I have already said, conceived that he was a true Socratic; if herein he missed the true Socratic spirit, one is forced to conclude that this spirit was rather easy to miss.

Stoicism was in general a paradoxical movement; it affirmed that the material order alone is real and then put supreme emphasis on a "virtue" that the material order does not give. In other words it sought to attain and to some extent actually did attain on monistic postulates the fruits that are normally associated with a genuinely dualistic philosophy. In spite of its many merits and partial successes, Stoicism was on the whole a failure; and the same must be said of the whole Greek attempt to deal critically with the problem of conduct, to work out, in other words, a sound type of individualism. This failure of Greek philosophy was due, I have suggested, to the fact that it is not quite adequate in its treatment of the closely allied problems of the imagination and the higher or ethical will. Anyone who believes that "illusion is an integral part of reality," and who also holds with the Asiatic that, if humility is to be secured, will must take precedence of mind, is forced to conclude that the danger of Greek philosophy was from the start a certain obstinate intellectualism.

Christianity supplied what was lacking in Greek philosophy. It set up doctrines that humbled reason and at the same time it created symbols that controlled man's imagination and through the imagination his will. On the basis supplied by this Oriental faith, it was possible to reconstruct European civilization after the Greco-Roman collapse and in the midst of the havoc of the barbarian invasions. But this work of regeneration was accomplished in no small degree at the expense of the critical spirit. It resulted in the triumph of an authority "anterior, exterior, and superior" to the individual. If the Greek confidence in reason proved in some respects fallacious, there are also, it must be admitted, dangers and difficulties in the worship of will in all its forms. On the danger of will-worship in its Nietzschean form it is scarcely necessary to dilate. But even the Oriental cult of the ethical will is beset with pitfalls. The Hindu ascetic who lies on a bed of spikes or holds his arm in the air until it withers away is exercising will in the Oriental sense, but he can scarcely be said to be exercising it intelligently. When the higher will again is conceived as a divine will that has been revealed once for all in words of literal and plenary inspiration, one has the drawbacks and difficulties that are most manifest, perhaps, in Muhammadanism. The effect is to force human life into a rigid and definitive mold. It is not safe to overlook the element of flux and relativity in favor of absolute will any more than it is to overlook it in favor of absolute reason. The Muhammadan has his own way of forgetting that illusion is an integral part of reality. Moreover, when will is conceived as absolute and irresponsible and at the same time as transcendent, the individual is made humble, indeed, but he is so far from being made self-reliant that he is prone to fall into the Oriental form of fatalism.

We need to consider in the interests of our present subject not merely the difficulties of the Oriental worship of will in general, but of this worship as practiced by Christians in particular—above all, the form that appears in the doctrine of grace. Saint Augustine, it is scarcely necessary to say, did more than any other one man to develop the Pauline teaching on this subject; and Saint Augustine was destined, here as elsewhere, to exercise an influence great almost beyond reckoning on medieval

and later Christianity. Now Saint Augustine is considered with some truth the Christian Plato. The supreme contrast for him as for Plato is that between *fluxa
et caduca*, on the one hand, and, on the other, *certa et
aeterna*. A further comparison of the two men will, however, reveal a profound shifting of emphasis as regards
the relative importance of intellect and will. Saint Augustine's desire, as he tells us, is to know only two things
—God and the soul. (*Deum et animam scire cupio. Ni-
hilne plus? nihil omnino.*) God is envisaged primarily
not as mind, but as will. The soul of man is also reduced
in its essential aspect to will (*nihil aliud habeo quam
voluntatem*). The human will is, however, hopelessly
alienated from the divine will by the Fall. The gap between the two can be traversed only by a miracle of
grace, a miracle that itself depends on the miracle of the
redemption. Man not only needs the mediation of Christ
if his will is to be brought into harmony with the divine
will, but also of the church and the sacraments and the
elaborate priestly hierarchy that is required to administer them. So far from right will following upon right
knowledge, as Plato thought, fallen man delights in evil
for its own sake. What was so delicious upon his tongue,
says Saint Augustine in speaking of the pears that he
stole when a boy, was not the flavor of the pears themselves, but of his sin. Moreover, this perversity of will
sprang originally from the intellect and its pride: man
wished to be as a God, *knowing* good and evil. The intellect was thus not only put in its proper subordinate
place, but brought under positive suspicion. The way
was opened for obscurantism. Man was humbled and his

will regenerated, but more or less, as I have said, at the expense of the critical spirit. The historical explanation of this uncritical element in Christianity is no doubt that, more than most other doctrines, it worked its way up from the bottom of society toward the top. At all events, men were asked to believe a thing because it was absurd,[12] and ignorance was declared to be the mother of devotion. The church was enabled to carry on all the more effectively its work of regeneration, it might be argued, from the fact that men had ceased to be self-reliant and above all had ceased like the Socratic Greek to rely on the intellect. "Is righteousness, then, the daughter of ignorance?" Rousseau inquires. "Are science and virtue incompatible?" The history of the Occident, it must be confessed, raises some doubt on this point. The so-called Dark Ages, says Lord Acton with some exaggeration, were spiritually full of light.[13] On the other hand, the intellectually "enlightened" eighteenth century was, as Burke complains, spiritually full of darkness.

---

[12] The phrase *Credo quia absurdum* does not actually occur in the famous fifth chapter of Tertullian's *De Carne Christi*, but sums up correctly the total sense of the chapter.

[13] "Then followed the ages which are not unjustly called the Dark Ages, in which were laid the foundations of all the happiness that has been since enjoyed, and of all the greatness that has been achieved by men. . . . It was not an age of conspicuous saints, but sanctity was at no time so general. The holy men of the first centuries shine with an intense brilliancy from the midst of the surrounding corruption. Legions of saints—individually for the most part obscure, because of the atmosphere of light around them—throng the five illiterate centuries, from the close of the great dogmatic controversies to the rise of a new theology and the commencement of new interests with Hildebrand, Anselm, and Bernard" (*History of Freedom*, p. 200).

The beginnings of "Enlightenment" in the eighteenth-century sense go back to the Middle Ages themselves—at least as far back as the thirteenth century. A significant coincidence is that between this incipient emancipation of intellect and the founding of the Inquisition. The real emancipation of intellect got fairly under way with the Renaissance. Men were becoming self-reliant again and in almost the same measure were losing humility. They were inclining, once more, like the ancient Greeks, to look on life primarily as a problem of knowledge. Only the knowledge that they sought increasingly was not the ethical knowledge at which Socrates aimed, but knowledge of the natural order. Ethical knowledge seemed to have become indissolubly associated with incomprehensible dogmas. An acute conflict was inevitable, often in the heart of the same individual, between the old humility and the new spirit of intellectual inquiry. Let us consider the case of Pascal, an eminent scientific investigator and also a religious writer at once profound and poignant. He recommends a full application of the critical and experimental spirit to the natural order, but in all that transcends the natural order he would have the critical spirit abdicate before a twofold outer authority—that of revelation and the church.[14] Spiritual truth he identifies with dogmas that are most repugnant to reason—for example, infant damnation.[15] To be sure, all the nobility of man is in reason, but this nobility is not in itself of much avail, inasmuch as rea-

---

[14] See his *Fragment d'un Traité du vide.*
[15] *Pensées,* 434.

son is the sport and plaything of the imagination. Here, I have already noted, is a supreme clash between Christian psychology and that of the Stoic, who holds that it is possible for reason to triumph over the imagination.

If reason is thus the plaything of the imagination, either the Stoical or any other form of self-reliance is vain. Man's only hope is in arbitrary will in the form of divine grace. To the sudden illumination of grace Pascal gives the name "heart." "The heart has reasons of which the reason knows nothing." Will in the form of grace is thus at odds with reason which is in turn at odds with imagination; whereas, if one is to be a sound individualist, it may be that reason and imagination need to cooperate in the service of the power in man that I have defined as the ethical will.

It is not to be inferred from what I have said that Pascal has ceased to have value for the individualist. Many of the arguments that he urges in favor of humility and against the pride of intellect are still valid for the simple reason that they are not dogmatic, but keenly psychological. Why should man be proud, seeing that he is, as Pascal shows, caught between two infinites, one of smallness and one of magnitude, and is equally unable to grasp either, so that the essence of things eludes him and must ever elude him? If at any time he thinks he has found a firm foundation on which to rear a tower that will reach even to the infinite, this foundation suddenly fails him and "the earth yawns open even to the abyss." Lacking some such firm foundation, man has no assurance that his knowledge is real knowledge or anything more than a dream within a dream. But there is some-

thing still more humbling to man than his ignorance, and
that is the inability of unaided reason to control effectively his outer impressions and expansive desires. Surely
realistic observation is here on the side of Pascal rather
than of the Stoics. Man's peculiar blindness arises from
the fact that he does not wish to be limited in his dominant desire, whatever that desire may be. He wishes to
be free to pursue his folly, as Erasmus would say, and
finally discovers the limits established in the nature of
things by the somewhat painful process of colliding with
them. This human proclivity is so universal, and yet
the punishment visited upon it is so harsh, that one's
final impression is that of a certain treachery in life itself. Under the circumstances one does not need to be a
Jansenist, or even perhaps a Christian, to see certain
merits in the older plan of working out one's salvation in
fear and trembling as compared with our modern plan
of "living dangerously," or, what amounts to the same
thing, of turning away from awe and humility in favor
of an endless reaching out of wonder and curiosity.
Man's expansive conceit, as the Greeks saw, produces
insolent excess (*hybris*) and this begets blindness (*atê*)
which in turn brings on Nemesis. Expansive conceit
tempered by Nemesis—this is a definition of an essential aspect of human nature that finds considerable
support in the facts of history. Man never rushes forward so confidently, it would sometimes seem, as when
he is on the very brink of the abyss. The malady of
Europe on the eve of the Great War was not so much
ignorance as blindness in the Greek sense. A clear perception of the workings of Nemesis is what gives distinc-

tion to the great Greek poets, even to Euripides, the least ethical of them:

Gold and Fair-fortune, with Power the victorious
Harnessed beside them, in folly vainglorious
  Hurry man to his doom:
Law he outpaceth, and lawlessness lasheth
  To speed; nor his heart doth incline
To take heed to the end — lo, his car sudden-crasheth
  Shattered in gloom![16]

A consideration of man's ignorance and blindness as they are revealed on a vast scale in the facts of history gives a positive basis to humility. One comes to feel that the great religious teachers may be right after all in their insistence that man needs to subordinate himself to some higher will; above all that it is needful that his intellect should recognize some such control. The peril that results from intellectual unrestraint (*libido sciendi*) is perhaps the most fundamental of all. "What must be the face-to-face antagonist," asks Cardinal Newman, "by which to withstand and baffle . . . the all-corroding, all-dissolving energy of the intellect?" Cardinal Newman has at all events asked the essential question, whatever one may think of his own solution of it. Unfortunately, in getting rid of the pride of intellect the Christian has often tended to get rid of the intellect itself or at least to depreciate it unduly.[17] Hence the obscurantist vein

---

[16] *The Madness of Hercules*, pp. 744 ff., trans. A. S. Way.

[17] One may illustrate from Cardinal Newman himself: "What is intellect itself," he asks, "but a fruit of the Fall, not found in paradise or in heaven, more than in little children, and at the utmost but tolerated by

that I have already noted in Christianity. To use the intellect to the utmost and at the same time to keep it in
its proper subordinate place is a task that seems thus far
to have been beyond the capacity of Occidental man.
The warfare between a reason that presumes unduly
and a faith that has got itself more or less identified with
credulity may turn out to be the true disease of Western
culture from the Greeks to the present day. This strife
between the head and the heart has left its marks even
on the forms of language. Thus, to take a few examples,
to be a person of "strong mind" (*esprit fort*) was about
equivalent in older French usage to being an atheist;
to be "blessed," on the other hand, was to be a "block-
head" (*benêt*, from *benedictus*). An "innocent," again, is
an idiot, in contradistinction, no doubt, to the person
who is said to be as "bright as the devil." The English
"silly" is the same word etymologically as the German
"holy" (*selig*).

When Rousseau said that his heart and his head did
not seem to belong to the same individual, he simply
introduced a new and, as I shall try to show presently,
worse form of obscurantism. In its Rousseauistic form
the conflict between head and heart has continued to
our own day. Philosophers, who are under no suspicion
of being Christians, still assume that there is a more or
less complete opposition between intellect and intuition,

---

the church, and only not incompatible with the regenerate mind? . . .
Reason is God's gift, and so are passions. . . . Eve was tempted to follow
passion and reason, and she fell" (*Parochial and Plain Sermons*, v, p.
112).

so that to be vital in the Bergsonian sense is about the same as being anti-intellectual.[18]

The more significant contrast, however, still remains that between the partisan of grace and the man who, in some form or other, asserts the primacy of mind. It can be shown that the doctrine of grace was the keystone of the whole edifice of European society in its medieval form. It is not as clear as one might wish that European civilization can survive the collapse of this doctrine. In any case the problem for the individualist who believes that it is not enough to be self-reliant, but that one should also be humble, is to discover some equivalent for grace. It is here that we may find it profitable to take into account the total experience of Asia. While no sensible person would claim for the Far East a general ethical superiority over the West, the Far East had at least enjoyed a comparative immunity from that great disease of Occidental culture—the warfare between reason and faith. Buddha and Confucius both managed to combine humility with self-reliance and a cultivation of the critical spirit. They may, therefore, be of help to those who wish to restore to their lives on modern lines the element for which Asia has stood in the past, who believe that without some such restoration the Occident is in danger of going mad with the lust of speed and power. In describing the element of peace as the Asiatic element, I do not mean to set up any geographic or

---

[18] "L'intelligence est caractérisée par une incompréhension naturelle de la Vie" (Bergson, *Evolution créatrice*, p. 179).

other fatalism. China, for example, may under pressure from the Occident have an industrial revolution (Hankow is already taking on the aspect of an Oriental Pittsburgh) and this revolution is likely to be accompanied by a more or less rapid crumbling of her traditional ethos with the attendant danger of a lapse into sheer moral chaos. The Occident, on the other hand, may not only reaffirm the truths of the ethical will, but may reaffirm these truths in some appropriately modern way and with an emphasis distinctly different from anything that has been seen in the Orient. In dealing with this topic we can best take our point of departure from the fact that all who profess to be modern are, in some sense or other of the word, liberals. If there has been any vital omission in the passage from old to new, this omission is likely to be most visible in one's definition of liberty. Lord Acton was planning to begin his *History of Liberty* with a hundred such definitions. It is not certain that any one of the hundred would exactly have met our present requirement, which is to secure in some thoroughly critical fashion what I have termed the centripetal element in liberty. If one fails in this task, one ceases to be a complete modern and becomes a mere modernist. The modernist is wont to assume that the really important conflict is that between liberals, on the one hand, and reactionaries, on the other; a more important conflict, however, may turn out to be that between true and false liberals.

CHAPTER 6

True and False Liberals

The choice to which the modern man will finally be reduced, it has been said, is that of being a Bolshevist or a Jesuit. In that case (assuming that by Jesuit is meant the ultramontane Catholic) there does not seem to be much room for hesitation. Ultramontane Catholicism does not, like Bolshevism, strike at the very root of civilization. In fact, under certain conditions that are already partly in sight, the Catholic church may perhaps be the only institution left in the Occident that can be counted on to uphold civilized standards. It may also be possible, however, to be a thoroughgoing modern and at the same time civilized. Before considering this possibility more in detail, it will be helpful to trace the process by which the present situation has grown up, a situation that seems, at least superficially, to impose the extreme choice I have just mentioned.

In tracing this process everything will be found to

hinge ultimately on the idea of liberty in its relation to
the principle of control. Under the old order, spiritual
control, I have said, had its final source and sanction in
the doctrine of grace. We need, therefore, to follow to
some extent the fortunes of this doctrine as affected by
the progressive emancipation, since the Renaissance, of
the individual from outer authority and by the concomitant growth of naturalistic tendencies. Certain
groups within the church itself, notably the Jansenists,
sought to revive, in opposition to the incipient naturalistic movement, the doctrine of grace in its full Augustinian rigor. This doctrine originally marked the very
apex of Christian otherworldliness, whereas, at the time
of the Jansenist revival, men were turning more and
more resolutely to this world. Saint-Evremond estimates that there were not ten men in France who could
satisfy the Jansenist test of holiness. All other Frenchmen the Jansenists seemed to consign to outer darkness.
In standing for a more moderate interpretation of grace
the Catholic church simply showed its good sense. What
was more dubious was its tendency to substitute for the
inner dependence of man on God that the Jansenist desired, his outer dependence on the priest. My present
subject does not require me to consider the truth of the
charge that the church, in the effort to induce the individual to submit to its authority, dissimulated unduly
the austerity of Christian doctrine; that, in short, it gave
countenance to a casuistical relaxation, the upshot of
which was, in Bossuet's phrase, to put "cushions under
the elbows of sinners." All I need to point out here is
that the reply of the church to individualistic tenden-

cies of every kind has been an ever-increasing papal centralization. It may be said of the ultramontane Catholic,
as of the extreme partisan of grace, though in a very different sense, that he has simply repudiated self-reliance.

If one wishes to understand the types of individualism
to which ultramontane Catholicism is such an uncompromising answer, one needs to study also the doctrine
of grace in its relation to the Protestant Reformation.
Both Luther and Calvin, it is scarcely necessary to say,
put prime emphasis on this doctrine, though not quite
the same emphasis. Now the Reformation is, by its underlying postulates, a critical movement; it sought to
recover the authentic Christian doctrine that seemed to
it to have been perverted by the Roman theocracy. It
urged the individual to take a critical attitude toward
this theocracy, or, what amounts to the same thing, it
urged him to exercise the right of private judgment,
which is only another way of encouraging him to be self-
dependent and self-reliant. But the Protestant was involved in peculiar difficulties as soon as he set out to be
self-reliant and at the same time to defend the doctrine
of grace; for the doctrine, in the Pauline and Augustinian
form that a Luther and a Calvin sought to revive, was
the very negation of self-reliance; it was designed to
make man feel his utter and helpless dependence on the
divine will. If a man is to be self-reliant, two things, it
should seem, are necessary: he must have sound standards and must then be free to act on them. To secure
the standards he needs intellect and to act on them he
needs will. Luther, for his part, wishes to be an individualist and at the same time to follow the early Christian

obscurantists in flouting the intellect and denying the
freedom of the will. Since the "covenant of work" was
abrogated by the Fall, man's will is in helpless bondage
to sin,[1] so that God alone is capable of any salutary
working; man's only hope, therefore, is in the covenant
of grace and the scheme of redemption. To hold any
other view is subversive of humility. Luther's extreme
hostility to work is, of course, due also to the identification of work with the performance of rites and ceremonies, especially in connection with penance (*satisfactio
operis*).

Luther and the other reformers had by their separation from the church cut themselves off more or less
from the traditional symbols by which the truths of
humility and of the higher will were interpreted to the
imagination; so that, in their defense of these truths,
they were thrown back, almost in spite of themselves, on
reason. Erasmus with his fine psychological tact felt in
the Reformation, almost from the outset, an element of
intellectual presumption. If the impression that Calvin
produces in his preaching of man's utter dependence on
the divine will is not precisely that of humility, one suspects that the explanation is that he presumes to know
too much about that will. Jonathan Edwards, again, in
his anxiety to justify rationally God's absolute and arbitrary will, finally seems to have insinuated himself as a
fourth into the council chamber of the Trinity.

It is fair to say that the difficulty that confronted a
Calvin and an Edwards and has led to at least a partial

---

[1] See Luther's *De servo arbitrio* (1526).

breakdown of Protestantism is no slight one: it must confront in some measure anyone who seeks to combine a free play of the critical spirit with the acceptance of traditional Christianity. If one starts, as the traditional Christian has been wont to start, with the hypothesis of an omnipotent God with "foreknowledge absolute," the question almost inevitably arises why such a being has permitted evil at all. Furthermore, strict logic would seem to impose the conclusion that this being has doomed a multitude of his creatures to everlasting torments simply for doing what, in the last analysis, he himself has willed.[2] In short, the critical crux at the heart of historical Christianity is how to reconcile God's omnipotence and omniscience with his justice and mercy. The portion of the world that piques itself on its modernity has simply turned its back on this theological nightmare. Unfortunately, in getting rid of the nightmare, it has also tended to get rid of the inner life, of the truth, namely, that man needs in his natural self (which includes the intellect) to look up to some higher will in awe and humility. With the decline of the inner life, there has been a weakening of control over the expansive lusts of the natural man—whether the lust of knowledge or the lust of sensation or the lust of power.

In the development I have been following, the idea of work in the spiritual sense is either very much subordi-

---

[2] "Dieu non seulement a prévu la chute du premier homme et en elle la ruine de toute sa postérité, mais il l'a ainsi voulu" (Calvin, *Inst. chrét.*, liv. 3, chap. 23, par. 7). Melancthon declares in his *Commentary on Epistle to Romans* (1525) that "God works all things. . . . He is the author of the treason of Judas as well as of the conversion of Paul."

nated to grace or else is more or less identified with the
performance of rites and ceremonies.[3] We need to trace
at this point the rise of a very different doctrine of work.
The last scholastics, notably Duns Scotus, inclined to
divorce religious truth from reason and to identify it
with absolute, arbitrary will and unintelligible theological mysteries. A man like Francis Bacon takes theologians of this type at their word and, after a more or
less sincere obeisance to a spiritual truth that is immeasurably beyond man's grasp, he turns an intellect
that is left without other occupation to a study of the
natural order. He aims to establish upon this order a
philosophy, not of vain words, but of works and fruits.
The Baconian conception of work can be followed down
through the utilitarian movement. It appears, for example, in an extreme form in Locke's second *Treatise
of Government*. Work is practically identified by Locke
with physical effort and is made the sole legitimate
source of property. Adam Smith tends to a very similar
conception of work in its relation to property. In thus
reducing the idea of work to its lowest terms, the orthodox political economy opened the way for political
economy of the unorthodox type. Karl Marx was especially influenced in his definition of work by Ricardo.
Why should not the man who, on the showing of the
orthodox political economists themselves, does the real
work, get all the reward? Why should he turn over such
a large part of this reward to that mere idler and para-

---

[3] The church was supposed to be able to work efficaciously in this sense
because of the grace that had been delegated to it.

site, the capitalist? Though the orthodox economist makes work in an unduly restricted sense the source of wealth, he does not, to do him justice, fall, like the Marxian, into the further fallacy of identifying work with value. That, he insists, is largely determined by the law of supply and demand and by competition. The extreme Marxian not only takes a purely quantitative view of work, so much so that he tends, as has been said, to put the work of a Raphael and that of a common sign painter on the same level, but in evaluating the product of work he aims to eliminate the competitive element. Recent Marxians have come to take a somewhat less quantitative view of work, but the fallacies that result from a total or partial suppression of competition are built into the very foundations of socialism.

One should note at this point that in their views as to the nature of work there is much underlying agreement between the Rousseauist and the Baconian. Rousseau himself tends to reduce work to the lowest terms and to identify it with manual labor. All who do not work in this outward and visible sense are, it would seem, hangers-on and parasites and not worthy to live.[4] The attempt to apply the utilitarian-sentimental conception of work and at the same time to eliminate competition has resulted in Russia in a ruthless despotism, on the one hand, and in a degrading servitude, on the other.

A conception of work that means practically a return to barbarism evidently suffers from some serious flaw.

---

[4] "Un rentier que l'Etat paie pour ne rien faire ne diffère guère à mes yeux d'un brigand qui vit aux dépens des passants," etc., *Emile*, liv. 3.

The man who wishes to be at once modern and civilized will not oppose to the Baconian or Rousseauistic one-sidedness a mere appeal to the past, but a more accurate definition. Aristotle was, according to Bacon, the "vile plaything of words." As a matter of fact, the surest way to become the vile plaything of words is, like both Bacon and Rousseau, to look on visible and concrete objects as "real" and on words, in contrast with these objects, as unreal. Words, especially abstract words, have such an important relation to reality because they control the imagination which in turn determines action and so "governs mankind." The way to escape from the tyranny of words is not to dismiss them as unreal in favor of objects of sense, but to submit them to a searching Socratic dialectic. The only way, for instance, not to be the dupe of the general term "work" is to divide or "dichotomize" it Socratically and so become aware of the different meanings of which it is susceptible. The fallacies involved in a purely quantitative definition of work are almost too gross to need refuting. As Mencius remarked long ago, it is both proper and inevitable that the man who works with his mind should hold sway over the man who works only with his hands. As a result of the concentrated mental effort of the gifted few, an effort displayed either in invention or in organization and management, the common laborer may today enjoy comforts that were out of the reach even of the opulent only two or three generations ago. If the laborer wishes to add to these comforts or even to keep them, he should not listen to the agitator who seeks to stir up his envy of every form of superiority. He should be the first to recognize that exceptional capacity should receive exceptional rewards.

The laborer, to be sure, has a grievance: this grievance is that those who have been set over him have concentrated so exclusively in their mental working on the material order. The real problem is to subordinate to some adequate end the enormous mass of machinery of power and comfort that has been the fruit of working of the utilitarian type; and here a specifically ethical type of working is needful. Now this specifically ethical working has been associated traditionally in the Occident with the doctrine of grace; for man to substitute his work for that of God seemed to be subversive of humility. Yet thus to emphasize God's working led, I have tried to show, to an impossible theological dilemma; so that men tended, in getting rid of the dilemma, to get rid of the true work of the spirit in favor of a merely Baconian working. The problem would seem to be to recover the truths of grace in some individualistic form. We may be aided in this task by turning for a moment to the Far Eastern teacher who combined humility with the ultimate degree of spiritual self-reliance. The word *karma* (work) has come to have in the Occident a sort of mystical glamour. But it is well to remember that this word is employed by Buddha himself in the most businesslike fashion. The man who wishes, he says, to be a carpenter must do the work of a carpenter; the man who wishes to be a king must do the work of a king; the man who wishes to be a saint must do the work of a saint. One simply passes, as one mounts in the scale, from an outer to an inner working. The individual is to impose progressively his ethical will, affirmed as an immediate fact of consciousness, upon his outgoing desires. He is to perform this work of the spirit with a view to his own happiness, or, what amounts to the same thing in the eyes of the Buddhist, with a view to his own peace. "By rousing himself," says Buddha, "by strenuousness, by restraint and control, the wise man may make for himself an island which no flood can overwhelm." The supreme contrast in this faith is always that between the spiritually strenuous person and the spiritual idler.

Though probably no other teacher of the past has dealt with the idea of work so thoroughly as Buddha, the Buddhist emphasis does not seem just what we need today. Buddha was, like Christ, very otherworldly. The work in which he was primarily interested was of the type that leads to saintliness. It may show a lack of imagination on my part, but I cannot imagine my contemporaries in the role of saints. Perhaps no age was ever more lacking in otherworldliness or showed a greater incomprehension of religion. We have converted Buddha into a sort of heavy-eyed pessimistic dreamer, and, following Rousseau, have sentimentalized the figure of Christ. It might be well, therefore, for us to undertake something more within our capacity than religion. In general, for one person who has even an inkling of the nature of a genuinely religious working and of the strenuous peace at which religion aims, at least a hundred persons can be found who can grasp to some extent the type of work that has its fruition in the mediatory or humanistic virtues. Now humanism must, like religion, rest on the recognition, in some form or other, of the inner life, or, what amounts to the same thing, on the opposition between a law of the spirit and a law of the members. It must also, like religion, subordinate intellect to the ethical will and so put its ultimate emphasis on humility. In this matter of humility the Western humanist has something to learn, as I have already hinted, from Confucian China.

Though religion and the best type of humanism are at one in stressing humility, they diverge widely in their attitude toward the expansive desires. In its pursuit of the otherworldly virtue of peace, religion tends to renounce these desires completely, whereas humanism would simply moderate and harmonize them with a view to living to the best advantage in this world. As a result of this particular confusion of the things of God and the things of Caesar, the humanitarian would have us set up peace as a primary good in the secular order. He hopes to secure this peace by some form of machinery (such as a league of nations) or else by an appeal to emotion. "Peace is my passion," exclaimed the expansive Thomas Jefferson. But the person who turns peace into a passion is not entering upon the pathway of peace either within himself or in the outer world. It is possible to show that the pacifist is not only a materialist, but a very objectionable type of materialist. In the name of the fairest of virtues, he is actually engaged in breaking down ethical standards. It is a matter of common sense and everyday experience that there can be no peace with the unrighteous and the unrighteous always have been and are extremely numerous. As another instance of the humanitarian confusion of values, one may cite the assertion of Woodrow Wilson that a nation may be "too proud to fight." An individual may be too *humble* to fight, but a nation that is too proud to fight may, in a world like this, be too proud to survive as a nation. The virtue that sums up all other virtues in the secular order is, as every thinker worthy of the name has always seen, not peace but justice. Now anyone who deals positively with the idea of justice will almost inevitably be led to define it: To every man according to his works; and the adequacy of this definition will depend in turn on the adequacy of one's definition of work.

The humanitarians, I have pointed out, from Bacon down, are extraordinarily superficial in their definition of work. Even when they do not fall into the cruder quantitative fallacies, they conceive of work in terms of the natural law and of the outer world and not in terms of the inner life.[5] They do not take account of that form of work which consists in the superimposition of the ethical will upon the natural self and its expansive desires. The very notion of this form of work has, I have said, tended to disappear with the decline of the doctrine of grace.

---

[5] The writer of some verses in an Ohio newspaper, after complaining of the failure of the millennium to arrive in spite of the efforts of "many scores of dreamers, poets, orators, and schemers," concludes as follows:

> And so I hold it is not treason
> To advance a simple reason
> For the sorry lack of progress we decry.
> It is this: instead of working
> On himself, each man is shirking,
> And trying to reform some other guy.

The author of this doggerel is nearer to the wisdom of the ages than some of our college presidents.

If we grant, then, that what is needed just now is a revival of the ethical will on the secular level, where it is felt as a will to justice, rather than on the religious level, where it is felt as a will to peace, and if we grant further that justice, positively defined, consists in giving to every man according to his works, let us seek to restore to the idea of work the elements that have been omitted by the humanitarians. We may be aided in such a restoration by Greek philosophy, even though we do not agree with the tendency of the Socratic group to identify right reason and right will. The Platonic definition of justice as doing one's own work or minding one's own business has perhaps never been surpassed. It brings one straight back to the truths of the inner life. Justice results when every part of a man is performing its proper function and especially when his higher self is performing its proper function of coordinating and controlling the inferior parts of his nature. An echo of this Platonic conception is found in the Senecan definition of justice: *Animus quodam modo se habens.* Justice in the outer world must, in the last analysis, be only a reflection of the harmony and proportionateness that have resulted in certain individuals from the working of the spirit upon itself.

Aristotle's view of justice has much in common with the Platonic view. In defining justice he starts, not from society, but from the individual who limits desires that are in themselves insatiable and imposes upon them the law of measure. A state in which such individuals are sufficiently numerous to set the tone is a just state. Justice, whether retributive or distributive, must be proportionate in its rewards and penalties, and it can be thus proportionate only by taking account of the higher form of working. The disciplining of the expansive desires to the law of measure which constitutes this higher form of working must, to be effective, begin early and become habitual. The necessary basis, therefore, of an ethical type of state is an ethical type of education.

Aristotle makes not only justice but happiness depend on what he calls "energizing according to virtue." He finally carries his conception of work from the humanistic to the religious level, from mediation to meditation or the life of "vision," defining God himself as pure act. It has seemed to some that the activity the individual displays in the life of vision is so disassociated from the activity that he displays in his relations with his fellow men as to encourage the ascetic excess of the Middle Ages. The altruist, indeed, would maintain that both the Platonic and Aristotelian definitions of justice, encouraging a man as they do to put his own work before the world's work, are selfish and antisocial. A man should renounce self and give himself up to sympathy and service. But there is something, we should remind the altruist, that the world needs even more than our service, and that is our example. "Example," as Burke says, "is the school of mankind; it will learn at no other." Now a man becomes exemplary only as a result of either a religious or a humanistic working. The man who works religiously helps the world, one is tempted to affirm, by the very act of renouncing it. He sets his fellow men the most important of all examples—that of unworldliness. If Buddha has dealt profoundly with the form of work by which one becomes exemplary on the religious level, Confucius has shown, even more adequately, perhaps, than Aristotle, the benefits that accrue to society and civilization from a humanistic working. Confucius has summed up his teaching in a sentence: Loyalty to oneself and charity toward one's neighbor. The altruist might accept this formula provided he were allowed to give the first place to the charity toward one's neighbor. But to do so is entirely un-Confucian. The individual must first of all look up to something higher than either himself or his neighbor in order that he may be worthy to be looked up to in turn. Of his ideal ruler, Shun, Confucius says: "Shun was one who did nothing, yet governed well. For what, in effect, did he do? Religiously self-observant, he sat gravely on his throne, and that is all." All that Confucius means to affirm by this passage is the superiority of inner over outer action (of which, as we learn from other passages, his monarch was also capable). Shun was, in short, minding his own business in the Platonic sense, and such was the persuasiveness of his example that others were led to do likewise; whereas, with the present trend toward "social justice," the time is rapidly approaching when everybody will be minding everybody else's business. For the conscience that is felt as a still small voice and that is the basis of real justice, we have substituted a social conscience that operates rather through a megaphone. The busybody, for the first time perhaps in the history of the world, has been taken at his own estimate of himself. We are in fact, as someone remarked, living in the Meddle Ages; inasmuch as the meddling is itself only an outcome of our confused definition of justice, the cynic might suggest, as an even more correct description of the time, the Muddle Ages.

Perhaps, indeed, the meddling and the muddling are not quite so widespread as one is at times tempted to suppose. There are probably still a few persons left who realize the importance of minding their own business, even though not in the full Platonic or Confucian sense. There is probably an element of exaggeration in a recent assertion that to the question, "Am I my brother's keeper?" the whole American people had replied in an "ecstatic affirmative." One should note in passing the intolerable dilution of the principle of obligation that is implied in extending to men indiscriminately what one owes to one's own brother. At all events, no small issues are involved in the question whether one should start with an expansive eagerness to do something for humanity or with loyalty to one's self. There may be something after all in the Confucian idea that if a man only sets himself right, the rightness will extend to his family first of all, and finally in widening circles to the whole community.

One's definition of work and of justice in terms of work will be found to be inseparably bound up with one's definition of liberty. The only true freedom is freedom to work. All the evidence goes to show that there is no safety in the nature of things for the idler and that the most perilous of all forms of idling is spiritual idling. The failure to take account of the subtler forms of working is what vitiates the attempts of the utilitarian to define liberty—for example, the attempt of J. S. Mill.

If a man is only careful not to injure his fellow men, he should then, according to Mill, be free to cultivate his idiosyncrasy. One cannot grant in the first place that any such sharp division between the altruistic and the self-regarding elements in human nature is possible; and even if one did grant it, one should have to insist that the self-regarding virtues are the most important even from the point of view of society; for it is only by the exercise of these virtues that one becomes exemplary and so, as I have tried to show, truly helpful to others.

If society should in its own interests encourage those who work with their minds as compared with those who work with their hands, how much more should it give recognition to those who are engaged in a genuinely ethical working. It is in fact the quality of a man's work that should determine his place in the hierarchy that every civilized society requires. In short, from the positive point of view, work is the only justification of aristocracy. "By work," says Buddha, "a man is noble, by work he is an outcast."[6] The principle, though sound, is not, one must confess, altogether easy to apply. Though justice require that every man receive according to the quantity and the quality of his work, there is in this competition a manifest inequality from the start. One man has an innate capacity that another cannot acquire by any amount of effort. God, according to the Platonic myth, has mingled lead with the nature of some and with the nature of others silver and gold. Stress unduly the initial differences between men and one will tend to fall

---

[6] *Sutta-Nipâta*, v. 135.

into some system of caste, as Plato himself tends to do, or else one will incline to fatalism, whether naturalistic or predestinarian. On the other hand, deny these differences in favor of some egalitarian theory and one runs counter to the most palpable facts. Genuine justice seems to demand that men should be judged, not by their intentions or their endeavors, but by their actual performance; that in short the natural aristocrat, as Burke terms him, should receive his due reward, whether one attribute his superiority, with the man of science, to heredity, or, with the Christian, to grace, or, with the Buddhist, to his past working.

One's view of work and of the rewards that it deserves will determine necessarily one's attitude toward property. From the point of view of civilization, it is of the highest moment that certain individuals should in every community be relieved from the necessity of working with their hands in order that they may engage in the higher forms of working and so qualify for leadership. If the civilization is to be genuine, it must have men of leisure in the full Aristotelian sense. Those who in any particular community are allowed to enjoy property that is not the fruit of their own outer and visible toil cannot, therefore, afford to be idlers and parasites. An aristocratic or leading class, however the aristocratic principle is conceived, must, if it hopes in the long run to preserve its property and privileges, be in some degree exemplary. It is only too clear that the members of the French aristocracy of the Old Regime failed, in spite of many honorable exceptions, to measure up to this test. Some have argued from the revelations of recent writers like Colonel Repington and Mrs. Asquith that the English aristocracy is also growing degenerate. People will not consent in the long run to look up to those who are not themselves looking up to something higher than their ordinary selves. A leading class that has become Epicurean and self-indulgent is lost. Above all it cannot afford to give the first place to material goods. One may, indeed, lay down the principle that, if property as a means to an end is the necessary basis of civilization, property as an end in itself is materialism. In view of the natural insatiableness of the human spirit, no example is more necessary than that of the man who is setting limits to his desire for worldly possessions. The only remedy for economic inequality, as Aristotle says, is "to train the nobler sort of natures not to desire more";[7] this remedy is not in mechanical schemes for dividing up property; "for it is not the possessions but the desires of mankind which require to be equalized."[8] The equalization of desire in the Aristotelian sense requires on the part of individuals a genuinely ethical or humanistic working. To proclaim equality on some basis that requires no such working will result ironically. For example, this country committed itself in the Declaration of Independence to the doctrine of natural equality. The type of individualism that was thus encouraged has led to monstrous inequalities and, with the decline of traditional standards, to the rise of a raw plutocracy. A man who amasses a billion dollars is scarcely exemplary in the

---

[7] *Politics,* 1267b.
[8] *Ibid.,* 1266b.

Aristotelian sense, even though he then proceeds to lay out half a billion upon philanthropy. The remedy for such a failure of the man at the top to curb his desires does not lie, as the agitator would have us believe, in inflaming the desires of the man at the bottom; nor again in substituting for real justice some phantasmagoria of social justice. As a result of such a substitution, one will presently be turning from the punishment of the individual offender to an attack on the institution of property itself; and a war on capital will speedily degenerate, as it always has in the past, into a war on thrift and industry in favor of laziness and incompetence, and finally into schemes of confiscation that profess to be idealistic and are in fact subversive of common honesty. Above all, social justice is likely to be unsound in its partial or total suppression of competition. Without competition it is impossible that the ends of true justice should be fulfilled—namely, that every man should receive according to his works. The principle of competition is, as Hesiod pointed out long ago, built into the very roots of the world;[9] there is something in the nature of things that calls for a real victory and a real defeat. Competition is necessary to rouse man from his native indolence; without it life loses its zest and savor. Only, as Hesiod goes on to say, there are two types of competition—the one that leads to bloody war and the other that is the mother of enterprise and high achievement. He does not perhaps make as clear as he might how one may have the sound rivalry and, at the same time, avoid the type that degenerates

---

[9] See beginning of *Works and Days*.

into pernicious strife. But surely the reply to this question is found in such sentences of Aristotle as those I have just been quoting. The remedy for the evils of competition is found in the moderation and magnanimity of the strong and the successful, and not in any sickly sentimentalizing over the lot of the underdog. The mood of unrest and insurgency is so rife today as to suggest that our leaders, instead of thus controlling themselves, are guilty of an extreme psychic unrestraint.

One should note a certain confusion on the part of the advocates of social justice as to the nature of capital. Dr. Johnson is reported to have said at the sale of Thrale's brewery: "We are not here to sell a parcel of boilers and vats, but the potentiality of growing rich beyond the dreams of avarice." The realizing of the potentiality depended, of course, on the ability of the management, and this ability was not only a part, but the essential part, of the capital of the brewery. It is being assumed at present that the capital invested in our railways may be measured by what one may term their junk value. As a result of this and similar fallacies, both the owners and managers of the railways have been so treated of recent years as to discourage enterprise in this field of industry. It seems easy to convince the public that the railways are suffering from watered stock when what they are really suffering from is watered labor. If our apostles of service and social justice have their way, that considerable portion of the savings of the middle class that is now invested in the railways, either directly or indirectly through the insurance companies and savings banks, may undergo partial or total confiscation.

Every form of social justice, indeed, tends to confiscation and confiscation, when practiced on a large scale,
undermines moral standards and, in so far, substitutes
for real justice the law of cunning and the law of force.
To be on one's guard against these perils of social justice, one needs that cooperation of keen analysis and
imagination that can alone produce genuine vision;
whereas a great number of persons are weak in analysis,
and idyllic rather than ethical in their imagining. Not
being able, as a result, to get at underlying causes, they
are prone to doctor symptoms and to resort to what
Burke calls "tricking shortcuts, and little fallacious
facilities." The apparent good turns out to be evil in its
secondary consequences, and the apparent evil turns out
to be the necessary condition of some good. Things often change their aspect, not once but several times, when
thus traced in their ultimate effects. The ordinary laboring man, for instance, may not be able to see that the
"levy upon capital," for which he is urged to vote in
the name of social justice, will finally recoil upon himself. It is not yet clear that it is going to be possible to
combine universal suffrage with the degree of safety for
the institution of property that genuine justice and
genuine civilization both require. Taxation without
representation was the main grievance of the American
revolutionists; but that is precisely what an important
section of the community has to submit to today. Can
those who tax in the name of the sovereign people be
counted on to tax more equitably than those who alleged
the royal prerogative?

Among all the forms of dishonesty that assume the

idealistic mask, perhaps none is more diabolically effective in unsettling the bases of civilized life than those that involve a tampering with the monetary standard. If property stands for work in some sense or other of the word, and if money is the conventional symbol of property, the ends of justice tend to be subverted if this symbol fluctuates wildly; thrift and foresight become meaningless; no man can be sure that he will receive according to his works. Inflation of the currency amounts in practice to an odious form of confiscation, whether it is supposed, as in Germany, to promote national interests or, as in Russia, to advance internationalism. The radical, it has been pointed out, often errs in confounding money with property and in supposing that a division of money would be the same as a division of actual wealth. Though money is only a conventional token, the nature of this token is, nevertheless, not a matter of indifference. The reason for the gold standard is simple: gold involves in its production an amount of work equal approximately to the work involved in producing the various commodities for which it may be exchanged. If for any reason gold is produced more abundantly and with less effort, or if the reverse takes place, the monetary standard fluctuates; and this is an evil, but a trifling evil (human nature being what it is), compared with that which results from the substitution for gold of paper or some other medium of exchange that when, tested in terms of work, has little intrinsic value.

The modern man is as a matter of fact being whipsawed between two contradictory tendencies. On the one hand, he is being involved nationally and internationally in an ever more complex network of material relationships which rest in turn on an extraordinarily delicate mechanism of credit and exchange. On the other hand, the various idealistic schemes that are being put forward as a substitute for common honesty, or, again, the schemes, whether economic or political, that are openly imperialistic, are undermining the confidence that is the necessary basis of credit and exchange: so that the whole elaborate structure that has been reared by the industrial revolution is in danger of collapse. The political economists who promoted this revolution were, according to Carlyle, in favor of making cash payment the sole nexus between man and man. Cash payment, however, cannot serve as a nexus between men who are spiritually centrifugal. In various parts of eastern Europe, men have already become so suspicious of cash payment that they have been forced to revert in their economic contacts to barter.

The evils I have been enumerating derive in no small degree from the one-sided notion of work that has prevailed in the utilitarian movement. The interests of property itself require that at least some members of a community should work in a very different sense, that they should limit in short their own acquisitive instincts and so serve society by setting it a good example. It does not follow that the best way to secure such work from a man is to urge upon him the interests of society. Leslie Stephen, himself a utilitarian, says that "the doctrine that each man can only care for his own happiness is terribly plausible, and fits in admirably with individualism." It does indeed; so much so that the wisest way of reaching the individual may be to point out to him, not how his conduct will affect the happiness of others, but how it will affect his own happiness. Only in that case one must be careful to define happiness, not like the utilitarian and the Epicurean, in terms of pleasure, but like an Aristotle or a Buddha, in terms of work. One may apply this method not merely to the reining in of the acquisitive instincts, but to the control of the instinct of sex. Sexual unrestraint has wrought and is wreaking fearful havoc to society. The resultant diseases are, even more than alcoholism, a menace to the future of the white race. To approach the subject from another angle, there is an undoubted connection between a certain type of centrifugal and self-indulgent individualism and an unduly declining birthrate. The French and also the Americans of native descent are, if we are to trust statistics, in danger of withering from the earth. Where the population is increasing, it is, we are told, at the expense of quality. The stocks to which the past has looked for its leaders are dying out and the inferior or even degenerate breeds are multiplying.

The humanitarian remedies for evils of this order seem especially doubtful. Such schemes for regulating the relations of sex as have been put forward by the believers in eugenics are likely to lead to a tyranny at once grotesque and ineffectual. On the other hand, the evidence is slight that the individual can be induced to control himself on such general grounds as the good of country or the good of humanity or the good of the white race menaced by "the rising tide of color." Religion may be right after all in dealing with the whole question of sex in terms of the inner life. According to a French moralist, man is made up in his natural self of a little vanity and a little voluptuousness. The Christian would substitute chastity and humility. Though the humanist would moderate rather than deny entirely the most imperious form of the *libido sentiendi*, he agrees with the Christian in starting with the struggle between vital impulse and vital control. He would have the individual exercise the control not primarily for the good of society, but for his own good. Nowhere indeed is the opposition between pleasure and happiness more visible than in matters of sex.

The more one considers our modern emancipation, the more it becomes clear that it has been at the expense of what I have termed the centripetal element in liberty; and without this centripetal element or ethical will any genuine working of the spirit becomes impossible. How, one may ask, have men been able to deceive themselves as to the gravity of the error? One way in which they have deceived themselves, it may be replied, has been to offer work according to the natural law as a substitute for work according to the human law. As good an example as any is that of Faust, who is supposed to make up for moral delinquencies by reclaiming marshlands from the sea. Carlyle, who professes to be a follower of Goethe, is even more defective in his idea of work. Instead of the Socratic "Know thyself," he would adopt as his gospel: "Know thy work and do it."[10] Thus to disparage the effort at self-knowledge because man, as

---

[10] *Past and Present*, chap. 11 (beginning).

Carlyle goes on to say, is in the abstract and metaphysical sense unknowable, is simply, under existing conditions, to discredit the inner life in favor of a mere outer working. Work when conceived in this one-sided fashion degenerates into mere efficiency. Carlyle, as a matter of fact, exalts not only the efficiency of the "captain of industry" (a phrase that he apparently originated), but the military efficiency of a Frederick the Great or even of a Dr. Francia. In spite of his desperate efforts to prove to himself and others the contrary, he, therefore, tends in his philosophy to be imperialistic rather than genuinely ethical. His "hero" is at the very least a first cousin of the Nietzschean superman; they both have an authentic descent from the "original genius" of the eighteenth century.

A point worth considering is the position not merely of the "captain" but of the private in the modern army of industry. It is true that, like the rest of us, this private must find his happiness in work or not at all. One may, however, raise the question whether he may be expected to find his happiness in the type of efficiency that has been developed by the industrial revolution. This efficiency has been achieved by an endless subdivision of effort until the individual worker has tended to become a mere cog in a gigantic machine. He works with only an infinitesimal portion of himself. At times, indeed, he can scarcely be said to work at all; the machine does the working and seems to lead a less automatic life than the person who tends it. A workman in one of Henry Ford's factories is reported to have replied, when asked his name, that he was "bolt No. 29." A multitude of men are thus mechanized in order that the captain of industry may be "vital" and "dynamic," or, what amounts to the same thing as the words are now used, may live in a state of psychic unrestraint. For one may affirm with some confidence that a man who thinks it worthwhile to pile up an income said to be greater than that of J. D. Rockefeller is not engaged in a very energetic humanistic or religious working. If the ordinary industrial private follows the example of the "captain" and sets out to be "vital" and "dynamic" in his turn, either in his own person or through his unions and their leaders, the result will be chaos; for he will thus disturb the nice adjustment of parts on which the successful functioning of the whole mechanism depends.

I am not, indeed, affirming that the multiplication of machines is an unmixed evil. This multiplication has made it possible for one man to do work that would formerly have required a dozen or even a hundred men, and so has lifted a load of drudgery from the shoulders of many and opened up to them the opportunities of leisure. "No man," says Aristotle, "can practice virtue who is living the life of a mechanic or laborer." But the laborer now has opportunities such as have never before existed to become something more. Unfortunately, as we all know, he is not using his relief from drudgery to enjoy leisure in the Aristotelian sense, but to seek amusements, in which he is almost as much subordinated to machines as he is in his working moments (automobiles, phonographs, moving pictures and the like). Perhaps the fault is not so much in the laborer himself as in the pattern that is being offered him by the man "higher up."

The very unexemplary type of individualism I have been discussing can be shown to derive not only from the utilitarian conception of life in general, but from the political economy of the school of Adam Smith in particular. Let the state stand aside, says Adam Smith, and give the individual free swing (*laissez-faire*). He will not abuse this freedom, for he will be guided by an enlightened self-interest. Now the doctrine of enlightened self-interest is not in itself superficial. It has been held by really profound thinkers like Aristotle and Buddha. But the self that these thinkers have in mind is not the self that makes the pursuit of wealth its first aim, but the ethical self that exercises control over this acquisitive self. Leave the acquisitive self without this control and the right kind of competition will degenerate into the wrong kind, the ruthless kind which was actually encouraged by the Manchester school of economics and in which mill operatives become mere "cannon fodder" in the industrial warfare. Nor will competition of this sort have a sufficient counterpoise in sympathy or altruism. The efficiency of sympathy as a substitute for the ethical will is at all events the crucial issue in this whole movement. Everything will be found to hinge ultimately on this point in our current gospel of "service," a gospel in which most men seem to believe as unquestioningly nowadays as they once did in the Trinity. Yet the foundations of this gospel can be shown, on strictly psychological grounds, to be highly precarious.

In the first place, the idea of "service" as now understood is not Christian. The Christian serves not man
but God, and this service, as we learn from the Prayer
Book, is "perfect freedom." Service in the humanitarian
sense has, on the other hand, important points of
contact with Stoicism. The Stoic sought, like the humanitarian, to regulate his conduct with reference to the general welfare of mankind. Important differences need,
however, to be noted between the humanitarian and the
Stoic. The Stoic did not hold at all or held only in very
rudimentary form the doctrine of progress; he did not
think of men in the mass as moving forward almost
automatically toward "a far-off divine event." Progress
of this automatic type, when subjected to severe psychological scrutiny, will be found to resolve itself either into
a delight in change for its own sake or a delight in change
for the sake of power and comfort. The confusion between moral and material progress that the utilitarian has
promoted can be shown to involve a tampering with general terms similar to that which I have already noted in
speaking of Rousseau and the sentimentalists. Disraeli
says that the English-speaking peoples have been unable
to distinguish between comfort and civilization. The word
comfort itself is an excellent example of the illegitimate
transfer of a general term from one scheme of values to
another. "Blessed are they that mourn, for they shall be
comforted." The American of the present day wishes to
get his comfort without any preliminary mourning.

As a result of the confusion between moral and material progress the modern man has developed an inordinate confidence in organization and efficiency and in

general in machinery as a means for the attainment of ethical ends. If he is told that civilization is in danger, his first instinct is to appoint a committee to save civilization. The League of Nations is itself only a super-committee.

Progress in the utilitarian sense is, however, an even less essential element in the idealistic creed than sympathy. In this matter of sympathy one must note again a difference between the Stoic and the humanitarian. If, on the one hand, the Stoic had less confidence in machinery than the humanitarian, he was, on the other hand, less emotionally expansive. Interesting questions of this kind come up, as I have already noted, in dealing with Shaftesbury and his influence. The Stoical derivation of one whole side of Shaftesbury's philosophy is so manifest that some have sought to present him as a pure disciple of Epictetus and Marcus Aurelius. But the fact remains that the Stoics were not sentimentalists and that Shaftesbury can be shown to be a main source of sentimentalism in England and even more perhaps in Germany. The right reason of the Stoics is indeed already taking on an emotional coloring in an English precursor of Shaftesbury like Cumberland. In their tendency to identify happiness and pleasure the utilitarians remind us less of the Stoics than of the Epicureans. The Epicurean "ataraxy," however, did not any more than the Stoic "apathy" encourage effusiveness; neither Stoic nor Epicurean was prone to "let his feelings run in soft luxurious flow" and then call the result "virtue." Of Rousseau's exaltation of impulsive pity as a sufficient offset to egoistic impulse and the source of all the other virtues, I have already spoken. Of almost equal importance is Hume's assertion, professedly on strictly psychological grounds, of an element of sympathy in the natural man, anterior to reason and independent of self-love. Sympathy becomes in turn the basis of Hume's definition of justice. The just man for Hume is not the man who minds his own business in the Platonic sense, but the altruist.[11]

The crucial question, of course, is not whether a man in his spontaneous and natural self will sympathize with another's pleasure, but whether he will sympathize with another's pain,[12] at least to a degree that will be an adequate counterpoise to egoistic impulse. The confidence of the eighteenth-century moralist on this point is already beginning to seem to us singularly naive. Rousseau, it will be remembered, not only attempts to rear the whole edifice of ethics on the basis of man's innate pitifulness, but asserts that this quality increases in almost direct ratio as one descends in the social scale and so gets closer to "nature." When asked why, if the plain people were so pitiful, they crowded eagerly to see men broken on the wheel, he replied that pity is such a delicious emotion that they did not wish to miss any opportunity of experiencing it! It was no doubt for this reason that Chateaubriand's house porter, as he narrates, regretted Robespierre and the spectacles in the Place Louis XV, where women mounted the guillotine who had "necks as white as chicken's flesh." For a sim-

---

[11] Justice is, according to Hume, an "artificial" virtue; its immediate source is an enlightened self-interest. Its ultimate source, like that of all the other virtues, is "an extensive sympathy with mankind."

[12] "Laugh and the world laughs with you, weep and you weep alone."

ilar reason doubtless the Spanish populace frequents the bullring and the ancient Roman populace flocked to the gladiatorial arena. The truth is that the psychology of the plain people in matters of this kind is not ethical at all, but Epicurean. It is pleasant, as the Epicurean Lucretius pointed out some time ago, to witness another's dire peril of shipwreck from a safe position on the shore. In much the same way, the misery of the world, when properly dished up in the headlines, merely serves to give the ordinary citizen an agreeable fillip at his breakfast table. With the help of the sensational press, the men of today are indeed constantly lined up on the shore, witnessing an endless series of shipwrecks.

The outstanding trait, in short, of a populace that is "natural" in Rousseau's sense is its irresponsible quest of thrills. The success of the whole attempt to base ethics directly on the emotions has been due in no small measure to the fact that it seemed to offer an equivalent, not only for Christian charity, but for grace, a grace that did not, like the old variety, involve humility and the conviction of sin; inasmuch as the man who transgresses does so, not through any survival of the "old Adam" in him, but because of society and its institutions. The man who has not fallen from the grace of nature into social sophistication is spontaneously virtuous. "Heaven's rich instincts in him grew," says Lowell of a beautiful soul of this kind, "as effortless as woodland nooks send violets up and paint them blue." The difference between the new and the old grace is here obvious: the old grace involved a working, even though the recipient of it maintained that not he but God did the working.

The fact of the working was in any case indubitable, so
much so that it often imposed a severe and even ascetic
control upon the natural man. Goodness by the grace of
nature, on the other hand, does not require on the part
of the recipient anything more than a "wise passiveness."

Another striking contrast between Christian love and
grace and the parody of these doctrines by the Rousseauist should be noted. The love and grace of the
Christian lead to sharp exclusions and discriminations;
whereas the Rousseauist tends to blur all distinctions in
pantheistic revery. Contrast the "vision" of a Dante,
for example, with its clear-cut scale of moral values from
the peak of heaven to the pit of hell with the "vision"
of a Walt Whitman in which not merely men and women,
good, bad, and indifferent, but "elder, mullein, and
pokeweed" are all viewed on the same level in virtue of
what the pantheist calls love. Dante speaks of the "highest
love" that built the walls of hell. We shudder at the
medieval grimness. The opposite and more dangerous
extereme is to lavish what Bossuet calls a "murderous
pity" upon human nature and, under cover of promoting
love, to be ready to subvert justice.

An unselective love joined to a "wise passiveness"
and a return to "nature" might, indeed, be justified if,
as their votaries maintain, they tend to draw men to a
common center; but it can be shown that this communion is achieved, not in the real world, but in dreamland.
Let us consider from this point of view the "simple life"
that Rousseau and other primitivists have proposed as
a remedy for the luxury and self-indulgence that have
tended to increase with the breakdown of traditional

standards. True simplicity of life must, it would seem, be attained by the limitation of desire; whereas the luxurious life is one in which, as Montesquieu says, "the desires have become immense." Now the "nature" of the primitivist can be shown to be only a nostalgia of the romantic imagination so that the attempt to return to it not only expands desire instead of limiting it, but makes it infinite and indeterminate. Rousseau speaks of that "devouring but barren fire with which from my childhood up I have felt myself vainly consumed." Chateaubriand makes his René actually flee from European civilization to the American wilderness and take an Indian bride. René speaks for Chateaubriand himself when he writes to her: "There issue forth from this heart flames . . . which might devour creation without being satisfied." Chateaubriand posed as the champion of Christianity. Yet nothing is more certain than that Christian love makes for peace and communion, whereas nostalgic "love" of the type Chateaubriand has just described makes for restlessness and solitude. The ironical contrast between the ideal and the real appears even more clearly, perhaps, in Shelley than in Chateaubriand, inasmuch as Shelley did not, like Chateaubriand, pose as a traditionalist, but came out uncompromisingly for the new ethics. "The great secret of morals," he says, "is love." A characteristic note of his poetry, on the other hand, perhaps the most characteristic note is that of an acute spiritual isolation.

Many of the partisans of the new liberty, a liberty based, not upon work (in the sense of inner control), but upon "love" in the sense of expansive emotion, were

severely disillusioned by the French Revolution. Chateaubriand is himself one of the best types of the disillusioned
Rousseauist. In his "Essay on Revolutions" he still looks
upon romantic nostalgia as the true badge of the superior
spirit, though he admits that the aspiration toward the
"infinite" that it inspires is especially prevalent in epochs
of moral decline. As a result of this nostalgia, at all
events, man is never satisfied with what he has. He
shatters one political form after another from sheer
satiety and ennui. The movement of mankind is not
steadily forward in a straight line, as the apostles of
perfectibility maintain, but circular, like that of a squirrel
in a cage. From the point of view of the lover of liberty
society is hopeless. "If it is political truth we are looking
for, it is easy to find. Here a despotic minister gags me
and casts me into the depths of a dungeon where I remain for twenty years without knowing why: having
escaped from the Bastille, I plunge indignantly into democracy; an anthropophagus awaits me there at the foot
of the guillotine." As we should say nowadays, overthrow
the Czar and the Bolshevist has you by the throat.

Is there, then, no such thing as liberty? "Yes, there
is a delicious, a celestial liberty, that of nature." Let a
man betake himself to the "religious forest." In very
similar fashion, Coleridge, after discovering that the
French Revolution, theoretically a crusade for universal
brotherhood, was imperialistic in its essence, abandoned
hope of finding liberty among men. If a man wishes to
find true liberty, he says in substance, let him go out and
listen to what the wild waves are saying. Liberty is not
to be found in any human form. But if one "shoots his
being through earth, sea, and air" and "possesses all

things with intensest love," liberty will be revealed to him.[13]

It may be, however, that a man should look for true liberty neither in society nor in nature, but in himself— his ethical self; and the ethical self is experienced, not as an expansive emotion, but as an inner control. Liberty is associated, therefore, not primarily with "love," but with work. "It is work," as Buddha says, and not love, as the Western sentimentalist would have it, "that makes the world go round."[14] The man who works ethically grows more at one with himself and at the same time tends to enter into communion, not indeed with mankind at large, but with those who are submitting to a similar ethical discipline, and so are, in the Confucian phrase, moving toward the "universal center." So that even from the point of view of the man who desires love, the great secret of morals is work. Love is the fulfillment of the law and not, as the sentimentalist would have us believe, a substitute for it. The psychological truth at the basis of the Christian doctrine of charity is that men cannot come together expansively and on the level of their ordinary selves. The attempt to do so results, as we have seen in the case of a Rousseau and a Shelley, in an extreme psychic isolation.

Rousseau says that he founded "an indomitable spirit

---

[13] See *France: An Ode* (1798), pt. 5. The beginnings of this part of the poem are pure Burke:

> The Sensual and the Dark rebel in vain,
> Slaves by their own compulsion! etc.

After striking this Burkian note, Coleridge proceeds to fall into sheer pantheistic bewilderment.

[14] *Sutta-Nipâta*, v. 654.

of liberty" on an "indolence that is beyond belief." True liberty, it is hardly necessary to say, cannot be founded on indolence; it is something that must be won by high-handed struggle, a struggle that takes place primarily in oneself and not in the outer world. Possibly the ultimate distinction between the true and the false liberal, as I have suggested elsewhere, is that between the spiritual athlete and the cosmic loafer. If true liberty is to survive, it is important that ethical idling should not usurp the credit due only to ethical effort. This usurpation takes place if we accept the program of those who would substitute expansive emotion for the activity of the higher will. In the real world, as I have tried to show, the results of an expansion of this kind are not fraternal but imperialistic.

The confusion between true and false liberals, between the ethically strenuous and the ethically indolent, has also been promoted by the doctrine of natural rights. A liberty that is asserted as an abstract right, something anterior to the fulfillment of any definite obligation, will always, so far as the inner life is concerned, be a lazy liberty. From this point of view, all other "natural" rights are in a way summed up in the title of a book written by a grandson of Karl Marx: *The Right to Idleness*. We have heard asserted in our own time the abstract right of whole populations to self-determination as something anterior to their degree of moral development. To put forward a supposed right of this kind as a part of a program for world peace is to sink to the ultimate depth of humanitarian self-deception.

To be sure, the dogma of natural rights, though it

still controls the popular imagination, has been disavowed by the political theorists themselves. Unfortunately, some of these theorists, while disavowing the dogma, have retained the underlying fallacy. For example, Mr. Harold J. Laski says that, though we no longer believe in the rights of man in any abstract and metaphysical sense, we still accept them as a convenient expression of the truth that what men want corresponds in a rough way to what they need.[15] The first and very elementary step in any effective knowledge of human nature, a step that "liberals" of the type of Mr. Laski have failed to take, is the discovery of the lack of coincidence between man's wants and his needs. What man needs, if we are to believe the Lord's Prayer, is bread and wisdom. What man, at least Roman man, wanted about the time this prayer was uttered, was bread and the circus. The gap between man's wants and his needs has not diminished greatly, if at all, since Roman times. Whatever we may think of Christian theology, the Christian insight remains true that man suffers from a divided will: he needs to follow the law of the spirit and wants to follow the law of the members, so that he is a thoroughly paradoxical creature, for the most part at war with his own happiness.

Our endeavor at the present time, I have said, should be to deal with the law of the spirit positively and so be able to meet on their own ground those who have professed to be positive and are not. Let us take a glance from this point of view at the professional philosophers.

---

[15] *Political Thought from Locke to Bentham*, p. 270.

Hume, for example, set up as a pure positivist: he was in favor of getting rid of all apriorism and planting himself on what Bergson calls the "immediate data of consciousness." Strictly speaking, indeed, mere rationalism died with Hume. Unfortunately, Kant galvanized the corpse. His "pure reason" does not, as the reason of Descartes and the other great system builders of the seventeenth century was supposed to do, give reality, but only empty categories. In opposition to this pure reason Kant sets up a practical reason that is led to make certain affirmations that cannot be shown to correspond with the "thing-in-itself." By the divorce that is thus established between practice and reality, the way is opened for pragmatism which, instead of testing utility by truth, would test truth by utility; likewise for the closely allied theory of "useful fiction" and other philosophical vagaries of recent times.

Let us return from the insubstantial transcendence of Kant to Hume and his claim to be purely experimental. This claim cannot be allowed for two reasons: first, as I have already remarked, he asserts something that cannot be experimentally established—namely, an element of spontaneous sympathy in the natural man, strong enough to cope unaided with egoistic impulse. Second, he fails to assert something that is, nevertheless, one of the "immediate data of consciousness"—namely, an ethical will that is felt as a power of control over the natural man and his expansive desires. Deny this ethical will and the inner life disappears; assert it and one may dispense with numerous other assertions, or at least give them minor emphasis. Many other things are true, no doubt, in addition to what one may affirm positively; and "extra-beliefs" are in any case inevitable. It is desirable, however, under existing circumstances, to get at human-istic or religious truth with the minimum of metaphysical or theological complications. It is not even clear that, in order to preserve the integrity of the inner life, one needs to set up a world of entities, essences, or "ideas" above the flux. Much of the loftiest spirituality of the Occident has been associated with this Platonic idealism. On the other hand, the early Buddhists saw in a somewhat similar doctrine in India an obstacle rather than an aid to the achievement of the fruits of religion.

Kant, again, has from a strictly experimental point of view, gone too far in asserting "God, freedom, immor-tality"; and at the same time, from another point of view, he has not gone far enough, for the freedom of his "categorical imperative" is primarily a freedom to do, and not, like that of the ethical will, a freedom to refrain from doing. The first step surely is to plant oneself on the psychological fact of an opposition between a law of the spirit and a law of the members, a living and present fact that one neglects at one's peril in favor of what may seem superficially more useful and agreeable. Some persons, it may be urged, are conscious of no such oppo-sition in themselves. Some persons are also color-blind, and spiritual vision is subject to even more infirmities than physical vision.

The higher will in the dualism I have been sketching has, as I have tried to show, been very much bound up historically with the doctrine of grace and has tended to be obscured with the decline of this doctrine. It would be possible to go through the chief modern philosophers one after the other from Descartes down and show that they are least satisfactory in their treatment of the will.[16] Any one who wishes to recover the true dualism must begin by exalting the ethical will to the first place. Any attempt to give the primacy to "reason" in any sense of the word will result in the loss of humility and lead to a revival, in some form, of the Stoical error. One must in this matter not only side with the Christian against the Stoic, but in general with the Asiatic against the European intellectual. It does not follow because one gives the first place to will that one is to identify it with the absolute or, like Schopenhauer, with the "thing-in-itself"; for this is to fall from positive psychological observation into metaphysics; nor, because one insists that intellect is, as compared with will, secondary, need one conclude with Wordsworth and other romantic obscurantists that it is therefore "false."

To give the first place to the higher will is only another way of declaring that life is an act of faith. One may discover on positive grounds a deep meaning in the old Christian tenet that we do not know in order that we may believe, but we believe in order that we may know. What follows almost inevitably when the intellect ceases to be the servant of the higher will and sets up as an independent power is a lapse into the metaphysical illusion—the illusion of having confined the ocean in a cup. The most familiar form of this illusion in recent times is that of the pure mechanist or determinist. If the de-

---

[16] See Appendix A.

terminist is told in the words of the poet that "our wills
are ours, we know not how; our wills are ours to make
them thine," he answers in substance that our wills are
not ours and that he knows how. But his knowledge on
this point is only a conceit of knowledge. He is trying
with finite faculties to grasp factors that are at bottom
infinite, or, what amounts to the same thing, trying to
subject the higher element in human nature to the lower.
The proper reply to the determinist is not to appeal to
some dogma or other, but to experience. The decisive
word here has been uttered by Dr. Johnson, who has
claims to be regarded as the most sensible person of
recent times: "All theory," he says, "is against the
freedom of the will, all experience for it." Plant oneself
firmly on this fact of experience and the way is open
at one essential point for a return to common sense.
We escape at once from the vast web of intellectual and
emotional sophistry in which the naturalistic moralists
have sought to enmesh us. The answer to the enigma
of life, so far as there is any, is not for the man who
sets up some metaphysical theory, but for the man who,
in some sense or other of the word, acts. Now to act
according to the ethical will is, so far as the natural
man is concerned, to pull back, limit, and select. This
supremely human act of selection the rationalistic naturalist would turn over to physical nature. The emotional naturalist, refusing to be mechanized along either
Cartesian or Darwinian lines, emphasizes his vital unique-
ness, his spontaneous and temperamental "me," and its
right to get itself uttered. The natural will that is thus
released from control is conceived by Nietzsche as a

will to power, and this would seem to have some relation
to the facts. On the other hand, the notion of a Rousseau
or a Whitman, that "liberty" of this type is compatible
with fraternity, is very far from being experimental.

A French writer, M. Léon Daudet, has won a certain
notoriety by applying to the nineteenth century the
epithet "stupid." If the century deserves the epithet
at all, it is surely because of the aspect of it that I
have just been discussing. The determinist tends to
mechanize man and deny him genuine moral choice. The
partisans of romantic spontaneity from Rousseau to
Bergson have hoped to escape from this naturalistic
fatalism by setting up some cosmic urge or *élan vital*
as a substitute for moral effort. Yet a multitude of men
during the past century, who acquiesced in either one or
the other of these two main forms of ethical passiveness,
held at the same time a firm faith in "progress." They
were drifting, to be sure, but drifting toward a "far-off
divine event," usually conceived as a paradise of peace
and brotherhood. But if it is a question of drifting,
there is only one direction in which one can drift and
that is toward barbarism. Civilization is something that
must be deliberately willed; it is not something that
gushes up spontaneously from the depths of the unconscious. Furthermore, it is something that must be willed
first of all by the individual in his own heart. Men who
have thus willed civilization have never been any too
numerous; so that civilization always has been and, in
the very nature of the case, always must remain something precarious. In the words of Rivarol, barbarism is

always as close to the most refined civilization as rust is to the most highly polished steel.

As a result of the denial or dissimulation of the forms of inner action on which civilization finally depends, the naturalistic era in which we are living has been especially rich in dubious moralists, from the "beautiful souls" of the eighteenth century to the Freudians and behaviorists of our own day. If the behaviorist deserves censure for seeing only matter and material causes, the tendency that appears in Berkeleyan idealists and, in much cruder form, in the exponents of various brands of "new thought," to deny matter in favor of what they conceive to be spirit is also open to grave objection. As a result of this denial, they tend to lose their sense of the reality of the "civil war in the cave," and so to fall into materialism from the other side. The Freudian corruption of ethics illustrates interestingly another main naturalistic fallacy. Because outer and mechanical repression of desire may work injury, it is insinuated that the repression of desire is bad *per se*. If one says that what is needed is not outer control but inner control, even philosophers of some standing will reply that inner control or the ethical will is only the brake on personality; and that a vehicle cannot, after all, be propelled by its brake. The metaphor, however, is utterly misleading; the ethical will is nothing external and mechanical like a brake. The man who imposes this will upon the outgoing desires is moving away from what is peripheral in himself to what is central, to what is indeed at the very center. The humanist would not go beyond disciplining the "lusts" of the natural man to the law of measure. However, if one goes still further and "dies" entirely to the natural self and its impulses, what follows, if we are to believe the great religious teachers, is not mere emptiness, but the peace that passeth understanding.

The man who does not impose either religious or humanistic control upon his ordinary self does not usually avow that he is a mere materialist. The ethical problem would be comparatively simple if he did. The egocentric individualist is, however, prone to give fine names to his own unrestraint. As Plato says, he will call insolence breeding, anarchy liberty, and waste magnificence; and may even go to the point of deifying his own impulses. There are times when one must reply in the affirmative to the question of Virgil "whether each man's god is but his own fell desire." There is a sense in which one must agree with the scoffer that an honest God is the noblest work of man. We recognize readily that the God whom the Kaiser and many Germans worshipped during the War was only a projection into the religious realm of their own will to power. We are loath, however, to admit any equivalent of this imperialistic error in the champions of democracy. And yet it is not difficult to point out such an equivalent, for example, in the humanitarian illusionist Victor Hugo. Monckton Milnes relates that when he called on Hugo at Paris, "he was shown into a large room, with women and men seated in chairs against the walls, and Hugo at one end throned. No one spoke. At last Hugo raised his voice solemnly and said: 'Quant à moi, je crois en Dieu.' Silence followed. Then a woman responded as if in deep meditation: 'Chose sublime! un Dieu qui croit en Dieu.' '"[17] The sublimity diminishes somewhat when one observes to what an extent the God in whom Hugo believes reflects his ordinary self so that he is thus enabled to worship this self on a sort of cosmic scale. A man also frequently calls what is at bottom only an hypostasis of his ordinary self in its dominant desire either progress or justice. Thus Mr. Samuel Gompers complained that the New York Assembly of 1919 did not pass a single "progressive or forward-looking act." We all know what this means. The far-off divine event toward which the whole creation moves is for Mr. Gompers the domination of the laboring class, with the understanding that the laboring class itself is to be dominated by Mr. Gompers or his kind. As a result of the cowardice of our politicians, this more or less divine event has at times not seemed so far off as one might wish. The attempt to bestow the word justice on personal or class interests is too familiar to need illustration.

We are dealing here with the most ancient and still the most successful form of camouflage. During the War, the French did not fail to quote a passage of Tacitus to the general effect that the Germans give fine names to what is at bottom only their own lawlessness and love of plunder. But there is in this trait nothing specifically German. The barbaric Briton, the same Tacitus narrates, complained of his Roman conquerors that "they make a desolation and call it peace." This human proclivity, though universal, is especially marked in periods

---

[17] I take the anecdote from *The Education of Henry Adams*, p. 143.

of individualistic emancipation. It is especially at such
a period that one needs to remind oneself with Hobbes
that words are the counters of wise men and the coin of
fools, and that one is not to suppose, on hearing a fine
phrase, that it coincides necessarily with a fine thing.
We are put here on the track of the true office of the intellect in such a period. To set out like Rousseau to be
an individualist and at the same time to disparage intellect is to enter upon the pathway of madness. In
direct ratio, indeed, to the completeness of one's break
with the past must be the keenness of one's discrimination. Otherwise one runs the risk of setting up as an
"ideal" and decking out with fair phrases some unsub-
stantial dream—the mere ballooning out of the imagination into the void.

The imagination must, to be sure, be supreme, but it
should be an imagination disciplined to the facts. If the
imagination is not present, the facts will not be unified;
they will remain inert and isolated. But the intellect
must also be present—and by intellect I mean the power
in man that analyzes and discriminates and traces causes
and effects; for this power alone can determine whether
the unity the imagination has established among the facts
is real or whether it exists rather only in some "realm of
chimeras." The genuine man of science is not, on the one
hand, a metaphysical theorist nor, on the other, a mere
fact-grubber. His eminence is measured by the gift he
possesses for true vision in connection with some field
of facts on which he has long been fixing his attention.
What may have come to him originally in a flash of intuition he is careful to check up and test experimentally

by every means in his power; and at this stage he is not synthetic but analytic. His success is due to the correct relation he has established between the part of himself that perceives, the part that conceives, and the part that discriminates.

Now the true humanist deals with his facts in a somewhat similar fashion: only the facts on which he is fixing his attention are on an entirely different order. His imagination is disciplined to law, but this law is not the "law for thing." He is tracing cause and effect, but these causal sequences are not the ones that occur in physical nature. Because there is in us, in Lowell's phrase, something that refuses to be "Benthamized," the romantic idealist looks with suspicion on a cause-and-effect philosophy and the keen analysis by which it can be established; but any other than a cause-and-effect philosophy is likely to fall into sheer unreality; inasmuch as reality means practically the reality of law, and law in turn means that as a matter of positive observation there is a constant association between certain phenomena either in time or in space—an association that exists quite apart from the desires or opinions of the individual. If there is not a human law that is thus objective, so that the person who violates it exposes himself to certain consequences in much the same way that the person who puts his finger into the fire exposes himself to certain consequences, then the human law is not worth going in search of. A skeptic of the type of Hume would affirm, indeed, that the very idea of cause and effect is not objective but subjective, that it arises from man's "propensity to feign." But even if we go to the extreme of skepticism and look on life merely as a "dream whose shapes return," it remains true that these returning shapes bear a certain constant relationship to one another; so that they are susceptible of study from the point of view of the only problem that finally matters—the problem of happiness or unhappiness. Of cause and effect in any abstract and metaphysical sense, the critical humanist is willing to avow his ignorance; just as the true man of science admits that he cannot grasp the ultimate essence behind the phenomenal relationships he is busy in tracing.

The foregoing analysis, if it is correct, suggests that the type of material progress on which the Occident has been expending its main effort for some time past, so far from promoting moral progress, is likely rather to make against it. This type of progress has resulted from imaginative concentration on facts of an entirely different order from those of the moral law. The keen analytical discrimination in the service of actual perception that gives reality—such reality as man has access to—has become the more and more exclusive monopoly of the man of science or of the utilitarian who has been organizing scientific discovery into a vast machinery of material efficiency. In the meanwhile, in the distinctively human realm, the imagination has been left more or less free to roam at large. It has set up a unity, as I remarked at the outset, that has not been sufficiently tested from the point of view of its reality. The unity that the humanitarian hopes to achieve among men hinges almost entirely, I have tried to show, on the idea of "service." Men are to be brought together, one finds on analyzing this idea of service, by means that are either rationalistic and mechanical or else emotional. In either case, the humanitarian assumes that men can meet expansively and on the level of their ordinary selves. But if this notion of union should prove to be illusory, if men can really come together only in humble obeisance to something set above their ordinary selves, it follows that the great temple to humanity that has been in process of erection for several generations past is the modern equivalent of the Tower of Babel; and so we should not be surprised if it is being stricken with a confusion of tongues.

With the progressive weakening of traditional standards, the inability of the humanitarian to supply any adequate substitute is becoming apparent. The whole of the Occident seems to be at an impasse. The mere rationalist and the mere emotionalist are about equally bankrupt. It may be that our only hope is a return to the truths of the inner life. If we ourselves are unable to see the need of such a return, it is perhaps because we have reached the stage of the decadent Romans who, according to Livy, were unable to endure the evils from which they were suffering and also the remedies for those evils.

The loss of the truths of the inner life in their traditional form has involved, I have tried to show, a profound alteration in the idea of liberty. Liberty has come more and more to be conceived expansively, not as a process of concentration, as a submission or adjustment to a higher will. My whole argument thus far has been that we should seek to recover in some critical form the centripetal element in liberty that the modernist has allowed to drop out and so become thoroughgoing and complete moderns. It is a matter of no small importance in any case to be defective in one's definition of liberty; for any defect here will be reflected in one's definitions of peace and justice; and the outlook for a society which has defective notions of peace and justice cannot be regarded as very promising.

A good deal of the confusion about liberty, as I have endeavored to show, has been promoted by the pantheistic dreamers who have sought a substitute for the grace of God in the grace of nature, and so have obscured the distinction between the man for whom liberty is an ethical working and the man who, like Rousseau, seeks to found an indomitable spirit of liberty on an indolence that is beyond belief. The pure traditionalist, the Catholic, for example, not only avoids a particular confusion of this kind, but is in general relieved of the task of defining liberty that is imposed upon the individualist. The church will supply him with his definition: liberty, he will be told, is submission to the will of God; and the church will not only supply him with the general principle, but also give him guidance in the innumerable "cases" that arise in the application of it. Inasmuch as the pope is infallible (since 1870), at least in religion and morals, submission to the will of God tends to coincide practically, though not of course in theory, with submission to the pope.

Though the sound individualist must also have standards, it is plain that he cannot get at them in this way— not, namely, by leaning on outer authority, but rather by the cooperation of intellect and imagination I have tried to describe. The standards he has thus secured he will proceed to press into the service of the ethical will.

A program of this kind, in which imagination, intellect, and will cooperate, instead of flying asunder, as they tend to do in Pascal, for example, is, it must be confessed, easier to outline than to accomplish. Yet it is hard to see that our modern experiment can be carried through safely on any other terms. If this experiment shows signs of breaking down, the explanation is surely that it has failed thus far to achieve adequate equivalents for the traditional controls. Instead of setting up genuine standards and then selecting with reference to them, the man who professes to be modern has turned selection over to "nature" and sought to substitute for the working of the ethical will a diffuse, unselective sympathy. This tendency to put on sympathy a burden that it cannot bear and at the same time to sacrifice a truly human hierarchy and scale of values to the principle of equality has been especially marked in the democratic movement, nowhere more so perhaps than in our American democracy. It remains, therefore, to discuss democracy in its relation to standards. I shall attempt in the course of this discussion to elucidate still further, with the aid of a Socratic dialectic, my distinction between the true and the false liberal.

CHAPTER 7

Democracy and Standards

Judged by any quantitative test, the American achievement is impressive. We have ninety percent of the motors of the world and control seventy-five percent of its oil; we produce sixty percent of the world's steel, seventy percent of its copper, and eighty percent of its telephones and typewriters. This and similar statistical proof of our material preeminence, which would have made a Greek apprehensive of Nemesis, seems to inspire in many Americans an almost lyrical complacency. They are not only quantitative in their estimates of our present accomplishment, but even more so if possible in what they anticipate for the future. Now that we have fifteen million automobiles they feel, with Mr. Henry Ford, that we can have no higher ambition than to expand this number of thirty million. Our present output of fifty million tons of steel a year is, according to Mr. Schwab, a mere trifle compared with our probable output of twenty

years hence. In short, an age that is already immersed in
things to an unexampled degree is merely to prepare
the way for an age still more material in its preoccupations and still more subservient to machinery. This, we
are told, is progress. To a person with a proportionate
view of life it might seem rather to be full-blown commercial insolence.

The reasons for the quantitative view of life that prevails in America are far from being purely political. This
view has resulted in a large measure from the coming
together of scientific discovery with the opening up of a
new continent. It has been possible with the aid of science
to accomplish in a hundred years what even the optimistic
Thomas Jefferson thought might take a thousand. The
explanation, it has been said, of much that is obscure
to us in the Chinese may be summed up in the words
"lack of elbowroom." We in this country, on the other
hand, have received a peculiar psychic twist from the
fact that we have had endless elbowroom. A chief danger
both to ourselves and others is that we shall continue to
have a frontier psychology long after we have ceased to
have a frontier. For a frontier psychology is expansive,
and expansiveness, I have tried to show, is, at least in its
political manifestations, always imperialistic.

If quantitatively the American achievement is impressive, qualitatively it is somewhat less satisfying. What
must one think of a country, asks one of our foreign
critics, whose most popular orator is W. J. Bryan, whose
favorite actor is Charlie Chaplin, whose most widely
read novelist is Harold Bell Wright, whose best-known
evangelist is Billy Sunday, and whose representative

journalist is William Randolph Hearst? What one must evidently think of such a country, even after allowing liberally for overstatement, is that it lacks standards. Furthermore, America suffers not only from a lack of standards, but also not infrequently from a confusion or an inversion of standards. As an example of the inversion of standards we may take the bricklayer who, being able to lay two thousand bricks a day, is reduced by union rules to laying five hundred. There is confusion of standards, again, when we are so impressed by Mr. Henry Ford's abilities as organizer and master mechanic that we listen seriously to his views on money; or when, simply because Mr. Edison has shown inventive genius along certain lines, we receive him as an authority on education. One is reminded of the story of the French butcher who, having need of legal aid, finally, after looking over a number of lawyers, selected the fattest one.

The problem of standards, though not identical with the problem of democracy, touches it at many points and is not therefore the problem of any one country. Europeans, indeed, like to look upon the crudity and chaotic impressionism of people who are no longer guided by standards as something specifically American. "America," says the *Saturday Review*, "is the country of unbalanced minds, of provincial policies and of hysterical utopias." The deference for standards has, however, been diminished by a certain type of democracy in many other countries besides America. The resulting vulgarity and triviality are more or less visible in all of these countries— for example, if we are to believe Lord Bryce, in New Zealand. If we in America are perhaps preeminent in lack of distinction, it is because of the very completeness of our emancipation from the past. Goethe's warning as to the retarding effect of the commonplace is well known (*Was uns alle bändight, das Gemeine*). His explanation of what makes for the commonplace is less familiar: "Enjoyment," he says, "makes common" (*Geniessen macht gemein*). Since every man desires happiness, it is evidently no small matter whether he conceives of happiness in terms of work or of enjoyment. If he work in the full ethical sense that I have attempted to define, he is pulling back and disciplining his temperamental self with reference to some standard. In short, his temperamental self is, in an almost literal sense, undergoing conversion. The whole of life may, indeed, be summed up in the words diversion and conversion. Along which of these two main paths are most of us seeking the happiness to the pursuit of which we are dedicated by our Declaration of Independence? The author of this phrase, Thomas Jefferson, remarks of himself: "I am an Epicurean."[1] It cannot be gainsaid that an increasing number of our young people are, in this respect at least, good Jeffersonians. The phrase that reflects most clearly their philosophy of life is perhaps "good time." One might suppose that many of them see this phrase written in great blazing letters on the very face of the firmament. As *Punch* remarked, the United States is not a country, but a picnic. When the element of conversion with reference to a standard is eliminated from life, what remains is the irresponsible quest of thrills. The utilitarian and industrial side of the modern

---

[1] *Works* (ed. Ford), x, p. 143.

movement comes into play at this point. Commercialism is laying its great greasy paw upon everything (including the irresponsible quest of thrills); so that, whatever democracy may be theoretically, one is sometimes tempted to define it practically as standardized and commercialized melodrama. This definition will be found to fit many aspects of our national life besides the moving-picture industry. The tendency to steep and saturate ourselves in the impression of the moment without reference to any permanent pattern of human experience is even more marked, perhaps, in our newspapers and magazines. It was said of the inhabitants of a certain ancient Greek city that, though they were not fools, they did just the things that fools would do. It is hard to take a glance at one of our newsstands without reflecting that, though we may not be fools, we are reading just the things that fools would read. Our daily press in particular is given over to the most childish sensationalism. "The Americans are an excellent people," Matthew Arnold wrote from Boston in 1883, "but their press seems to me an awful symptom." This symptom was not so awful then as now; for that was before the day of the scarehead and the comic supplement. The American reading his Sunday paper in a state of lazy collapse is perhaps the most perfect symbol of the triumph of quantity over quality that the world has yet seen. Whole forests are being ground into pulp daily to minister to our triviality.

One is inclined, indeed, to ask, in certain moods, whether the net result of the movement that has been sweeping the Occident for several generations may not be a huge mass of standardized mediocrity; and whether in this country in particular we are not in danger of producing in the name of democracy one of the most trifling brands of the human species that the world has yet seen. To be sure, it may be urged that, though we may suffer loss of distinction as a result of the democratic drift, by way of compensation a great many average people will, in the Jeffersonian sense at least, be made "happy." If we are to judge by history, however, what supervenes upon the decline of standards and the disappearance of leaders who embody them is not some egalitarian paradise, but inferior types of leadership. We have already been reminded by certain developments in this country of Byron's definition of democracy as an "aristocracy of blackguards." At the very moment when we were most vociferous about making the world safe for democracy the citizens of New York refused to reelect an honest man as their mayor and put in his place a tool of Tammany, an action followed in due course by a "crime wave"; whereupon they returned the tool of Tammany by an increased majority. The industrial revolution has tended to produce everywhere great urban masses that seem to be increasingly careless of ethical standards. In the case of our American cities, the problem of securing some degree of moral cohesion is further complicated by the presence of numerous aliens of widely divergent racial stocks and cultural backgrounds.[2] In addition, not only is our population about half urban, but we cannot be said,

---

[2] For example, 41 percent of the residents of New York City are actually foreign-born; if we add those whose father or mother or both were born abroad, the more or less foreign element in its population amounts to 80 percent.

like most other countries, to have any peasantry or yeo-
manry. Those Americans who actually dwell in the country are more and more urban in their psychology. The
whole situation is so unusual as to suggest doubts even
from a purely biological point of view. "As I watch the
American nation speeding gaily, with invincible optimism
down the road to destruction," says Professor William
McDougall, an observer of the biological type, "I seem
to be contemplating the greatest tragedy in the history of
mankind."

We are assured, indeed, that the highly heterogeneous
elements that enter into our population will, like various
instruments in an orchestra, merely result in a richer
harmony; they will, one may reply, provided that, like
an orchestra, they be properly led. Otherwise the outcome may be an unexampled cacophony. This question
of leadership is not primarily biological, but moral. Leaders may vary in quality from the man who is so loyal
to sound standards that he inspires right conduct in
others by the sheer rightness of his example, to the man
who stands for nothing higher than the law of cunning
and the law of force, and so is, in the sense I have sought
to define, imperialistic. If democracy means simply the
attempt to eliminate the qualitative and selective principle
in favor of some general will, based in turn on a theory
of natural rights, it may prove to be only a form of the
vertigo of the abyss. As I have tried to show in dealing
with the influence of Rousseau on the French Revolution,
it will result practically, not in equality, but in a sort of
inverted aristocracy. One's choice may be, not between
a democracy that is properly led and a democracy that

hopes to find the equivalent of standards and leadership in the appeal to a numerical majority, that indulges in other words in a sort of quantitative impressionism, but between a democracy that is properly led and a decadent imperialism. One should, therefore, in the interests of democracy itself seek to substitute the doctrine of the right man for the doctrine of the rights of man.

The opposition between traditional standards and an egalitarian democracy based on the supposed rights of man has played an important part in our own political history, and has meant practically the opposition between two types of leadership. The "quality" in the older sense of the word suffered its first decisive defeat in 1829 when Washington was invaded by the hungry hordes of Andrew Jackson. The imperialism latent in this type of democracy appears in the Jacksonian maxim: "To the victors belong the spoils." In his theory of democracy Jackson had, of course, much in common with Thomas Jefferson. If we go back, indeed, to the beginnings of our institutions, we find that America stood from the start for two different views of government that have their origin in different views of liberty and ultimately of human nature. The view that is set forth in the Declaration of Independence assumes that man has certain abstract rights; it has therefore important points of contact with the French revolutionary "idealism." The view that inspired our Constitution, on the other hand, has much in common with that of Burke. If the first of these political philosophies is properly associated with Jefferson, the second has its most distinguished representative in Washington. The Jeffersonian liberal has faith in the goodness of the natural man, and so tends to overlook the need of a veto power either in the individual or in the state. The liberals of whom I have taken Washington to be the type are less expansive in their attitude toward the natural man. Just as man has a higher self that acts restrictively on his ordinary self, so, they hold, the state should have a higher or permanent self, appropriately embodied in institutions, that should set bounds to its ordinary self as expressed by the popular will at any particular moment. The contrast that I am establishing is, of course, that between a constitutional and a direct democracy. There is an opposition of first principles between those who maintain that the popular will should prevail, but only after it has been purified of what is merely impulsive and ephemeral, and those who maintain that this will should prevail immediately and unrestrictedly. The American experiment in democracy has, therefore, from the outset been ambiguous, and will remain so until the irrepressible conflict between a Washingtonian and a Jeffersonian liberty has been fought to a conclusion. The liberal of the type of Washington has always been very much concerned with what one may term the unionist aspect of liberty. This central preoccupation is summed up in the phrase of Webster: Liberty and union, one and inseparable. The liberty of the Jeffersonian, on the other hand, makes against ethical union like every liberty that rests on the assertion of abstract rights. Jefferson himself proclaimed not only human rights, but also state rights.[3] Later the doctrine of state rights was developed with logical rigor by Calhoun,

---

[3] He drafted, for example, the so-called Kentucky Resolutions (November 1799).

whereas the doctrine of human rights was carried through
no less uncompromisingly by the abolitionists. The result
was two opposing camps of extremists and fire-eaters;
so that the whole question of union, instead of being settled on ethical lines, had to be submitted to the arbitra-
ment of force.

The man who has grasped the full import of the conflict between the liberty of the unionist and that of the
Jeffersonian has been put in possession of the key that
unlocks American history. The conflict between the
two conceptions is not, indeed, always clear-cut in particular individuals. There is much in Jefferson himself
that contradicts what I have been saying about Jefferson. A chief business of criticism, however, is to distinguish, in spite of peripheral overlappings, between
things that are at the center different. For example, to
link together in a common admiration Jefferson and John
Marshall, our most eminent unionist after Washington
himself, is proof of lack of critical discrimination rather
than of piety toward the fathers. Jefferson and Marshall
knew perfectly that they stood for incompatible things,[4]
and it is important that we should know it also. "Marshall," says John Quincy Adams in his Diary, "has
cemented the Union which the crafty and quixotic democracy of Jefferson had a perpetual tendency to dis-
solve."

By his preoccupation with the question of the union,

---

[4] A similar opposition existed, of course, between Jefferson and Alexander Hamilton. The *Life of Hamilton*, by F. S. Oliver, is to be commended
for the clearness of the insight it displays into the nature of this opposition.

Lincoln became the true successor of Washington and Marshall. In making of Lincoln the great emancipator instead of the great unionist, in spite of his own most specific declarations on this point, we are simply creating a Lincoln myth, as we have already created a Washington myth.[5] We are sometimes told that the good democrat needs merely to be like Lincoln. But to be like Lincoln one must know what Lincoln was like. This is not only a task for the critic, but, in view of the Lincoln myth, a more difficult task than is commonly supposed. It is especially easy to sentimentalize Lincoln because he had a strongly marked vein of sentimentalism. Nevertheless, in spite of the peripheral overlappings between the democracy of Lincoln and that of Jefferson[6] or even between that of Lincoln and Walt Whitman, one should insist on the central difference. One has only to read, for example, the Second Inaugural along with the "Song of Myself" if one wishes to become aware of the gap that separates religious humility from romantic egotism. We should be careful again, in spite of peripheral overlappings, not to confound the democracy of Lincoln with that of Roosevelt. What we feel at the very center in Roosevelt is the dynamic rush of an imperialistic personality. What we feel at the very center of Lincoln, on the other hand, is an element of judicial control; and in close relation to this control a profound conception of the role of the

---

[5] A specially influential book in the creation of this myth was the *Life of Washington* (1800), by "Parson" Weems.

[6] Lincoln actually defended himself against the charge of having spoken disparagingly of Jefferson. See *Works* (ed. Nicolay and Hay), VI, p. 60.

courts in maintaining free institutions. The man who has studied the real Lincoln does not find it easy to imagine him advocating the recall of judicial decisions.

The Jeffersonian liberal is, as a rule, much more ostentatiously fraternal than the liberal in the other tradition. Yet he is usually inferior in human warmth and geniality to the unionist. Washington and Marshall and Lincoln at their best combined practical sagacity with a central benignity and unselfishness. Jefferson, on the other hand, though perhaps our most accomplished politician, did not show himself especially sagacious in dealing with specific emergencies. Furthermore, it is hard to read his *Anas* and reflect on the circumstances of its composition without concluding that what was central in his personality was not benignity and unselfishness but vindictiveness.

Statesmen who deserve the praise I have bestowed on our unionist leaders are, as every student of history knows, extremely rare. The type of constitutional liberty that we owe to these men before all others is one of the greatest blessings that have ever been vouchsafed to any people. And yet we are in danger of losing it. The Eighteenth Amendment is striking proof of our loss of grasp, not only on the principles that underlie our own Constitution, but that must underlie any constitution, as such, in opposition to mere legislative enactment.

Our present drift away from constitutional freedom can be understood only with reference to the progressive crumbling of traditional standards and the rise of a naturalistic philosophy that, in its treatment of specifically human problems, has been either sentimental or utilitarian. The significant changes in our own national temper in particular are finally due to the fact that Protestant Christianity, especially in the puritanic form, has been giving way to humanitarianism. The point is worth making because the persons who have favored prohibition and other similar "reforms" have been attacked as Puritans. Genuine puritanism was, however, a religion of the inner life. Our unionist leaders, Washington, Marshall, and Lincoln, though not narrowly orthodox, were still religious in the traditional sense. The struggle between good and evil, as they saw it, was still primarily not in society, but in the individual. Their conscious dependence on a higher or divine will could not fail to be reflected in their notion of liberty. Jefferson, on the contrary, associated his liberty, not with God, but with "nature." He admired, as is well known, the liberty of the American Indian.[7] He was for diminishing to the utmost the role of government, but not for increasing the inner control that must, according to Burke, be in strict ratio to the relaxation of outer control. When evil actually appears, the Jeffersonian cannot appeal to the principle of inner control; he is not willing again to admit that the sole alternative to this type of control is force; and so he is led into what seems at first a paradoxical denial of his own principles; he has recourse to legislation. It should be clear at all events that our present attempt to substitute social control for self-control is Jeffersonian rather than puritanical. So far as we are true children of the Puri-

---

[7] See *Works* (ed. Ford), III, p. 195.

tans, we may accept the contrast established by Professor Stuart P. Sherman[8] between our own point of view and that of the German: "The ideal of the German is external control and 'inner freedom'; the government looks after his conduct and he looks after his liberty. The ideal of the American is external freedom and inner control; the individual looks after his conduct and the government looks after his liberty. Thus *Verboten* in Germany is pronounced by the government and enforced by the police. In America *Verboten* is pronounced by public opinion and enforced by the individual conscience. In this light it should appear that puritanism, our national principle of concentration, is the indispensable check on democracy, our national principle of expansion. I use the word 'puritanism' in the sense given to it by German and German-American critics: *the inner check upon the expansion of natural impulse.*"

Professor Sherman's contrast has been true in the past and still has some truth—at least enough for the purposes of wartime propaganda. But what about our main drift at present? It is plainly away from the point of view that Professor Sherman ascribes to the Puritan[9] and toward the point of view that he ascribes to the

---

[8] *American and Allied Ideals* (War Information Series, No. 12), p. 9.

[9] Strange things have been happening to the Puritan conscience of late even in the most authentic descendants of the Puritans. Thus Henry Adams inserts in a hymn to the Virgin a hymn to the dynamo. The whole conception has little relation to medieval Christianity and none at all to puritanism. It is, however, closely related to the tendency of the nineteenth century to see in a sympathy that is emancipated from justice the proper corrective of a power that is pursued without regard to the law of measure.

German. "The inner check upon the expansion of natural impulse" is precisely the missing element in the Jeffersonian philosophy. The Jeffersonian has therefore been led to deal with the problem of evil, not vitally and in terms of the inner life, but mechanically. Like the Jesuit he has fallen from law into legalism. It has been estimated that for one *Verboten* sign in Germany we already have a dozen in this country; only, having set up our *Verboten* sign, we get even by not observing it. Thus prohibition is pronounced by the government, largely repudiated by the individual conscience, and enforced (very imperfectly) by the police. The multitude[10] of laws we are passing is one of many proofs that we are growing increasingly lawless.

There are, to be sure, peripheral overlappings between the point of view of the Puritan and that of the humanitarian legalist. The Puritan inclined from the start to be meddlesome, as anyone who has studied the activities of Calvin at Geneva will testify. But even here

---

[10] It is estimated that 62,014 statutes were passed by our national and state legislatures in the period 1909–13. Some of these laws—for example, those regulating finger bowls and the length of sheets in hotels—remind one of the minute prescriptions indulged in by the ancient city-states at their worst. Cf. Fustel de Coulanges, *La Cité antique*, p. 266: "L'Etat exerçait sa tyrannie jusque dans les plus petites choses; à Locres, la loi défendait aux hommes de boire du vin pur; à Rome, à Milet, à Marseille, elle le défendait aux femmes. Il était ordinaire que le costume fût fixé invariablement par les lois de chaque cité; la législation de Sparte réglait la coiffure des femmes, et celle d'Athènes leur interdisait d'emporter en voyage plus de trois robes. A Rhodes la loi défendait de se raser la barbe; à Byzance, elle punissait d'une amende celui qui possédait chez soi un rasoir; à Sparte, au contraire, elle exigeait qu'on se rasât la moustache."

one may ask whether the decisive arguments by which we have been induced to submit to the meddling of the prohibitionist were not utilitarian rather than puritanical. "Booze," says Mr. Henry Ford, "had to go out when modern industry and the motor car came in." The truth may be that we are prepared to make any sacrifice to the Moloch of efficiency, including, apparently, that of our federal Constitution.

The persons who have been carrying on of late a campaign against the Puritans like to look on themselves as "intellectuals." But if the primary function of the intellect is to make accurate distinctions, it is plain that they do not deserve the title. For in dealing with this whole subject they have fallen into a twofold confusion. So far as they identify with puritanism the defense of the principle of control in human nature, they are simply attacking under that name the wisdom of the ages and all its authentic representatives in both East and West. To bestow, on the other hand, the name of Puritans on the humanitarian legalists who are now sapping our spiritual virility is to pay them an extravagant and undeserved compliment. Let us take as a sample of the attacks on the Puritans that of Mr. Theodore Dreiser, culminating in the grotesque assertion regarding the United States: "No country has such a peculiar, such a seemingly fierce determination to make the Ten Commandments work." We are murdering one another at the rate of about ten thousand a year (with very few capital convictions)[11] and are in general showing our-

---

[11] In 1885 there were 1,808 homicides in the United States with 108 executions; in 1910, 8,975 homicides with 104 executions.

selves more criminally inclined than any other nation that is reputed to be civilized.[12] The explanation is that we are trying to make, not the Ten Commandments, but humanitarianism work—and it is not working. If our courts are so ineffective in punishing crime, a chief reason is that they do not have the support of public opinion, and this is because the public is so largely composed of people who have set up sympathy for the underdog as a substitute for all the other virtues, or else of people who hold that the criminal is the product of his environment and so is not morally responsible. Here as elsewhere there is a cooperation between those who mechanize life and those who sentimentalize it.

The belief in moral responsibility must be based on a belief in the possibility of an inner working of some kind with reference to standards. The utilitarian, as I have sought to show, has put his main emphasis on outer working. The consequence of this emphasis, coinciding as it has with the multiplication of machines, has been the substitution of standardization for standards. The type of efficiency that our master commercialists pursue requires that a multitude of men should be deprived of their specifically human attributes, and become mere

---

[12] "In 1918 Chicago had 22 robberies for every one robbery in London and 14 robberies for every one robbery in England and Wales. . . . Cities like St. Louis and Detroit, in their statistics of robbery and assault with intent to rob, frequently show annual totals varying from three times to five times greater than the number of such crimes reported for the whole of Great Britain. Liverpool is about one and a third times larger than Cleveland, and yet in 1919 Cleveland reported 31 robberies for every one reported in Liverpool" (Raymond B. Fosdick, *Crime in America and the Police*, 1920, p. 18). Mr. Fosdick ascribes our imperfect administration of justice to our legalism (p. 48) and our sentimentalism (p. 44).

cogs in some vast machine. At the present rate even
the grocer in a remote country town will soon not be
left as much initiative as is needed to fix the price of a
pound of butter.

Standardization is, however, a less serious menace to
standards than what are currently known as "ideals."
The person who breaks down standards in the name of
ideals does not seem to be impelled by base commercial
motives, but to be animated, on the contrary, by the
purest commiseration for the lowly and the oppressed.
We must have the courage to submit this humanitarian
zeal to a close scrutiny. We may perhaps best start with
the familiar dictum that America is only another name
for opportunity. Opportunity to do what? To engage in
a scramble for money and material success, until the
multimillionaire emerges as the characteristic product
of a country dedicated to the proposition that all men
are created equal? According to Napoleon, the French
Revolution was also only another name for opportunity
(*la carrière ouverte aux talents*). Some of our commercial
supermen have evidently been making use of their opportunity in a very Napoleonic fashion. In any case,
opportunity has meaning only with reference to some
true standard. The sentimentalist, instead of setting up
some such standard by way of protest against the wrong
type of superiority, inclines rather to bestow an unselective sympathy on those who have been left behind
in the race for economic advantage. Even when less
materialistic in his outlook, he is prone to dodge the
question of justice. He does not ask whether a man is
an underdog because he has already had his opportunity

and failed to use it, whether, in short, the man that he takes to be a victim of the social order is not rather a victim of his own misconduct[18] or at least of his own indolence and inattention. He thus exposes himself to the penalties visited on those who set out to be kinder than the moral law.

At bottom the point of view of the "uplifter" is so popular because it nourishes spiritual complacency; it enables a man to look on himself as "up" and on some one else as "down." But there is psychological if not theological truth in the assertion of Jonathan Edwards that complacent people are a "particular smoke" in God's nostrils. A man needs to look, not down, but up to standards set so much above his ordinary self as to make him feel that he is himself spiritually the underdog. The man who thus looks up is becoming worthy to be looked up to in turn, and, to this extent, qualifying for leadership. Leadership of this type, one may add, may prove to be, in the long run, the only effectual counterpoise to that of the imperialistic superman.

No amount of devotion to society and its supposed interests can take the place of this inner obeisance of the spirit to standards. The humanitarian would seem to be caught here in a vicious circle. If he turns from

---

[18] "This is a chain of galley slaves," cried Sancho, "who are going to the galleys." . . . "Be it how it may," replied Don Quixote, "these people, since they are being taken, go by force and not of their own will. . . . Here comes in the exercise of my office, to redress outrages and to succor and aid the afflicted." "Let your worship reflect," said Sancho, "that justice, which is the king's self, does no violence or wrong to such people, but chastises them in punishment of their crimes" (*Don Quixote*, pt. 1, chap. 22).

the inner life to serve his fellow men, he becomes a busy-body. If he sets out again to become exemplary primarily with a view to the benefit of others, he becomes a prig. Nothing will avail short of humility. Humility, as Burke saw, is the ultimate root of the justice that should prevail in the secular order, as well as of the virtues that are specifically religious. The modern problem, I have been insisting, is to secure leaders with an allegiance to standards, now that the traditional order with which Burke associated his standards and leadership has been so seriously shaken. Those who have broken with the traditional beliefs have thus far shown themselves singularly ineffective in dealing with this problem of leadership, even when they have admitted the need of leaders at all. The persons who have piqued themselves especially on being positive have looked for leadership to the exponents of physical science. Auguste Comte, for example, not only regarded men of science as the true modern priesthood, but actually disparaged moral effort on the part of the individual. I scarcely need to repeat here what I have said elsewhere —that the net result of a merely scientific "progress" is to produce efficient megalomaniacs. Physical science, excellent in its proper place, is, when exalted out of this place, the ugliest and most maleficent idol before which man has as yet consented to prostrate himself. If the essence of genuine science is to face loyally all the facts as they present themselves without dogmatic prepossessions, one is justified in asking whether the man who forgets that physical science is, in Tennyson's phrase, the second, not the first, is genuinely scientific; whether the very sharpest discrimination does not need to be established between science and utilitarianism. Aristotle, for example, was a true man of science; he was not a utilitarian.[14] Francis Bacon, on the other hand, is the prophet of the whole utilitarian movement, but one may doubt his eminence as a man of science. Quite apart from the fact that he failed to make important scientific discoveries, one may question the validity of the Baconian method. His failure to do justice to deduction as part of a sound scientific method has often been noted. A more serious defect is his failure to recognize the role of the imagination, or, what amounts to the same thing, the role of exceptional genius in the making of scientific discoveries.[15]

One cannot grant that an aristocracy of scientific intellectuals or indeed any aristocracy of intellect is what we need. This would mean practically to encourage the *libido sciendi* and so to put pride in the place of humility. Still less acceptable would be an aristocracy of artists; as the word art has come to be understood in recent times, this would mean an aristocracy of aesthetes who would attempt to base their selection on the *libido sentiendi*. The Nietzschean attempt, again, to found the aristocratic and selective principle on the sheer expansion of the will to power (*libido dominandi*) would lead in

---

[14] "To be always seeking after the useful does not become free and exalted souls" (*Politics*, 1338b).

[15] To suppose, as Bacon did, not only that nature is exhaustible, but that it may be exhausted by the accumulated observations of a number of essentially commonplace specialists is to be wrong at the center. Cf. *Novum Organum*, bk. 1, aphorism 122: "My way of discovering sciences goes far to level men's wits, and leaves but little to individual excellence."

practice to horrible violence and finally to the death of civilization. The attempts that were made during the past century to establish a scale of values with reference to the three main lusts of the human heart often took on a mystical coloring. Man likes to think that he has God as an ally of his expansive conceit, whatever this conceit may chance to be. When, indeed, one has passed in review the various mysticisms of the modern movement, as they are set forth, for example, in the volumes of M. Seillière, one is reminded of the saying of Bossuet: "True mysticism is so rare and unessential and false mysticism is so common and dangerous that one cannot oppose it too firmly."

If one discovers frequently a pseudomystical element in the claims to leadership of the aesthetes, the supermen and the scientific intellectuals, this element is even more visible in those who would, in the name of democracy, dispense with leadership altogether. Thus Walt Whitman, as we have seen, would put no check on his "spontaneous me"; he would have every one else indulge his "idiocrasy" to the same degree, be a "genius," in short, in the full romantic sense of the term. A liberty thus anarchical is to lead to equality and fraternity. If one tells the democrat of this type that his program is contrary to common sense and the facts of experience, he is wont to take refuge in mystical "vision." One needs in effect to be very mystical to suppose that men can come together by flying off each on his temperamental tangent. Whitman does not admit the need of the leader who looks up humbly to some standard and so becomes worthy to be looked up to in turn. The only leadership he contemplates apparently is that of the ideal democatic bard who flatters the people's pride and chants the divine average.[16] He represents in an extreme form the substitution for vital control of expansive emotion under the name of love. Pride and self-assertion when tempered by love, will not, he holds, endanger the principle of union.[17] The Union, though "always swarming with blatherers, is yet," he says, "always sure and impregnable." The records of the past are not reassuring as to the maintenance of ethical union in a community that is swarming with "blatherers." At all events, the offset to the blatherers will be found, not in any divine average, but in the true leader— the "still strong man in a blatant land." We come here to another opposition that is one of first principles and is not therefore subject to mediation or compromise—the opposition, namely, between the doctrine of the saving remnant and that of the divine average. If one deals with human nature realistically one may find here and there a person who is worthy of respect and occasionally one who is worthy of reverence. Anyone, on the other hand, who puts his faith in the divinity of the average is destined, if we are to trust the records of history, to pass through disillusion to a final despair. We are reaching

---

[16] "The American demands a poetry . . . that will place in the van and hold up at all hazards the banner of the divine pride of man in himself (the radical foundation of the new religion). Long enough have the people been listening to poems in which common humanity, deferential, bends low, humiliated, acknowledging superiors. But America listens to no such poem. Erect, inflated, and fully self-esteeming be the chant; and then America will listen with pleased ears" (*Democratic Vistas*).

[17] ". . . the American Soul, with equal hemispheres, one Love, one Dilation or Pride."

the stage of disillusion in this country at the present moment. According to the author of *Main Street,* the average is not divine but trivial; according to the author of the *Spoon River Anthology,* it is positively hideous. It can scarcely be gainsaid that contemporary America offers an opening for satire. A great many people are gradually drifting into materialism and often cherishing the conceit at the same time that they are radiant idealists. But satire, to be worthwhile, must be constructive. The opposite of the trivial is the distinguished; and one can determine what is distinguished only with reference to standards. To see Main Street on a background of standards would be decidedly helpful; but standards are precisely what our so-called realists lack. They are themselves a part of the disease that they are attempting to define.

The democratic idealist is prone to make light of the whole question of standards and leadership because of his unbounded faith in the plain people. How far is this appeal to the plain people justified and how far is it merely demagogic? There is undoubted truth in the saying that there is somebody who knows more than anybody, and that is everybody. Only one must allow everybody sufficient time to sift the evidence and add that, even so, everybody does not know very much. Burke told the electors of Bristol that he was not flattering their opinions of the moment, but uttering the views that both they and he must have five years thence. Even in this triumph of the sober judgment of the people over its passing impression, the role of the true leader should not be underestimated. Thus in the year 1795 the plain

people of America were eager to give the fraternal acco-
lade to the French Jacobins. The great and wise Washington opposed an alliance that would almost certainly have
been disastrous, and as a result he had heaped upon him
by journals like the *Aurora,* the forerunner of our modern
"journals of opinion," epithets that, as he himself complained, would not have been deserved by a common pick-
pocket. In a comparatively short time Washington and his
group were seen to be right, and those who seemed to be
the spokesmen of the plain people were seen to be wrong.
It is not clear that one can have much faith even in the
sober second thought of a community that has no enlightened minority. A Haitian statesman, for example,
might not gain much in appealing from Haitian opinion
of today to Haitian opinion of five years hence. The democratic idealist does not, however, mean as a rule by an
appeal to the plain people an appeal to its sober second
thought. He means rather the immediate putting into
effect of the will of a numerical majority. Like the man
in the comic song the people is supposed to "want what
it wants when it wants it." Our American drift for a
number of years has unquestionably been toward a democracy of this radical type, as is evident from the increasing vogue of the initiative, referendum, and recall
(whether of judges or judicial decisions) as well as from
popular primaries and the direct election of senators.
The feeling that the people should act directly on all
measures has led to the appearance in certain states of
ballots thirty feet long! Yet the notion that wisdom re-
sides in a popular majority at any particular moment
should be the most completely exploded of all fallacies.

If the plain people at Jerusalem had registered their will with the aid of the most improved type of ballot box, there is no evidence that they would have preferred Christ to Barabbas. In view of the size of the jury that condemned Socrates, one may affirm confidently that he was the victim of a "great and solemn referendum." On the other hand, the plain people can be shown to have taken a special delight in Nero. But the plain people, it will be replied, has been educated and enlightened. The intelligence tests applied in connection with the selective draft indicate that the average mental age of our male voters is about fourteen.[18] The intelligence testers are, to be sure, under some suspicion as to the quality of their own intelligence. A more convincing proof of the low mentality of our population is found, perhaps, in the fact that the Hearst publications have twenty-five million readers.

"There is nothing," says Goethe, "more odious than the majority; for it consists of a few powerful leaders, a certain number of accommodating scoundrels and subservient weaklings, and a mass of men who trudge after them without in the least knowing their own minds." If there is any truth in this analysis the majority in a radical democracy often rules in name only. No movement, indeed, illustrates more clearly than the supposedly democratic movement the way in which the will of highly organized and resolute minorities may prevail

---

[18] For a tabulation of these tests, see vol. 15 of the *Memoirs of the National Academy of Sciences.*

over the will of the inert and unorganized mass. Even though the mass does not consent to "trudge" after the minority, it is at an increasing disadvantage in its attempts to resist it. Physical science is on the side of the tyrannical minority. The ordinary citizen cannot have a machine gun by his fireside or a "tank" in his back yard. The most recent type of revolutionary idealist, though his chief concern is still to bestow benefit on the people, does not, to do him justice, hope to achieve this benefit through the majority, but rather through the direct action of organized minorities. He feels that he is justified in cramming his nostrum down the throat of the people, if necessary by force.

The radical of this type is coming round to the doctrine of the saving remnant and recognizing in his own way that everything finally hinges on the quality of the leadership. His views, however, as to this quality differ strangely from the traditional views. One must admit that, whatever theories of leadership may have been held traditionally, actual leadership has never been any too good. One scarcely suspects, as John Selden remarked, "what a little foolery governs the world." Moreover, the folly which has prevailed at the top of society, and that from the time of the Trojan War, has ever been faithfully reflected in the rank and file (*Quidquid delirant reges*—). One who surveys the past is at times tempted to acquiesce in the gloomy judgment of Dryden: "No government has ever been or ever can be wherein timeservers and blockheads will not be uppermost. The persons are only changed, but the same juggling in state, the same hypocrisy in religion, the same self-interest and mismanagement will remain forever. Blood and money will be lavished in all ages only for the preferment of new faces with old consciences." One should note, however, a difference between the bad leadership of the past and that of the modern revolutionary era. The leaders of the past have most frequently been bad in violation of the principles they professed, whereas it is when a Robespierre or a Lenin sets out to apply his principles that the man who is interested in the survival of civilization has reason to tremble.

Dryden's passage seems to suggest that what is really needed is not new faces with old consciences, but a transformation of conscience itself. It is precisely such a transformation that a revolutionary idealist like Robespierre hopes to effect. For the corrupt conscience of the old type of aristocratic leader he would substitute a social conscience. The popular will that is inspired by this conscience is so immaculate, as we have seen, that it may safely be put in the place not merely of the royal but of the divine will. I have already tried to show that a leader who sets out to be only the organ of a "general will" or "divine average," that is conceived at times as essentially reasonable and at other times as essentially fraternal, will actually become imperialistic. It may be well at this point to submit this democratic idealism to still further analysis with special reference to its probable effect on our own international relations. The tendency for some time past has been to treat international law, not theoretically as an embodiment of reason, but positively as an embodiment of will.[19] In that case, if international law is to reflect any improvement in the relations between states, it must be shown that the substitution of the popular will for the divine will has actually tended to promote ethical union among men even across national frontiers. If we analyze realistically the popular will, we find that it means the will of a multitude of men who are more and more emancipated from traditional standards and more and more given over to what I have termed the irresponsible quest of thrills. These thrills are, as we all know, supplied by sensational newspapers and in international affairs involve transitions, often disconcertingly sudden, from pacifism to jingoism. Anyone who can recollect the period immediately preceding our conflict with Spain will be sufficiently aware of the role that this type of journalism may play in precipitating war. Let us ask ourselves again whether the chances of a clash between America and Japan are likely to diminish if Japan becomes more democratic, if, in other words, the popular will is substituted for the will of a small group of "elder statesmen." Anyone who knows what the Japanese sensational press has already done to foment suspicion against America is justified in harboring doubts on this point.

A democracy, the realistic observer is forced to conclude, is likely to be idealistic in its feelings about itself,

---

[19] In *Le Droit international public positif* (1920), I, pp. 77 ff., J. de Louter has traced historically the opposition between those who base international law on "jus naturale," conceived as universal reason, and those who incline rather to see in it an expression of will ("just voluntarium").

but imperialistic in its practice. The idealism and the imperialism, indeed, are in pretty direct ratio to one another. For example, to be fraternal in Walt Whitman's sense is to be boundlessly expansive, and a boundless expansiveness, is, in a world like this, incompatible with peace. Whitman imagines the United States as expanding until it absorbs Canada and Mexico and dominates both the Atlantic and the Pacific—a program that would almost certainly involve us in war with the whole world. If we go, not by what Americans feel about themselves, but by what they have actually done, one must conclude that we have shown ourselves thus far a consistently expansive, in other words, a consistently imperialistic, people.[20] We have merely been expanding, it may be replied, to our natural frontiers; but we are already in the Philippines, and manifestly in danger of becoming involved in Asiatic adventures. Japan, a country with fifty-seven million inhabitants (increasing at the rate of about six hundred thousand a year), on a group of islands not as large as the state of California, only seventeen percent of which is arable, has at least a plausible pretext for reaching out beyond her natural frontiers. But for us, with our almost limitless and still largely undeveloped resources, to risk the horrors of war under modern conditions for anything we are likely to gain from expanding eastward, would be an extreme example of sheer restlessness of spirit and of an intemperate commercialism. It is a part of our psychology that each main

---

[20] This consistent imperialism has been traced by H. H. Powers in his volume *America Among the Nations*.

incident in our national history should take on a highly idealistic coloring. For example, we were on the verge of a conflict with Mexico a few years ago as the result of an unwarranted meddling with her sovereignty. President Wilson at once described the incipient struggle as a war of "service." Cicero says that Rome gained the mastery of the world by coming to the aid of her allies. In the same way it may be said some day of us that, as the result of a series of outbursts of idealism, we changed from a federal republic to a highly centralized and bureaucratic empire. We are willing to admit that all other nations are self-seeking, but as for ourselves, we hold that we act only on the most disinterested motives. We have not as yet set up, like revolutionary France, as the Christ of Nations, but during the late war we liked to look on ourselves as at least the Sir Galahad of Nations. If the American thus regards himself as an idealist at the same time that the foreigner looks on him as a dollar-chaser, the explanation may be due partly to the fact that the American judges himself by the way he feels, whereas the foreigner judges him by what he does.

This is not, of course, the whole truth. Besides our tradition of idealism there is our unionist tradition based on a sane moral realism. "It is a maxim," says Washington, "founded on the universal experience of mankind, that no nation is to be trusted further than it is bound by its interests; and no president, statesman or politician will venture to depart from it." All realistic observation confirms Washington. Those who are inspired by his spirit believe that we should be nationally prepared, and then that we should mind our own business. The tendency of our idealists, on the other hand, is to be unprepared and then to engage in more or less general meddling. A third attitude may be distinguished that may properly be associated with Roosevelt. The follower of Roosevelt wants preparedness, only he cannot, like the follower of Washington, be counted on to mind his own business. The humanitarian would, of course, have us meddle in foreign affairs as part of his program of world service. Unfortunately, it is more difficult than he supposes to engage in such a program without getting involved in a program of world empire. The term sentimental imperialism may be applied to certain incidents in ancient Roman history.[21] Some of the motives that we professed for entering the Great War remind one curiously of the motives that men like Flamininus professed for going to the rescue of Greece. Cicero, writing over a century later and only a few months before his assassination by the emissaries of the Triumvirs, said that he himself had once thought that Rome stood for world service rather than for world empire, but that he had been bitterly disillusioned. He proceeds to denounce Julius Caesar, the imperialistic leader *par excellence,* as a demon in human form who did evil for its own sake. But Caesar had at least the merit of seeing that the Roman ethos was changing, that as the result of the breakdown of religious restraint (for which Stoical "service" was not an adequate substitute), the Romans were rapidly becoming unfit for republican institutions.

---

[21] See Tenney Frank's *Roman Imperialism,* especially chap. 8 ("Sentimental Politics").

Some persons, indeed, are inclined to go beyond particular comparisons of this kind and develop a general parallel between decadent Rome and modern America. Such a parallel is always very incomplete and must be used with great caution. We need, in the first place, to define with some precision what we mean by decadence. The term is often used vaguely by persons who are suffering from what one may call the illusion of the "good old times."[22] Livy is surely a bit idyllic when he exclaims: "Where will you now find in one man this modesty and uprightness and loftiness of spirit that then belonged to a whole people?" Yet if one compares the Rome of the Republic with the Rome of the Empire one is conscious of a real decline. The Senate that had seemed to Cineas, the adviser of Pyrrhus, an assembly of demigods, had become by the time of Tiberius a gathering rather of cringing sycophants. Horace was uttering only the sober truth when he proclaimed the progressive degeneracy of the Romans of his time.[23] The most significant symptom of this degeneracy seemed to Horace and other shrewd observers to be the relaxation of the bonds of the family.

Are we witnessing a similar moral deliquescence in this country, and, if so, how far has it gone? One of our foreign critics asserts that we have already reached the "Heliogabalus stage"—which is absurd. But at the

---

[22] As the rural philosopher remarked: "Things ain't what they used to be—in fact they never was."

[23] Aetas parentum peior avis tulit
  Nos nequiores, mox daturos
  Progeniem vitiosiorem.

  Carminum, Lib. iii, 6

same time it is not to be denied that the naturalistic notion of liberty has undermined in no small measure the two chief unifying influences of the past—the church and the family. The decline in the discipline of the family has been fairly recent. Persons are still living who can remember the conditions that prevailed in the Puritan household.[24] The process of emancipation from the older restraint has not usually presented itself as a lapse into mere materialism. Idealism in the current sense of that term has tended to take the place of traditional religion. The descendants of the Puritans have gone in for commercialism, to be sure, especially since the Civil War, but it has been commercialism tempered by humanitarian crusading. As I have pointed out, the humanitarian does not, like the genuine Puritan, seek to get at evil in the heart of the individual, so that he is finally forced to resort to outer regulation. The egoistic impulses that are not controlled at their source tend to prevail over an ineffectual altruism in the relations of man with man and class with class. The special mark of materialism, which is to regard property, not as a means to an end, but as an end in itself, is more and more visible. The conservative nowadays is interested in conserving property for its own sake and not, like Burke, in conserving it because it is an almost indispensable support of personal liberty, a genuinely spiritual thing. As for the progressive, his preoccupation with property and what he conceives to be its just distribution amounts to a morbid obsession. Orderly party

---

[24] Professor G. H. Palmer has written from his own memories an article on "The Puritan Home" (*Atlantic Monthly*, November 1921).

government will become increasingly difficult if we continue to move in this direction, and we shall finally be menaced by class war, if, indeed, we are not menaced by it already. Every student of history is aware of the significance of this particular symptom in a democracy. One may sum up what appears to be our total trend at present by saying that we are moving through an orgy of humanitarian legalism toward a decadent imperialism.

The important offsetting influence is our great unionist tradition. One should not, however, underestimate the difficulties in the way of maintaining this tradition. The idea that the state should have a permanent or higher self that is felt as a veto power upon its ordinary self rests ultimately upon the assertion of a similar dualism in the individual. We have seen that this assertion has in the Occident been inextricably bound up with certain Christian beliefs that have been weakened by the naturalistic movement. We are brought back here to the problem with which we have been confronted so often in the course of the present argument, how, namely, to get modern equivalents for the traditional beliefs, above all some fresh basis for the affirmation of a *frein vital* or centripetal element in liberty. What the men of the French Revolution wanted, according to Joubert, was not religious liberty, but irreligious liberty. In that case, the French modernist retorts bitterly, you would have us give up revolutionary liberty and become Jesuits. Similarly, if one points out to an American modernist the inanity of his idealism as a substitute for the traditional controls, he will at once accuse you of wishing to revert to puritanism. Strictly speaking, however, one does not need to revert to anything. It is a part of my own method to put Confucius behind Aristotle and Buddha behind Christ. The best, however, that even these great teachers can do for us is to help us to discover what is already present in ourselves.[25] From this point of view they are well-nigh indispensable.

Let us begin, therefore, by ridding our minds of unreal alternatives. If we in America are not content with a stodgy commercialism, it does not follow that we need, on the one hand, to return to puritanism, or, on the other, to become "liberals" in the style of *The New Republic;* nor, again, need we evolve under the guidance of Mr. H. L. Mencken into second-rate Nietzscheans. We do need, however, if we are to gain any hold on the present situation, to develop a little moral gravity and intellectual seriousness. We shall then see that the strength of the traditional doctrines, as compared with the modernist position, is the comparative honesty with which they face the fact of evil. We shall see that we need to restore to human nature in some critical and experimental fashion the "old Adam" that the idealists have been so busy eliminating. A restoration of this kind ought not to lead merely to a lapse from naturalistic optimism into naturalistic pessimism; nothing is easier than such a lapse and nothing at bottom is more futile. Both attitudes are about equally fatalistic and so undermine moral responsibility. A survey

---

[25] Cf. Pascal, *Pensées,* 64: "Ce n'est pas dans Montaigne, mais dans moi que je trouve tout ce que j'y vois."

of the facts would suggest that man is morally responsible, but that he is always trying to dodge this responsibility; that what he suffers from, in short, is not fate in any sense of the word, but spiritual supineness. There may be truth in the saying that the devil's other name is inertia. Nothing is more curious than to trace historically the way in which some great teaching like that of Christ or Buddha has been gradually twisted until man has adjusted it more or less completely to his ancient indolence. Several centuries ago there was a sect of Japanese Buddhism known as the Way of Hardships; shortly after there arose another sect known as the Easy Way which at once gained great popularity and tended to supplant the Way of Hardships. But the Japanese Way of Hardships is itself an easy way if one compares it with the original way of Buddha. One can follow, indeed, very clearly the process by which Buddhist doctrine descended gradually from the austere and almost inaccessible height on which it had been placed by its founder to the level of the prayer mill. It was announced in the press not long ago that as a final improvement some of the prayer mills in Tibet are to be operated by electricity. The man who hopes to save society by turning the crank of a legislative mill or who sets up as a "socioreligious engineer" may call himself a Christian, but he is probably as remote from the true spirit of Jesus as some Eastern votary of the Easy Way is from the true spirit of Buddha.

The essence of man's spiritual indolence, as I have already pointed out, is that he does not wish to look up to standards and discipline himself with reference to them. He wishes rather to expand freely along the lines of his dominant desire. He grasps eagerly at everything that seems to favor this desire and so tends, as the saying is, to keep him in good conceit with himself. Disraeli discovered, we are told, that the best way to get on with Queen Victoria was to flatter her and not to be afraid of overdoing the flattery, but "to lay it on with a trowel." Demos, as was pointed out long ago, craves flattery like any other monarch, and in his theory of popular sovereignty Rousseau has, it must be admitted, laid this flattery on with a trowel. In general, his notion that evil is not in man himself, but in his institutions, has enjoyed immense popularity, not because it is true, but because it is flattering.

Observations of the kind I have been making are likely to lay one open to the charge of cynicism. One needs, however, to cultivate a wholesome cynicism as the only way of avoiding the unwholesome kind—that of the disillusioned sentimentalist. When I speak of a wholesome cynicism, I mean that of Aristotle who says that "most men do evil when they have an opportunity," or that of Bossuet, expressing the moderate Christian view, when he speaks of "the prodigious malignity of the human heart always inclined to do evil." There is no harm in cynicism provided the cynic does not think of himself as viewing human nature from the outside and from some superior pinnacle. In the sense I have just defined, cynicism, indeed, has many points in common with religious humility.

Let us pursue then our realistic analysis without fear

of the charge of cynicism. Man would not succumb so easily to flattery if he did not begin by flattering himself; his self-flattery is closely related in turn to his moral indolence. I have said that the whole of life may be summed up in the words diversion and conversion. But man does not want conversion, the adjustment in other words of his natural will to some higher will, because of the moral effort it implies. In this sense he is the everlasting trifler. But, though he wishes diversion, he is loath at the same time to admit that he is missing the fruits of conversion. He wills the ends, because they are plainly desirable, but he does not will the means because they are difficult and disciplinary. In short, he harbors incompatible desires and so listens eagerly to those who encourage him to think that it is possible to have the good thing without paying the appointed price.

Two main modes in which men are thus flattered may be distinguished. First, in an age of authority and accepted standards, they are induced to substitute for the reality of spiritual discipline some ingenious art of going through the motions. An extreme example is that of the fashionable lady described by Boileau who (with the aid of her spiritual director) had convinced herself that she could enjoy all the pleasures of hell on the way to paradise. What concerns us now, however, is not the mode of flattery that is based on exaggerated respect for outer authority, but the other main mode that flourishes in an age of individualism. The cushions that, according to Bossuet, the Jesuits put under the sinner's elbows are as nothing compared to the cushions that the sinner puts under his own elbows when left to himself. In a period like the present every man is his own Jesuit.[26] Rousseau's sycophancy of human nature proved to be particularly suited to the requirements of the individualistic era. By his sophistry of feeling he satisfied in a new and fetching fashion man's permanent desire, especially in the realm of moral values, to have his cake and eat it too. The self-flattery that encourages the huddling together of incompatible desires has never been pushed further than in this movement. When one considers, for instance, the multitude of those who have hoped to combine peace and brotherhood with a return to nature, one is forced to conclude that an outstanding human trait is a prodigious and pathetic gullibility.

The chief corrective of gullibility is, in an age of individualistic emancipation, a full and free play of the critical spirit. The more critical one becomes at such a time, the more likely one is to achieve standards and avoid empty conceits. Now to criticize is literally to discriminate. The student of both the natural and the human law needs to be very discriminating; one should note, however, an important difference between them. The discrimination of the man of science is exercised primarily upon physical phenomena, that of the humanist primarily upon words. "The beginning of genuine culture," Socrates is reported to have said, "is the scrutiny of general terms."[27] Socrates himself was so ac-

---

[26] Cf. Confucius: "Alas! I have never met a man who could see his own faults and arraign himself at the bar of his own conscience."

[27] See Epictetus, *Dissert.* I, 17.

complished in this type of scrutiny that he still deserves
to be the master of those who are aiming at criticism. I
have said that the hope of civilization lies not in the divine average, but in the saving remnant. It is plain that
in an age like the present, which is critical in every sense
of the word, the remnant must be highly Socratic.

Discrimination of the humanistic type is especially
needed in the field of political theory and practice.
Confucius, when asked what would be his first concern
if the reins of government were put into his hands, replied that his first concern would be to define his terms
and make words correspond with things. If our modern
revolutionaries have suffered disillusions of almost un-
paralleled severity, it is too often because they have
given their imagination to words, without making sure
that these words corresponded with things; and so they
have felt that they were bound for the promised land
when they were in reality only swimming in a sea of
conceit. "The fruit of dreamy hoping is, waking, blank
despair." The disenchantment of Hazlitt with the French
Revolution is typical of that of innumerable other "idealists." "The French Revolution," he says, "was the only
match that ever took place between philosophy and experience; and, waking from the trance of theory to the
sense of reality, we hear the words *truth, reason, virtue,
liberty* with the same indifference or contempt that the
cynic, who has married a jilt or a termagant, listens to the
rhapsodies of lovers."

The reason that the Rousseauist often alleges for his
attacks on the analytical intellect, the necessary instrument of a Socratic dialectic, is that it destroys unity.

His disparagement of analysis may be due, however, even less to his love of unity than to his dislike of effort. It may be that, like Rousseau himself, he is seeking to give to indolence the dignity of a philosophical occupation.[28] If it is a strenuous thing to concentrate imaginatively on the facts of the natural order, the concentration on the facts of the human order that enables one to use one's terms correctly is even more strenuous. What a monstrous inequality, said Lincoln, to pay an honest laborer seventy cents a day for digging coal and a President seventy dollars a day for digging abstractions! The argument that Lincoln thus puts forth ironically, a follower of Karl Marx would be capable of employing seriously. But if the President does honest work, if he digs his abstractions properly, instead of substituting some art of going through the motions, he must display the utmost contention of spirit. There have been moments in recent years when a President of this kind would have been worth to the country many times seventy dollars a day. Did the idealistic abstractions, one must make bold to ask, that Mr. Woodrow Wilson poured forth so profusely when President, satisfy the Socratic and Confucian test—did they correspond with things? The late Mr. Walter H. Page concluded, after unusual opportunities of observation, that Mr. Wilson was "*not* a leader, but rather a stubborn phrasemaker." Fine words, according to the homely adage, butter no parsnips. They may, however, it would seem,

---

[28] Cf. Joubert on the writings of Rousseau: "La paresse y prend l'attitude d'une occupation philosophique."

put a man in the White House. Mr. Wilson, it should be remembered, was not only an ex-college president himself, but in his main policies he had the eager support of practically the whole corporation of college presidents. If Mr. Page's estimate of Mr. Wilson should prove to be correct, it would follow that our American remnant—and college presidents should surely belong to the remnant— is not sufficiently critical. The question is one of some gravity, if it be true, as I said at the outset, that democracy will in the long run have to be judged, like any other form of government, by the quality of its leadership and if it be true, furthermore, that under existing conditions we must get our standards and our leadership along Socratic rather than traditional lines. "What the Americans most urgently require," said Matthew Arnold, "is a steady exhibition of cool and sane criticism." That is precisely what they require and what they have never had.

If we had a Socratic remnant one of its chief concerns would be to give a civilized content to the catchwords that finally govern the popular imagination. The sophist and the demagogue flourish in an atmosphere of vague and inaccurate definition. With the aid of the Socratic critic, on the other hand, Demos might have some chance of distinguishing between its friends and its flatterers— something that Demos has hitherto been singularly unable to do. Let one consider those who have posed with some success as the people's friends from Cleon of Athens to Marat; and from Marat to William Randolph Hearst. It would sometimes seem, indeed, that the people might do very well were it not for its "friends." The demagogue has been justified only too often in his assumption that men may be led, not by their noses, but by their ears as tenderly as asses are. The records of the past reveal that the multitude has frequently been persuaded by a mirage of words that the ship of state was steering a straight course for Eldorado, when it was in reality drifting on a lee shore; and the multitude has not been apprised of the peril until it was within the very sound of the breakers.

It is only too evident that we are not coping adequately with this special problem of democracy; that we are, on the contrary, in danger of combining the strength of giants with the critical intelligence of children. Millions of Americans were ready not so very long ago to hail William Jennings Bryan as a "peerless leader." Other millions are ready apparently to bestow a similar salute on Henry Ford—in spite of the almost incredible exhibition he made of himself with his "Peace Ship." If our Socratic critics were sufficiently numerous, the followers of such leaders would finally become conscious of something in the air that was keen, crisp, and dangerous; they might finally be forced to ask themselves whether the ideals with which they were being beguiled really mean anything, or at all events anything more than the masking in fine phrases of the desire to get one's hand into the other citizen's pocket. The devil, as is well known, is a comparatively harmless person unless he is allowed to disguise himself as an angel of light. An unvarnished materialism is in short less to be feared than sham spirituality. Sham spirituality is especially promoted by the blurring of distinctions, which is itself promoted by a tampering with general terms. A dialectical scrutiny of such terms is therefore indispensable if one is to determine whether what a man takes to be his idealism is merely some windy inflation of the spirit, or whether it has support in the facts of human experience.

I have already made some application of the Socratic method to idealism, a term that has come to be almost synonymous with humanitarianism. I have pointed out, for instance, how the utilitarian has corrupted the word "comfort" and the sentimentalist the word "virtue." The idealist may, indeed, retort that I have myself admitted that certain elements essential to salvation are omitted in the Socratic scheme of things, and that for these elements we need to turn from Socrates to Christ; and he will proceed to identify the gospel of Christ with his own gospel of sympathy and service. Humanitarian idealism unquestionably owes much of its prestige, perhaps its main prestige, to the fact that it has thus associated itself with Christianity. I have sought to show, however, on strictly psychological grounds, that humanitarian service does not involve, in either its utilitarian or its sentimental form, the truths of the inner life and that it cannot therefore be properly derived from Christ. The transformation, indeed, of this great master of the inner life into a master of "uplift" must seem to austere Christians, if there are any left, a sort of second crucifixion. In substituting the love of man for the love of God the humanitarian is working in a vicious circle, for unless man has in him the equivalent of the love of God he is not lovely. Furthermore, it is important that man should not only love but fear the right things. The question was recently raised at Paris why medical men were tending to usurp the influence that formerly belonged to the clergy. The obvious reply is that men once lived in the fear of God, whereas now they live in the fear of microbes. It is difficult to see how one can get on humanitarian lines the equivalent of the truth that the fear of the Lord is the beginning of wisdom.

Perhaps there is no better way of dealing with the humanitarian movement than to take one's point of departure in certain sayings of Jesus and at the same time so to protect them by a Socratic dialectic as to bring out their true meaning. For the present desideratum, it may be, is not to renounce Socrates[29] in favor of Christ, but, rather, to bring Socrates to the support of Christ.

Three sayings of Jesus would seem especially relevant, if we wish to bring out the contrast between his inspired and imaginative good sense and humanitarianism: (1) "Render unto Caesar the things that are Caesar's and unto God the things that are God's." (2) "By their fruits ye shall know them." (3) One should build one's house upon the rock.

I have already glanced at a violation of the first of these maxims—that, namely, which has taken place in connection with the humanitarian attempt to abolish war even at the expense of justice, and the closely related attempt to convert the prince of peace into a prince of pacifism. Americans often fear that the Roman Catholic church may use the machinery of democracy

---

[29] In his *Life of Christ* Papini not only attacks Socrates specifically, but bases his whole point of view on an abdication of the critical spirit.

to its own ends; and in parts of the country where Catholic voters are in the majority such apprehensions —for example, the apprehension regarding the Catholic domination of the schools—may not be entirely without foundation. It was not, however, a Catholic but a Protestant who recently felt it necessary to recall to his fellow believers that the kingdom of heaven is within us and not at Washington. The Protestant churches seem to be turning more and more to social service, which means that they have been substituting for the truths of the inner life various causes and movements and reforms and crusades. If W. J. Bryan had been born fifty years earlier he would very likely have been a religious revivalist; the religion of the revivalist was still in a fashion a religion of the inner life. Bryan's protest, however, in connection with his crusade for free silver, against the crucifixion of the people on a cross of gold, not only involves an unusually mawkish mixture of the things of God and the things of Caesar, but might have led to political action that, so far from being religious, would have been subversive of common honesty.

One should face frankly the question whether the crusading spirit is in any of its manifestations genuinely Christian. The missionary spirit, the purely spiritual appeal from man to man, is unquestionably Christian. By the crusading spirit I mean, on the other hand, the attempt to achieve spiritual ends collectively through the machinery of the secular order. If one takes a long-range view, the question is one that should be of special interest to Frenchmen, for France has been more than any other country the crusading nation. It has been said that the religious crusading of the Middle Ages in which France played the leading part showed that Europe was already sloughing off genuine Christianity. The contrast is striking in any case between the Christianity of this period and that of the first centuries. The more or less legendary account of the Theban Legion that was ready to fight bravely for the emperor when he kept within the temporal domain, but allowed itself to be martyred to the last man unresistingly rather than worship him as a God, reflects accurately enough the attitude of the early Christian. The ruthless massacre that marked the first entrance of the crusaders into Jerusalem (July 15, 1099) is sufficient proof that they did not maintain any such distinction between the spiritual and the temporal order.[30] It seems hardly necessary to ask which of the two, the crusader or the member of the Theban Legion, was nearer in spirit to the Founder. By his confusion of the things of God with the things of Caesar the crusader was in danger of substituting a will to power for the will to peace that is at the heart of genuine Christianity.[31] The emergence of the will to power is even more obvious in the humanita-

---

[30] "It was an easier thing to consecrate the fighting instinct than to curb it. . . . [The crusader] might butcher all day till he waded ankle deep in blood and then at nightfall kneel sobbing for very joy at the altar of the Sepulchre—for was he not red from the winepress of the Lord? One can readily understand the popularity of the Crusades when one reflects that they permitted men to get to the other world by fighting hard on earth and allowed them to gain the fruits of asceticism by the way of hedonism" (Ernest Baker, "Crusades," *Encyclopedia Britannica* [11th ed.]).

[31] The predominance of the imperialistic over the religious motif is especially conspicuous in the fourth Crusade (1202–04).

rian crusader, as I attempted to show in my study of the Rousseauistic side of the French Revolution. The revolutionary formula, "liberty, equality, fraternity," is in itself only a portentous patter of words.[32] These words may, no doubt, be so defined both separately and in their relation to one another as to have a genuinely religious meaning. Understood in the fashion of Rousseau, that is, as summing up the supposed results of a return to "nature," they encouraged one of the most virulent forms of imperialism. The French themselves are growing more and more doubtful about the "idealistic" side of their Revolution (it goes without saying that the Revolution had other sides). They are growing more realistic in temper.[33] The great problem for them as for all of us is, that, on being disillusioned regarding this type of idealism, they should not become merely Machiavellian realists.

At all events, France can no longer be looked upon as the crusading nation. It is becoming the dangerous privilege of the United States to display more of the crusading temper than any other country in both its domestic and its foreign policies. Yet if one may properly question the religious crusading of which the French were once so fond (*Gesta Dei per Francos*), how much more properly may one question the activities of our

[32] Fitzjames Stephen has submitted this formula to a drastic analysis in *Liberty, Equality, Fraternity*. This book contains also a refutation of Mill's essay *On Liberty*.
[33] This tendency was noted by various observers even before the war, for example, by J.E.C. Bodley in his essay *The Decay of Idealism in France* (1912).

314 *Democracy and Leadership*

"uplifters" (*Gesta humanitatis per Americanos*). We are being deprived gradually of our liberties on the ground that the sacrifice is necessary to the good of society. If we attend carefully to the psychology of the persons who manifest such an eagerness to serve us, we shall find that they are even more eager to control us. What one discovers, for example, under the altruistic professions of the leaders of a typical organization for humanitarian crusading, like the Anti-Saloon League, is a growing will to power and even an incipient terrorism. Let one consider again Mr. Woodrow Wilson, who, more than any other recent American, sought to extend our idealism beyond our national frontiers. In the pursuit of his scheme for world service, he was led to make light of the constitutional checks on his authority and to reach out almost automatically for unlimited power. If we refused to take his humanitarian crusading seriously we were warned that we should "break the heart of the world." If the tough old world had ever had a heart in the Wilsonian sense, it would have been broken long ago. The truth is that this language, at once abstract and sentimental, reveals a temper at the opposite pole from that of the genuine statesman. He was inflexible and uncompromising in the defense of his "ideal," the League of Nations, which, as a corrective of the push for power on the national scale, is under the suspicion of being only a humanitarian chimera. At the same time he was only too ready to yield to the push for power of the labor unions (Adamson Act), a form of the instinct of domination so full of menace to free institutions that, rather than submit to it, a genuine statesman would have died in his tracks. One may contrast profitably the way in which Mr. Wilson faced this issue with the way in which Grover Cleveland, perhaps the last of our Presidents who was unmistakably in our great tradition, faced the issue of free silver.

The particular confusion of the things of God and the things of Caesar promoted by Mr. Wilson and the other "idealists" needs to have brought to bear on it the second of the sayings of Jesus that I have cited ("By their fruits ye shall know them"). The idealists so plainly fail to meet the test of fruits that they are taking refuge more and more, especially since the war, in their good intentions. The cynic might, indeed, complain that they already have hell paved at least twice over with their good intentions. We can no more grant that good intentions are enough in dealing with men than we can grant that they suffice a chemist who is handling high explosives. Under certain conditions, human nature itself may become one of the highest of high explosives. Above all, no person in a position of political responsibility can afford to let any "ideal" come between him and a keen inspection of the facts. It is only too evident that this true vision was found before the war in imperialists of the type of Lord Roberts rather than in liberals of the type of Asquith and Grey. It does not follow that the realism that one should oppose to the "idealists" need be of a merely imperialistic type; it may be a complete moral realism. The moral realist will not allow himself to be whisked off into any cloud-cuckoo-land in the name of the ideal. He will pay no more attention to the fine phrases in which an ideal of this kind is clothed than he would to the whistling of the wind around a corner. The idealist will, therefore, denounce him as "hard." His hardness is in any case quite unlike that of the Machiavellian realist. If the moral realist seems hard to the idealist, this is because of his refusal to shift, in the name of sympathy or social justice or on any other ground, the struggle between good and evil from the individual to society. If we restore the moral struggle to the individual, we are brought back at once to the assertion in some form or other of the truths of the inner life. The question that may properly be raised at present is not whether this or that cause or movement or reform is breaking down, but whether humanitarian crusading in general as a substitute for the inner life is not breaking down. The failure of humanitarianism might be even more manifest than it is were it not for the survival—and that even in the humanitarians themselves—of habits that derive from an entirely different view of life. The ethos of a community does not disappear in a day, even when the convictions that sustain it have been undermined. This slow decline of an ethos adds to the difficulty of judging any particular doctrine by its fruits. These fruits are often slow to appear. For example, no one has been more successful in breaking down American educational tradition in favor of humanitarian conceptions than President Eliot, who is himself an unusually fine product of the Puritan discipline.[34] He has owed his great influ-

---

[34] If one wishes to measure the wideness of the gap between President Eliot's doctrine and that of the Puritans, let him read together Jonathan Edwards's sermon "A Divine and Supernatural Light," a bit of quintessential puritanism, and "Five American Contributions to Civilization."

ence largely to the fact that many men are sensitive to a dignified and impressive personality, whereas very few men are capable of weighing the ultimate tendencies of ideas. One might have more confidence in the elective system if it could be counted on to produce President Eliots.

Though the traditional habits survive the traditional beliefs, they do not survive them indefinitely. With the progressive weakening, not merely of the Puritan ethos, but of the Christian ethos of the Occident in general, it may become harder and harder to justify humanitarianism experimentally. This movement has from Bacon's time stood for fruits and, in all that concerns man's power and material comfort and utility, it has as a matter of fact been superlatively fruitful. But it has also professed to give the fruits of the spirit—for example, peace and brotherhood—and here its failure is so conspicuous as to lead one to suspect some basic unsoundness.

At this point the third saying of Jesus that I have quoted comes into play—the saying as to the importance of building on the rock. The storm has come and it is not clear that our modern house is thus firmly established. The impression one has is rather that of an immense and glittering superstructure on insecure foundations.

The basis on which the whole structure of the new ethics has been reared is, as we have seen, the assumption that the significant struggle between good and evil is not in the individual but in society. If we wish once more to build securely, we may have to recover in some form the idea of "the civil war in the cave." If one ad-

mits this "war," one may admit at the same time the
need of the work of the spirit, if one is to bring forth the
fruits of the spirit. If one denies this war, one transfers
the work to the outer world or substitutes for it a sympathy that involves neither an inner nor an outer working. A main problem of ethics, according to Cicero, is
to prevent a divorce between the honorable (*honestum*)
and the useful (*utile*). If these terms are not sophisticated, he says, the honorable and the useful will be
found to be identical. But such a sophistication has taken
place as a result of the emphasis on an outer rather than
on an inner working about which I have already had so
much to say in this volume. The fruitful has thus come to
be identified with the useful and finally (in a narrow and
doctrinal sense) with the utilitarian. The whole problem
has assumed a gravity that it did not have in the time of
Cicero because of the way in which we have got ourselves
implicated, by our one-sided pursuit of utility, in an
immense mass of interlocking machinery.

One needs, however, if one is to recover a firm basis
for the spiritual life, to get behind even the word "work."
The sophistication of this word would not have been
possible had it not been for the previous sophistication
of the word "nature." This word should receive the first
attention of anyone who is seeking to defend on Socratic
lines either humanistic or religious truth. Apply a sufficiently penetrating dialectic to the word "nature," one is
sometimes tempted to think, and the sophist will be put
out of action at the start. The juggling with this word
can be traced from the ancient Greek who said that the
distinction between the honorable and the shameful has

no root in nature, but is merely a matter of convention, to Renan who said that "nature does not care for chastity." This juggling has always been the main source of an unsound individualism. The contrast between the natural and the artificial that has flourished since the eighteenth century and underlies the romantic movement is especially inadmissible. "Art," as Burke says, "is man's nature." I have already referred to Diderot's dismissal of the opposition between a law of the spirit and a law of the members as "artificial," and have said that the proper reply to such sophistry is not to take refuge in theology, but to insist upon this opposition as one of the "immediate data of consciousness"; that we shall thus get experimentally the basis we require if we are to do the work of the spirit and bring forth its fruits. A confusion like that of Diderot is so serious that the defining of the one word "nature" would justify a dialectical battle along Socratic lines the like of which has never been seen in the history of the world. When it was over, the field of conflict would be covered thick with dead and dying reputations; for there can be no doubt that many of the leaders of the present time have fallen into the naturalistic error.

On one's definition of work, which itself depends on one's definition of nature, will depend in turn one's definition of liberty. One is free to work and not to idle. Only when liberty is properly defined according not merely to the degree, but to the quality of one's working, is it possible to achieve a sound definition of justice (to every man according to his works). One's definition of justice again will be found to involve one's definition of peace in the secular order: for men can live at peace with one another only in so far as they are just. As for religious peace, it is not subject to definition. In the scriptural phrase, it passeth understanding.

Above all, if one is to achieve a sound philosophy of will, there must be no blurring of the distinction between the spiritually inert and the spiritually energetic. The point is one that should be of special interest to Americans. The European has tended in his typical moments, and that from the time of the Greeks, to be an intellectual. There are signs, on the other hand, that if America ever achieves a philosophy of its own, it will be rather a philosophy of will. We have been called the "people of action." Under the circumstances it is a matter of some moment both for ourselves and for the rest of the world whether we are to be strenuous in a completely human or in a merely Rooseveltian sense.

One may grant, indeed, that in a world like this the Rooseveltian imperialist is a safer guide than the Jeffersonian or Wilsonian "idealist." But there is no reason why one should accept either horn of this dilemma. The most effective way of dealing with the Jeffersonian idealism is to submit to a Socratic dialectic the theory of natural rights that underlies it. This theory rests on the sophistical contrast between the natural and the artificial of which I have just spoken, a contrast that encourages a total or partial suppression of the true dualism of the spirit and of the special quality of working it involves. With this weakening of the inner life it becomes possible to assert a lazy or, what amounts to the same thing, an anarchical liberty. For true liberty is not liberty to do as one likes, but liberty to adjust oneself, in some sense of that word, to law. "The Abbé Coigniard," says Anatole France, "would not have signed a line of the declaration of the rights of man because of the excessive and unjust discrimination it establishes between man and the gorilla." The true objection to the declaration of the rights of man is the exact opposite of the one stated by M. France: it does not establish a sufficiently wide gap between man and the gorilla. This gap can be maintained only if one insists that genuine liberty is the reward of ethical effort; it tends to disappear if one presents liberty as a free gift of "nature."

It may, indeed, be urged that the theory of natural rights, though false, may yet be justified as a "useful fiction," that it has often shown itself an effective weapon of attack on the iniquities of the existing social order. One may doubt, however, the utility of the fiction, for what it tends to oppose to the existing order is not a better order but anarchy. No doubt the established order of any particular time and place that the partisan of "rights" would dismiss as conventional and artificial is, compared with true and perfect order, only a shadow; but such as it is, it cannot be lightly abandoned in favor of some "ideal" that, when critically examined, may turn out to be only a mirage on the brink of a precipice. The "unwritten laws of heaven"[35] of which the great humanist

---

[35] The passage of the *Antigone* (vv. 450 ff.) needs to be associated with the passage of the *Oedipus* (vv. 863 ff.): ". . . laws that in the highest empyrean had their birth, of which Heaven is the father alone, neither did the race of mortal men beget them, nor shall oblivion ever put them to sleep. The power of God is mighty in them and groweth not old."

Sophocles speaks are felt in their relation to the written law, not as a right, but as a stricter obligation.

The tendency of the doctrine of natural rights to weaken the sense of obligation, and so to undermine genuine liberty, may be studied in connection with its influence on the common law which has prevailed among the English-speaking peoples. The spirit of this law at its best is that of a wholesome moral realism. Under the influence of the school of rights the equity that is often in conflict with strict law was more or less identified with a supposed law of "nature."[36] This identification encouraged an unsound individualism. The proper remedy for an unsound individualism is a sound individualism, an individualism that starts, not from rights, but from duties. The actual reply to the unrestraint of the individual has been another doctrine of rights, the rights of society, which are sometimes conceived almost as metaphysically as the older doctrine of the rights of man. The representatives of this school of legal thinking tend to identify equity with the principle of social utility. Judges have already appeared who have so solicited the strict letter of the law in favor of what they deemed to be socially expedient as to fall into a veritable confusion of the legislative and judicial functions. Unfortunately, those who represent society at any particular moment and who

---

[36] See chap. 4 ("The Rights of Man") in *The Spirit of the Common Law* (1921), by Roscoe Pound. Professor Pound is in sympathy with the second tendency to which I refer—the tendency toward what he terms the "socialization of justice." His point of view is closely related to that of the German Jhering, who may himself be defined as a sort of collectivistic Bentham.

are supposed to overflow with a will to service will be found by the realistic observer (insofar at least as they are mere humanitarian crusaders in whom there is no survival of the traditional controls) to be developing, under cover of their altruism, a will to power. On the pretext of social utility they are ready to deprive the individual of every last scrap and vestige of his freedom and finally to subject him to despotic outer control. No one, as Americans of the present day are only too well aware, is more reckless in his attacks on personal liberty than the apostle of "service." He is prone in his further-ance of his schemes of "uplift" not only to ascribe un-limited sovereignty to society as against the individual, but also to look on himself as endowed with a major portion of it, to develop a temper, in short, that is plainly tyrannical.

We seem, indeed, to be witnessing in a different form the emergency faced by the early Christians. The time may come again, if indeed it has not come already, when men will be justified in asserting true freedom, even, it may be, at the cost of their lives, against the monstrous encroachments of the materialistic state.[37] The collectiv-istic ideal suffers, often in an exaggerated form, from

---

[37] "Individuals and families, associations and dependencies were so much material that the sovereign power consumed for its own purposes. What the slave was in the hands of his master, the citizen was in the hands of the community. The most sacred obligations vanished before the public advantage. The passengers existed for the sake of the ship. By their dis-regard for private interests, and for the moral welfare and improvement of the people, both Greece and Rome destroyed the vital elements on which the prosperity of nations rests, and perished by the decay of fam-ilies and the depopulation of the country. They survive not in their in-

the underlying error of *laissez-faire* against which it is so largely a protest. It does not reveal an adequate sense of the nature of obligation and of the special type of effort it imposes. As a result of its shallowness in dealing with the idea of work, it is in danger of substituting for real justice the phantasmagoria of social justice. Some of the inequalities that the collectivist attacks are no doubt the result of the unethical competition promoted by *laissez-faire*. But the remedy for these inequalities is surely not the pursuit of such chimeras as social or economic equality, at the risk of sacrificing the one form of equality that is valuable—equality before the law.

Equality as it is currently pursued is incompatible with true liberty; for liberty involves an inner working with reference to standards, the right subordination, in other words, of man's ordinary will to a higher will. There is an inevitable clash, in short, between equality and humility. Historically humility has been secured more or less at the expense of the intellect. I have myself been trying to show that it is possible to defend humility, and in general the truths of the inner life, by a critical method and in this sense to put Socrates in the service of Christ. The question of method is, in any case, all-important if

---

stitutions but in their ideas, and by their ideas, especially on the art of government, they are—

The dead, but sceptred sovereigns who still rule
Our spirits from their urns.

To them, indeed, may be tracked nearly all the errors that are undermining political society—communism, utilitarianism, the confusion between tyranny and authority, and between lawlessness and freedom" (Lord Acton: *History of Freedom and Other Essays*, p. 17).

one is to heal the feud between the head and the heart that has subsisted in the Occident in various forms from Greco-Roman times. Intellect, though finally subordinate to will, is indispensable in direct ratio to the completeness of one's break with traditional standards. It is then needed to test from the point of view of reality the unity achieved by the imagination and so to supply new standards with reference to which the higher will may exercise its power of veto on the impulses and expansive desires. When will and intellect and imagination have been brought into right relation with one another, one arrives at last at the problem of the emotions, to which the Rousseauist, in his misplaced thirst of immediacy, gives the first place. To have standards means practically to select and reject; and this again means that one must discipline one's feelings or affections, to use the older word, to some ethical center. If the discipline is to be effective, so that a man will like and dislike the right things, it is as a rule necessary that it should become a matter of habit, and that almost from infancy. One cannot wait until the child has reached the so-called age of reason, until, in short, he is in a position to do his own selecting, for in the meanwhile he may have become the victim of bad habits. This is the true prison house that is in danger of closing on the growing boy. Habit must, therefore, as Aristotle says, precede reason. Certain other ideas closely connected with the idea of habit, need to receive attention at this point. The ethos of a community is derived in fact, as it is etymologically, from habit. If a community is to transmit certain habits to its young, it must normally come to some kind of agreement as to what habits are desirable; it must in the literal meaning of that word achieve a convention. Here is a chief difference between the true and the false liberal. It has been said of our modernists that they have only one convention and that is that there shall be no more conventions. An individualism that is thus purely temperamental is incompatible with the survival of civilization. What is civilized in most people is precisely that part of them which is conventional. It is, to be sure, difficult to have a convention without falling into mere conventionalism, two things that the modernist confounds; but then everything that is worthwhile is difficult.

The combining of convention with a due respect for the liberty of the individual involves, it must be admitted, adjustments of the utmost delicacy. Two extremes are about equally undesirable: first, the convention may be so rigid and minute as to leave little scope for the initiative of the individual. This formalistic extreme was reached, if Occidental opinion be correct, in the China of the past, and also in the older French convention that Rousseau attacked. At the opposite pole is the person who is spontaneous after the fashion encouraged by Rousseau and who, in getting rid of conventions, has also got rid of standards and abandoned himself to the mere flux of his impressions. The problem of standards would be simple if all we had to do was to oppose to this anarchical "liberty" a sound set of general principles. But so far as actual conduct is concerned, life resolves itself into a series of particular emergencies, and it is not always easy to bridge the gap between these emergencies or con-

crete cases and the general principle. It has been held in
the Occident, at least from the time of Aristotle, and in
the Orient, at least from the time of Confucius, that one
should be guided in one's application of the general
principle by the law of measure. The person who thus
mediates successfully seems, in the phrase of Pascal, to
combine in himself opposite virtues and to occupy all the
space between them. As a general principle, for example,
courage is excellent, but unless it be tempered in the
concrete instance by prudence, it will degenerate into
rashness. According to Bossuet, "Good maxims pushed
to an extreme are utterly ruinous" (*Les bonnes maximes
outrées perdent tout*). But who is to decide what is the
moderate and what the extreme application of a good
maxim? The casuist or legalist would not only lay down
the general principle, but try to deal exhaustively with
all the cases that may arise in the application of it, in
such wise as to deprive the individual, so far as possible,
of his autonomy. The cases are, however, inexhaustible,
inasmuch as life is, in Bergson's phrase, a perpetual gushing forth of novelties. A Jesuitical casebook or the equivalent is after all a clumsy substitute for the living intuition
of the individual in determining the right balance to strike
between the abiding principle and the novel emergency.
While insisting, therefore, on the need of a convention,
one should strive to hold this convention flexibly, imaginatively, and, as it were, progressively. Without a convention of some kind it is hard to see how the experience of
the past can be brought to bear on the present. The uncon-
ventional person is assuming that either he or his age is

so unique that all this past experience has become obsolete. This very illusion has, to be sure, been fostered in many by the rapid advance of the physical sciences.

So much experience has accumulated in both the East and the West that it should seem possible for those who are seeking to maintain standards and to fight an anarchical impressionism, to come together, not only as to their general principles, but as to the main cases that arise in the application of them. This convention, if it is to be effective, must, as I have already suggested, be transmitted in the form of habits to the young. This is only another way of saying that the civilization of a community and ultimately the government of which it is capable is closely related to the type of education on which it has agreed. (One should include in education the discipline that children receive in the family.) "The best laws," says Aristotle, "will be of no avail unless the young are trained by habit and education in the spirit of the constitution."[38] Aristotle complains that this great principle was being violated in his time. Is it being observed in ours? It will be interesting in any case to make a specific application of the Aristotelian dictum to our American education in its relation to American government. Assuming that what we wish to preserve is a federal and constitutional democracy, are we training up a class of leaders whose ethos is in intimate accord with this type of government? The older type of American college reflected faithfully enough the convention of its time. The classical element in its curriculum was appropri-

---

[38] *Politics*, 1310a. Cf. also *ibid.*, 1337a.

ately subordinated to the religious element, inasmuch as the leadership at which it aimed was to be lodged primarily in the clergy. It would have been possible to interpret more vitally our older educational convention, to give it the broadening it certainly needed and to adapt it to changed conditions. The new education (I am speaking, of course, of the main trend) can scarcely be said to have developed in this fashion from the old. It suggests rather a radical break with our traditional ethos. The old education was, in intention at least, a training for wisdom and character. The new education has been summed up by President Eliot in the phrase: training for service and power. We are all coming together more and more in this idea of service. But, though service is supplying us in a way with a convention, it is not, in either the humanistic or the religious sense, supplying us with standards. In the current sense of the word it tends rather to undermine standards, if it be true, as I have tried to show, that it involves an assumption hard to justify on strictly psychological grounds—the assumption that men can come together expansively and on the level of their ordinary selves. The older education was based on the belief that men need to be disciplined to some ethical center. The sentimental humanitarian opposes to a definite curriculum which aims at some such humanistic or religious discipline the right of the individual to develop freely his bent or temperamental proclivity. The standard or common measure is compromised by the assertion of this supposed right, and in about the same measure the effort and spirit of emulation that the standard stimulates disappear. The very word curriculum implies a running together. Under the new educational dispensation, students, instead of running together, tend to lounge separately. Interest is transferred from the classroom to the athletic field, where there is a standard of a kind and, with reference to this standard, something that human nature craves—real victory or real defeat. The sentimentalist also plays into the hands of the utilitarian, who likewise sets up a standard with reference to which one may strive and achieve success or failure. Anything that thus has a definite air tends to prevail over anything that, like a college of liberal arts under the elective system, is comparatively aimless. One cannot admit the argument sometimes heard that, because the older education had a definite end, it was therefore vocational in the same sense as the schools of business administration, for example, that have been developing so portentously of late in our educational centers. The older education aimed to produce leaders and, as it perceived, the basis of leadership is not commercial or industrial efficiency, but wisdom. Those who have been substituting the cult of efficiency for the older liberal training are, of course, profuse in their professions of service either to country or to mankind at large. The question I have been raising throughout this volume, however, is whether anything so purely expansive as service, in the humanitarian sense, can supply an adequate counterpoise to the pursuit of unethical power, whether the proper counterpoise is not to be sought rather in the cultivation of the principle of vital control, first of all in the individual and finally in the state.

I have said that one's attitude toward the principle of control will determine one's definition of liberty, and that the Jeffersonians inclining, as they did, to the new myth of man's natural goodness, looked askance, not merely at the traditional restraints, but at everything that interfered with a purely expansive freedom. Jefferson himself saw to some extent the implications of his general position for education in particular. He is, for example, one of the authentic precursors of the elective system.[39] The education that the Jeffersonian liberty has tended to supplant set up a standard that limited the supposed right of the individual to self-expression as well as the inbreeding of special aptitudes in the interests of efficiency; it was not, in short, either sentimental or utilitarian. There is a real relation between the older educational standard that thus acted restrictively on the mere temperament of the individual and the older political standard embodied in institutions like the Constitution, Senate, and Supreme Court, that serve as a check on the ordinary or impulsive will of the people. It follows from all I have said that the new education does not meet the Aristotelian requirement: it is not in intimate correspondence with our form of government. If the veto power disappears from our education there is no reason to anticipate that it will long survive in the state. The spirit of the leaders will not be that which should preside over a constitutional democracy.

---

[39] See Herbert B. Adams: *Thomas Jefferson and the University of Virginia* (1888), especially chap. 9 ("The University of Virginia and Harvard College"). Cf. also letter of Jefferson to George Ticknor, July 16, 1823. Superficially, Jefferson was friendly to classical study; his underlying philosophical tendency (of which his encyclopedic inclusiveness and encouragement of specialization are only symptoms) was unfavorable to it.

The best of our elder statesmen, though they opposed a standard to the mere flux of popular impulse and made sure that the standard was appropriately embodied in institutions, did not associate their standard with any theory of the absolute. Herein they showed their sagacity. One cannot separate too carefully the cause of standards from that of the absolute. Standards are a matter of observation and common sense, the absolute is only a metaphysical conceit. In political thinking this conceit has led to various theories of unlimited sovereignty. Judged by their fruits all these theories are, according to John Adams, "equally arbitrary, cruel, bloody, and in every respect diabolical." They can be shown, at all events, to be hard to reconcile with a proper respect for personal liberty.[40] It is a fortunate circumstance that the very word "sovereignty" does not occur in our Constitution. The men who made this Constitution were for granting a certain limited power here and another limited power somewhere else, and absolute power nowhere. The best scheme of government they conceived to be a system of checks and balances. They did not, however, look on the partial powers they bestowed as being on the same level. They were aware that true liberty requires a hierarchy and a subordination, that there must be something central in a state to which final appeal may be made in case of conflict. The complaint has, indeed, been made that they left certain ambiguities in the articles of union that had finally to be clarified on the battlefield. If they had been more explicit, however, it is not probable that

---

[40] See Appendix B.

they would have been able to establish a union at all. They were confronted with the difficult task of gaining recognition for the centripetal element in government in the face of the most centrifugal doctrine the world has ever known—the doctrine that encourages men to put their rights before their duties.

John Marshall deserves special praise for the clearness with which he saw that the final center of control in the type of government that was being founded, if control was to have an ethical basis and not be another name for force, must be vested in the judiciary, particularly in the Supreme Court. This court, especially in its most important function, that of interpreting the Constitution, must, he perceived, embody more than any other institution the higher or permanent self of the state. With a sound and independent judiciary, above all with a sound and independent supreme bench, liberty and democracy may after all be able to coexist. Many people are aware that personal liberty and the security of private property, which is almost inseparable from it, are closely bound up with the fortunes of the Supreme Court. Their ideas are, however, often vague as to the nature of the menace that overhangs our highest tribunal. We are familiar with the rant of Gompers and his kind against the courts; we also know what to expect from the radical press. We are not surprised, for example, when a socialistic periodical, published at Girard, Kansas, devotes a special issue of five million copies to an assault on the federal judiciary. A menace that is perhaps more serious than this open hostility may be defined as a sort of "boring from within." This phrase seems to fit the professors in our law schools who are departing from the traditional standards of the law in favor of "social justice." Social justice, it is well to remind these "forward-looking" professors, means in practice class justice, class justice means class war and class war, if we are to go by all the experience of the past and present, means hell.

The inadequacy of social justice with its tendency to undermine the moral responsibility of the individual and at the same time to obscure the need of standards and leadership may be made clearer if we consider for a moment the problem of government with the utmost degree of realism. Thus considered, government is power. Whether the power is to be ethical or unethical, whether in other words it is subordinated to true justice, must depend finally on the quality of will displayed by the men who administer it. For what counts practically is not justice in the abstract, but the just man. The just man is he whose various capacities (including the intellect) are acting in right relation to one another under the hegemony of the higher will. We are brought back here to the problem of the remnant. Those who strive for the inner proportion that is reflected in the outer world as justice have always been few. The remark of Aristotle that "most men would rather live in a disorderly than in a sober manner" remains true, at least in the subtler psychic sense. Though one agree with Aristotle as to the ethical unsoundness of the majority, it does not follow that the ethical state is impossible. Human nature, and this is its most encouraging trait, is sensitive to a right example. It is hard, indeed, to set bounds to the persuasiveness of a right example, provided only it be right enough. The ethical state is possible in which an important minority is ethically energetic and is thus becoming at once just and exemplary. Such a minority will also tend to solve the problem of union. The soul of the unjust man is, according to Aristotle, torn by every manner of faction.[41] The just man, on the contrary, is he who, as the result of his moral choices based on due deliberation, choices in which he is moved primarily by a regard for his own happiness, has quelled the unruly impulses of his lower nature and so attained to some degree of unity with himself. At the same time he will find that he is moving toward a common center with others who have been carrying through a similar task of self-conquest. A state that is controlled by men who have become just as the result of minding their own business in the Platonic sense will be a just state that will also mind its own business; it will be of service to other states, not by meddling in their affairs on either commercial or "idealistic" grounds, but by setting them a good example. A state of this kind may hope to find a basis of understanding with any other state that is also ethically controlled. The hope of cooperation with a state that has an unethical leadership is chimerical. The value of political thinking is therefore in direct ratio to its adequacy in dealing with the problem of leadership. The unit to which all things must finally be referred is not the state or humanity or any other abstraction, but

---

[41] *Eth. Nic.* 1166b.

the man of character. Compared with this ultimate human reality, every other reality is only a shadow in the mist.[42]

It follows from what I have said that ethical union, whether in the single man or among different men or on the national or international scale, is attainable so far as it is attainable at all, not by expansive emotion nor by any form of machinery or organization (in the current sense of the word), but only by the pathway of the inner life. Some persons will remain spiritually anarchical in spite of educational opportunity, others will acquire at least the rudiments of ethical discipline, whereas still others, a small minority, if we are to judge by past experience, will show themselves capable of the more difficult stages of self-conquest that will fit them for leadership. Our traditional education with all its defects did something to produce leaders of this ethical type, whereas the utilitarian-sentimental education which has been tending to supplant it is, as I have been trying to show, lacking in the essentials of the inner life and so is not likely to produce either religious or humanistic leaders. Most Americans of the present day will, indeed, feel that they have refuted sufficiently all that I have said, if they simply utter the word "service." One may suspect, however, that the popularity of the gospel of service is due to the fact that it is flattering to unregenerate human nature. It is pleasant to think that one may dispense with

---

[42] Cf. Confucius: "The moral man, by living a life of simple truth and earnestness, alone can help to bring peace and order in the world." "When the men are there, good government will flourish, but when the men are gone, good government decays and becomes extinct."

awe and reverence and the inner obeisance of the spirit to standards, provided one be eager to do something for humanity. "The highest worship of God," as Benjamin Franklin assures us blandly, "is service to man." If it can be shown experimentally—and a certain amount of evidence on this point has accumulated since the time of Franklin—that service in this sense is not enough to chain up the naked lusts of the human heart, one must conclude that the supreme exemplar of American shrewdness and practicality did not, in the utterance I have just cited, show himself sufficiently shrewd and practical. The gospel of service is at all events going to receive a thorough trial, if nowhere else, then in America. We are rapidly becoming a nation of humanitarian crusaders. The present reign of legalism is the most palpable outcome of this crusading. It is growing only too evident, however, that the drift toward license is being accelerated rather than arrested by the multiplication of laws. If we do not develop a sounder type of vision than that of our "uplifters" and "forward-lookers," the history of free institutions in this country is likely to be short, and, on the whole, discreditable. Surely the first step is to perceive that the alternative to a constitutional liberty is not a legalistic millennium, but a triumph of anarchy followed by a triumph of force. The time may come, with the growth of a false liberalism, when a predominant element in our population, having grown more and more impatient of the ballot box and representative government, of constitutional limitations and judicial control, will display a growing eagerness for "direct action." This is

the propitious moment for the imperialistic leader.
Though the triumph of any type of imperialistic leader
is a disaster, especially in a country like our own that has
known the blessings of liberty under the law, nevertheless there is a choice even here. Circumstances may arise
when we may esteem ourselves fortunate if we get the
American equivalent of a Mussolini; he may be needed
to save us from the American equivalent of a Lenin.
Such an emergency is not to be anticipated, however,
unless we drift even further than we have thus far from
the principles that underlie our unionist tradition. The
maintenance of this tradition is indissolubly bound up
with the maintenance of standards. The democratic contention that everybody should have a chance is excellent
provided it mean that everybody is to have a chance to
measure up to high standards. If the democratic extension
of opportunity is, on the other hand, made a pretext
for lowering standards, democracy is, insofar, incompatible with civilization. One might be more confident of the
outcome of the struggle between a true and a false
liberalism that has been under way since the founding
of the Republic, if the problem of standards was being
dealt with more adequately in our education, above all in
our higher education. The tendency here, however, is,
as I have noted, to discard standards in favor of "ideals";
and ideals, as currently understood, recognize very imperfectly, if at all, that man needs to be disciplined to a
law of his own, distinct from the law of physical nature.
One might view this idealistic development with more
equanimity if one were convinced with Professor John
Dewey that the growing child exudes spontaneously a will

to service.[43] If we look, however, on this form of spontaneity as a romantic myth, we shall be forced to conclude
that we have been permitting Professor Dewey and his
kind to have an influence on our education that amounts
in the aggregate to a national calamity; that with the
progress of ideals of this kind our higher education in
particular is, from the point of view of a genuinely liberal training, in danger of becoming a vast whir of
machinery in the void; finally, that, in the interest of our
experiment in free institutions, we need educational
leaders who will have less to say of service and more
to say of culture and civilization, and who will so use
these words as to show that they have some inkling of
their true meaning.

This book has been written to no purpose unless I
have made plain that the problem of standards and
leadership is by no means merely American. The American situation can be understood only with reference to
the larger background—the slow yielding in the whole
of the Occident of traditional standards, humanistic and
religious, to naturalism. I have defined in its main aspects
the movement that has supervened upon this emancipation from the past as Baconian, Rousseauistic, and
Machiavellian; in other words, as utilitarian, sentimental,
and imperialistic. The individualist should, however,
make a better use of his liberty; the less traditional he becomes, the more he should strive to get at standards
positively and critically. The result of such a striving

---

[43] See his *Moral Principles in Education*, p. 22: "The child is born with a
natural desire to give out, to do, to *serve*." (My italics.)

would, I have tried to show, be a movement that might
be best defined as Socratic, Aristotelian, and Christian,
that would, in short, put prime emphasis in its different
stages on definition, habit, and humility. What has actually been witnessed in the Occident, as a result of the
failure to work out critical equivalents of traditional
standards, has been a series of violent oscillations between
a humanitarian idealism and a Machiavellian realism.
Humanitarian idealism is still firmly entrenched in this
country, especially in academic circles, where it seems
to be held more confidently, one is almost tempted to
say more smugly, with each succeeding year. Europeans,
on the other hand, have suffered certain essential disillusions. It is becoming increasingly difficult for them
to believe that the idealists have discovered any effective
counterpoise to the push for power. "We are much be-
holden," says Bacon, "to Machiavel and others that wrote
what men do, and not what they ought to do." The gap
between what men do and what they ought to do is
turning out to be even wider under the humanitarian dispensation than under that of medieval Christianity.

Yet the Machiavellian solution is in itself impossible.
If the Occident does not get beyond this type of realism,
it will simply reenact all the pagan stupidities and hasten
once more to the pagan doom. Moreover, the latter stages
of the naturalistic dissolution of civilization with which
we are menaced are, thanks to scientific "progress," likely
to be marked by incidents of almost inconceivable horror.
The danger of power without wisdom, of a constantly
increasing material organization combined with an ever-
growing spiritual anarchy, is already so manifest that

unless there is a serious search for a remedy we may conclude that the instinct for self-preservation that is supposed to inhere in mankind is a myth. Surely the first step will be to put in his proper subordinate place the man of science with his poison gases[44] and high explosives, and that without a particle of obscurantism. The tendency of physical science to bring the whole of human nature under a single law can be shown to be at the bottom of some of the most dangerous fallacies of the present time—for example, the socialistic dream of "scientific" politics. "Thus the whole of society," says Mr. J. Ramsay MacDonald, "its organization, its institutions, its activities, is brought within the sway of natural law, not merely on its descriptive and historical side, but on its experimental side, and administration and legislation become arts pursued in the same way as the chemist works in his laboratory."[45] The man of science is flattered in the conceit of his own importance by this inordinate exaltation of the "law for thing." Yet he should, in the interest of science itself, reject the whole point of view as pseudoscientific; for science needs the support of civilization and the chief force that is now making against civilization is, next perhaps to emotional unrestraint, pseudoscience.

Mr. MacDonald and his kind almost invariably look upon themselves as "idealists." This should serve to

---

[44] The statement has been made by those who should be in a position to know that poison gases have recently been invented at least a thousand times more deadly than any employed during the war.

[45] *The Socialist Movement*, p. 90.

remind us that the terms idealism and realism as now
employed, however much they may clash superficially,
have at least this much in common: they are both rooted
in a naturalistic philosophy. Anyone who transcends
this philosophy ceases in about the same measure to be
either a humanitarian idealist or a Machiavellian realist.
He becomes aware of a quality of will that distinguishes
man from physical nature and is yet natural in the sense
that it is a matter of immediate perception and not of
outer authority. I have said that the neglect of this quality
of will by both utilitarians and sentimentalists has encouraged a sophistical definition of liberty; that this type
of liberty has owed its appeal to its flattery of spiritual
indolence, perhaps the most fundamental human trait
that is open to direct observation. Anyone who has once
perceived this trait in himself and others, and followed
it out in even a few of its almost innumerable ramifica-
tions, will be in no danger of overlooking the old Adam
after the fashion of the "idealists." The insistence on the
putting aside of spiritual indolence and the exercise of
the higher will is found in every genuinely spiritual doctrine, above all in genuine Christianity. Traditionally the
Christian has associated his liberty and his faith in a
higher will with grace. "Where the Spirit of the Lord is,
there is liberty." I myself have been trying to come at
this necessary truth, not in terms of grace, but in terms
of work, and that on the humanistic rather than on the
religious level. I am not so arrogant as to deny the validity
of other ways of affirming the higher will, or to dismiss as
obsolete the traditional forms through which this will has
been interpreted to the imagination. I am attempting a

contribution, I cannot remind the reader too often, to a specific problem—to the distiction, namely, between a sound and an unsound individualism. My argument should appeal primarily, so far as it appeals to anyone, to those who, as a result of having broken with the traditional forms on grounds insufficiently critical, are in danger of losing the truths of the higher will entirely; who are mere modernists at a time when there is a supreme need of thoroughgoing and complete moderns.

APPENDIX A

Theories of the Will

I append with some hesitation a few notes on the more technical aspects of a question the proper treatment of which would require a volume. The whole problem of the will is inextricably bound up with that of dualism. The true dualism I take to be the contrast in man between two wills, one of which is felt as vital impulse (*élan vital*) and the other as vital control (*frein vital*). The crucial point would seem to be the proper place of intellect in its relation to the higher will. It is hard, on the one hand, to be reasonable without becoming rationalistic, and on the other, to have faith without falling into credulity. The Christian form of the difficulty grew up in connection with the Pauline opposition between a law of the spirit and a law of the members; if the law of the spirit is to exercise its control effectually, it needs, according to the Christian, a greater or lesser degree of divine cooperation. So that if one wishes to get at a Christian's views of man's will, the best method is frequently to ascertain his views of God's will.

One of the first to proclaim the superiority of the divine will over the divine mind was Origen. The most important of Christian voluntarists is, however, Saint Augustine. He asserts the primacy of will in both man and God and on psychological as well as on theological grounds. One of the arguments that he employs was influential on later voluntarists like Duns Scotus.[1] Will, says Augustine, reveals itself above all in the act of attention or concentration; it therefore takes precedence of intellect because it selects the field of facts or order of perceptions to which the intellect attends and of which it acquires knowledge.[2]

With the influence of Aristotle from the latter part of the twelfth century on, there was a tendency to revert to Greek intellectualism and to reverse the Augustinian position in regard to will. Saint Thomas Aquinas, for example, not only grants a superior dignity to man's intellect as compared with his will,[3] but holds that the divine will is subordinate to the divine wisdom. It is hardly necessary to add that Saint Thomas is far from being a pure rationalist: a man's intellect, though superior to his will, is infinitely transcended by the divine will.

---

[1] The work of Wilhelm Kahl, *Die Lehre vom Primat des Willens bei Augustinus, Duns Scotus und Descartes,* is a useful repertory of material for the whole subject.

[2] See his *De Trinitate* for this and other subtle psychological observations on the will.

[3] P. H. Wicksteed has collected passages from Saint Thomas in illustration of the relation between intellect and will in his *Reactions Between Dogma and Philosophy,* pp. 582–620.

To be sure the working of God's will as it had been affirmed traditionally with the support of revelation had been felt from the outset, especially in connection with the more extreme forms of the doctrine of grace, to be a stumbling block to man's reason. The central preoccupation of the scholastic philosophy may indeed be said to have been the reconciliation of faith in this sense with reason.[4] This great effort culminated in Saint Thomas, in whose system reason and faith seem to cooperate harmoniously. Theological truth, he maintained, though beyond reason, is not contrary to it.

The outstanding trait of the later scholasticism is the tendency of reason and faith once more to separate and to appear as irreconcilable. The "realist," Duns Scotus, develops the thesis that "will is superior to intellect"[5] (*Voluntas est superior intellectu*) in both man and God. The nominalist William of Occam affirms in a still more uncompromising fashion that God's will is absolute and arbitrary. God does not will a thing because it is just, but it is just because he wills it. Theology may not hope to find support in reason. It must be accepted on the authority of revelation and the church.

This last stage of scholasticism is the point of departure

---

[4] For this struggle between faith and reason during the scholastic period see *La Philosophie au moyen âge*, par E. Gilson (the point of view is on the whole that of a scientific intellectual); also *History of Medieval Philosophy*, by M. de Wulf (the point of view is Catholic).

[5] According to M. Gilson (*op. cit.*, II, pp. 83–84), "Duns Scot revendique les droits du Dieu chrétien et les défend instinctivement contre la contamination de la pensée hellénique." In view of Arabian influence on Duns Scotus, one may perhaps go further and say that in his treatment of the will an Asiatic is arrayed against a European psychology.

for various movements that seem at first sight to have
very little in common—for example, Lutheranism and
Jansenism as well as the philosophies of Bacon and
Descartes. The Jansenist and Lutheran exalt God's will
at the expense of reason by an extreme interpretation of
grace. Descartes and Bacon, on the other hand, are interested, though in very different ways, in the use that may
be made of reason in the natural order. They continue
to pay more or less sincere homage to religion conceived
as indissolubly bound up with incomprehensible theological mysteries. It is especially important to ascertain
Descartes's conception of the will in view of his position
as the father of modern philosophy. We need to discriminate sharply between his conceptions of man's will and
God's will. God's will he holds to be absolute and arbitrary and to this extent he reminds us of Duns Scotus.[6]
His ultimate temper, however, is not that of the Christian
voluntarist, inasmuch as he is interested above all in
working out a mechanical law for phenomenal nature.
His attitude toward God's will is to be explained in two
ways: first by his extreme caution, not to say timidity;
with the fate of Galileo fresh in mind he was almost
morbidly apprehensive of becoming embroiled with the
theologians. He was moved in the second place, according
to M. Gilson,[7] by the desire to get rid of final causes in
the interest of his own mechanistic hypothesis.

According to Descartes himself what he meant by his

---

[6] M. Gilson, however, disagrees with Kahl as to the nearness of Descartes's conception of the divine will to that of Duns Scotus. See his
work *La Doctrine cartésienne de la liberté et la théologie*, pp. 128–49.

[7] *Op. cit.*, chap. 3; also p. 210.

Cogito ergo sum was that one should start from the immediate data of consciousness.[8] Practically he relegates the higher will to God (as understood by the theologians) and gives the first place among these data to mind or reason. He proceeds to set up a sharp dualism between mind and matter conceived as separate substances. As for man's will, it is according to Descartes in itself infinite and to that extent reminds us of the divine will.[9] On closer scrutiny, however, this infinite liberty of the will turns out to be only a liberty to err. The will escapes from error only in so far as it is determined by reason.[10] In his tendency thus to make right will depend upon right reason, as well as in his practical ethics,[11] Descartes reminds us strongly of the Stoics.

By "reason," it is scarcely necessary to add, Descartes means logical and mathematical reason. The only ideas that should determine the will and that one can follow without danger of error are clear and distinct ideas. No tendency is more marked in the Cartesian system than to conceive as it were mathematically of the truth and reality of both the human and the natural order. An example of the same tendency is the geometrical form that Spinoza gives to his *Ethics*. Descartes would make of God himself a "clear" idea and demonstrate him in almost geometrical fashion.[12] He thus contradicts the

---

[8] *Principes de la philosophie*, liv. 2, 9.

[9] *Méditations métaphysiques*, IV (*Du vrai et du faux*).

[10] *Ibid.*

[11] See especially his *Lettres à la princesse Elizabeth*.

[12] ". . . par conséquent il est pour le moins aussi certain que Dieu . . . est ou existe, qu'aucune démonstration de géométrie le saurait être" (*Discours de la Méthode*).

universal experience of mankind which is that the truths on which the inner life depends are not clear in the logical or any other sense. These truths are rather a matter of elusive intuition.

Perhaps the first person to assert intuition against the abstract reasoning of Descartes was Pascal. A whole order of truths, to employ Pascal's own distinction, can be attained, not by *l'esprit de géométrie*, but only by *l'esprit de finesse*. To the rationalistic God of Descartes he opposes *Dieu sensible au coeur*. "Heart" means practically "grace," and grace Pascal associates with what was rapidly becoming an impossible theology. What is conspicuous indeed in the whole transition from the medieval to the modern period is the failure to disengage the truths of the higher will from theology and to deal with them experimentally as "immediate data of consciousness." On the contrary, as the result of the endless disputes of Jansenists with Jesuits, of Catholics with Protestants, and of the various Protestant sects with one another, these truths became involved in a mass of almost incredible theological subtleties. The final reply to these subtleties was Voltaire. Especially significant is his article "Grace" in the *Dictionnaire philosophique*, the third section of which concludes as follows: "Ah! supralapsaires, infralapsaires, gratuits, suffisants, efficaciens, jansénistes, molinistes, devenez enfin hommes et ne troublez plus la terre pour des sottises si absurdes et si abominables."

With the virtual substitution by Descartes of "reason" for what is truly transcendent in man, namely the higher will, the genuine dualism is compromised and the way opened for monistic developments. The tendency toward a rationalistic pantheism is manifest in Spinoza who reveals in many respects the Cartesian influence. Spinoza inclines to get rid of the Cartesian dualism between mind and matter by denying to mind any superiority of substance.[13] Man is in nature not as one empire in another empire but as a part in a whole. Man must adjust his will to the divine will, to be sure, but God is declared to be the same as "nature." When one has made an identification of this kind, it will not be possible by any number of subsidiary distinctions—for example, by setting up a sort of dualism in the cosmic process itself in the form of a *natura naturans* and a *natura naturata*—to maintain a sound doctrine of the will and to avoid pantheistic confusion. The God or "nature" to which Spinoza would have man conform his will is closely related to reason of a distinctly Cartesian type; so that to adjust one's will to God or nature is equivalent to adjusting it to reason. Reason and will are indeed for Spinoza identical.[14] Here as elsewhere Spinoza revives more completely perhaps than any other modern philosopher of the first rank the Stoical position.

Quite apart from Spinoza the followers of Descartes[15] tended to suppress the dualism between mind and matter

---

[13] See *Ethics*, II, prop. 7, scholium.

[14] "Voluntas et intellectus unum et idem sunt" (*Ethics*, II, prop. 49, corollary). In *Ethics*, III, prop. 9, scholium, a different view of the will appears; it is there identified with impulse, possibly, as has been conjectured, under the influence of Hobbes.

[15] I am dealing with the main influence. Certain Cartesians like Geulincx developed in connection with the doctrine known as "Occasionalism" a sense of man's dependence on the divine will that reminds one of medieval humility.

in favor of universal mechanism. Descartes himself had seen in animals only automata; the temptation proved irresistible to look on man in the same way.[16] A parallel tendency was that of the English empiricists and utilitarians to deny that mind is transcendent, to assert that there is "nothing in the intellect that was not previously in the senses." At the same time they fail to recognize a quality of will in man that sets him above the natural order and so incline strongly toward a naturalistic determinism. The denial of the freedom of the will is especially complete in Hobbes and Hume.[17] Philosophy in its main trend from Descartes to Hume seemed to exalt analysis at the expense of synthesis and to be ready to sacrifice spontaneity to mechanism. Of the world as envisaged by Hume in particular one might say with Mephistopheles: "Fehlt leider! nur das geistige Band!" Among those who sought to restore unity and freedom to philosophy, the most important is Immanuel Kant. In the matter of the will, he asserts that in the "noumenal" realm, the realm of the "thing-in-itself," man is perfectly free; as a phenomenon among other phenomena, on the contrary, man is, he admits, as thoroughly determined as Hume had maintained. The question arises as to the value of this

---

[16] La Mettrie, a disciple of the Cartesian Boerhaave, published *L'Homme-machine* in 1747.

[17] See *Free Will and Four English Philosophers* (Hobbes, Locke, Hume and Mill), by the Reverend Joseph Rickaby, S. J. Father Rickaby is of course a traditionalist, but makes remarks (see, for example, p. 205) that are decidedly perspicacious even from a strictly psychological point of view.

purely "noumenal" liberty in the actual emergencies of life. Huxley remarks apropos of this Kantian conception of the will: "Metaphysicians, as a rule, are sadly deficient in the sense of humor; or they would surely abstain from advancing propositions which, when stripped of the verbiage in which they are disguised, appear to the profane eye to be bare shams, naked but not ashamed."[18] The professional metaphysician often betrays an even more serious lack than that of a sense of humor—a lack, namely, of common sense. This lack appears in Huxley's own attitude toward the will when compared, let us say, with that of Dr. Johnson.

Kant's views regarding the "categorical imperative," as expounded in his *Critique of Practical Reason*, seem especially open to objection from the point of view of common sense. The categorical imperative is conceived as something a priori, not as based on experience. It is not a living intuition of a will that is set above the cosmic process (which includes a man's natural self) and that acts upon this cosmic process restrictively and selectively. It is rather a rigid metaphysical abstraction that operates without reference to the happiness of the individual[19] or the special circumstances to which he needs

---

[18] See his *Hume*, chap. 10 (end).

[19] Schiller wrote satirically of the categorical imperative from this point of view in his poem *Die Philosophen* (vv. 35 ff.). Elsewhere (*Werke*, ed. Goedeke, x. p. 101) he opposes to what seems to him the "Draconian" severity of the Kantian reason, the point of view of the "beautiful soul." Kant himself tended at the outset to base ethics on feeling. About 1770, however, he repudiated Shaftesbury and his followers on the ground that they were guilty of Epicureanism.

to adjust himself.[20] Moreover, it is, as I have pointed out, a will to act and not a will to refrain from acting. One may therefore raise the question whether it can be counted on to quell effectually the expansive "lusts" of the natural man—for example, the lust of domination. As an expression of cosmic reason, the categorical imperative reminds one of the reason-will of the Stoics. The reason, however, that the Stoic took as his guiding principle (τὸ ἡγεμονικόν) was conceived as one with reality; whereas the conclusions of the *Critique of Pure Reason*, so far as the relation between reason and reality is concerned, are largely skeptical. Kant therefore asks us to make certain important affirmations, not as necessarily true in themselves, but as postulates of the practical reason. He thus prepares the way for the *Philosophie des Als Ob* of Vaihinger. According to Vaihinger, you do not will a thing because it is true; you merely act *as if* it were true on the ground that it is a "useful fiction."[21] The "As-if" philosophy, again, is akin to the point of view of the pragmatist. The pragmatist does not conceive of truth as something that already exists: he makes his truth as he goes along, in other words he takes that to be true which seems useful or agreeable to his ordinary self. He thus tends to eliminate both the high impersonal standard and

---

[20] Jacobi has this aspect of the categorical imperative in mind when he exclaims: "Yes, I am that atheist and godless man who will lie as dying Desdemona lied; will lie and deceive as Pylades did when he feigned to be Orestes, will murder as Timoleon did, etc."

[21] Cf. p. 225. See also *Rousseau and Romanticism*, p. 370 n., where I touch on the philosophy of Vaihinger in its relation to the problem of the imagination.

the ethical will that, with reference to this standard, opposes bounds to the expansive desires.

Though the philosophy of Kant supplies the freedom and the synthetic element that were absent from a philosophy like that of Hume, it supplies them in an abstract and rationalistic way. It does not satisfy the craving for immediacy. Those who felt this craving sought to gratify it by basing ethics on the emotions. Kant's *Critique of Practical Reason* suggests that the ultimate reality, the "thing-in-itself," is very closely related to will. Schopenhauer actually pushes on to the identification of reality and will. Only the will that he sets up is very different from the categorical imperative.[22] It is a cosmic will conceived as a will to live and at the same time as the source of evil. Schopenhauer does not oppose to this cosmic *nisus* a higher will that may control it and even renounce it; if he had he might have achieved a true dualism. Instead he affirms expressly that the will, as he understands it, should include only that which is common to man and beast.[23] He hopes to get the equivalent of a true dualism by a recourse to the benevolent theory of ethics, especially, as we have seen (p. 96), to Rousseau's doctrine of natural pity. At the same time Schopenhauer inclines on occasion

---

[22] For Schopenhauer's attack on the categorical imperative see the first nine sections of his *Grundlage der moral.* The reconciliation of liberty with necessity that Huxley ridicules seems to Schopenhauer, however, to be, along with his "transcendental aesthetics," Kant's most distinguished achievement.

[23] *Neue Paralipomena.* Fouillée seems to have missed the point seriously when he affirms (*Descartes*, p. 198) that in giving the primacy to will, Schopenhauer continues Descartes. So far as Descartes' emphasis on the divine will is genuine, it is a survival of Christian voluntarism.

to see in actual nature not pity but ruthless struggle, thus anticipating Darwin. Nietzsche follows Schopenhauer in according the primacy to will but denies natural pity and affirms that the will that is fundamental in man is the will to power. He is thus related, on the one hand, to Hobbes and the Machiavellians, and, on the other, to the evolutionists.

One should note that those who gratify their thirst for immediacy by basing ethics on instinct or impulse, whether they conceive of the resulting "will" as a will to brotherhood or a will to power, agree in denying that the element of inhibition is primary or vital; they dismiss everything that interferes with the free expansion of "will" as artificial or conventional. Moreover, the attempt to recover the unity and spontaneity of instinct usually involves another dualism—that between a man's "heart" (in the sense of his impulsive and emotional self) and his "head" (in the sense of his analytical intellect) which destroys unity and leads him to see things, as Wordsworth phrases it, "in disconnection dead and spiritless."

The difficulties in the way of maintaining the benevolent theory of ethics have increased in direct measure as the nature "red in tooth and claw" of the evolutionist has been substituted for the idyllic nature of Rousseau. These difficulties may be illustrated from Huxley's attempt to deal with the problem of the will. In his *Evolution and Ethics* (Romanes Lecture, 1893) he develops the thesis that civilization and the cosmic process are sharply at variance with one another. A man should therefore in the interests of society seek to rise superior to this process. The lecture ends with an eloquent exhortation to effort and struggle along these anticosmic lines. At the same time Huxley denies that man has a will that transcends the cosmic process and moves in an opposite direction from it. He adopts unreservedly the determinism of Hume.[24] He proclaims that "man, physical, intellectual and moral, is as much a part of nature, as purely a part of the cosmic process as the humblest weed."[25] In that case, if one is to avoid the Nietzschean conclusion, it would seem necessary to affirm like Rousseau and the sentimentalists some principle of benevolence in Nature herself. On the contrary, Huxley declares in the most uncompromising fashion that Nature is ruthless.[26] When one confronts with one another passages of the kind I have been citing it is hard to avoid the conclusion reached by Mr. P. E. More[27] that Huxley is in his main trend a naturalistic sophist.

Recent philosophers like Bergson and James and Croce cannot be said to differ essentially in their dealings with the will from the older partisans of a subrational unity and spontaneity as a mode of escape from mechanism. Bergson exalts a type of "intuition" that involves a more or less complete turning away from the analytical intellect on the ground that it leads to the setting up of a "block universe"; at the same time he eliminates the will to refrain (*frein vital*) in favor of *élan vital*. He differs, however, from many of his romantic forebears, as I have already remarked (p. 39), by associating *élan vital* not with a will

---

[24] See *Hume,* chap. 10.
[25] *Works* (ed. Eversley, IX, p. 11).
[26] *Works* (ed. Appleton, IX, p. 200).
[27] *Shelburne Essays,* VIII, pp. 193 ff.

to brotherhood but with a will to power. Signor Piccoli
points out that Croce's view of the will has much in common with that of Bergson.[28] Croce is not, however, so
frankly imperialistic. James, again, though he felt himself
in intimate accord with the ideas of Bergson, is nearer
to the older romantic psychology. Consider, for example,
his essay *On a Certain Blindness in Human Beings*. Men
are not most human, it would seem, in their moments of
strenuous effort with reference to a human law that they
possess in common; on the contrary, they are most themselves in the reveries of their idle and irresponsible moments:[29] they should at least try to enter sympathetically
into one another's romantic dreams. In general the difficulty of discovering any basis for a genuine ethical
communion among men becomes acute if one seeks, like
James and Bergson, to prove freedom and spontaneity by
the "gushing forth" of novelty in the cosmic process.[30]
It is hard to see how men can come together in their differences. Moreover, Nature herself may be active in producing the vital variations that the intellect can neither fore-
see nor formulate, but the man in whom the "creative"
evolution is taking place is not active; from a truly human
point of view, he remains both passive and purposeless.

---

[28] *Benedetto Croce*, p. 198.

[29] "The holidays of life are its most vitally significant portions, because
they are, or at least should be, covered with just this kind of magically
irresponsible spell." The point of view is related to that of Schiller when
he says (*Werke*, ed. Goedeke, x, p. 327): "Der Mensch ist nur da ganz
Mensch, wo er spielt."

[30] For attempts of James to prove free will in this way, see *A Pluralistic
Universe*, p. 391 n.; also *Some Problems of Philosophy*, p. 145.

In the popular summing up of this whole philosophical trend, he does not know where he is going but merely that he is on the way. He may be sure in any case that, as a result of his failure to put forth a specifically human quality of will, he is not on the way to peace or brotherhood.

I have already said something about two contemporary doctrines, psychoanalysis and behaviorism, that, at least as popularly interpreted, tend to break down the principle of control in human nature, and to that extent to distintegrate civilization. It may be well to add a word about behaviorism. Man is an animal among other animals, and in so far is subject to laboratory methods. When, however, one attempts to base a complete explanation of conduct on such methods,[31] when, on the pretext that one must be "objective," one refuses to discriminate qualitatively between the behavior of a man and that of a frog, the result is naturalism gone mad. The behaviorist is not only pushing the mechanistic view of life to a point where he denies certain "immediate data of consciousness" but, in his eagerness to reduce everything to stimuli and physical reactions, he is in a fair way to eliminate consciousness itself. If, as Dr. Johnson says, all experience bears witness to the freedom of the will, one must conclude that the extreme behaviorist is turning his back on something that is highly experimental in favor of a theory.

In general, this very inadequate review of theories of

---

[31] For an attempt of this kind, see J. B. Watson, *Psychology from the Standpoint of a Behaviorist* (1919). For a discussion of the whole tendency, see Mary W. Calkins, "The Truly Psychological Behaviorism," *Psychological Review*, vol. 28, pp. 1–18.

the will held by the professional philosophers seems to confirm the wider survey I have attempted in the body of this volume. If the older treatment of the will led to a theological nightmare, the more recent treatment has only too often resulted in a metaphysical bewilderment. There has been a failure, on the whole, to assert in a positive and critical form certain truths of the inner life that were compromised by the interminable wranglings of the religious sects about God's will and its mode of operation.

APPENDIX B

Absolute Sovereignty

By their distrust of absolutism combined with their respect for standards and the discipline in the state that only standards can give, our liberals of the unionist type are, as I have remarked (p. 272), close to the English political tradition of which the best exponent is Burke. Much of the Englishman's concern for personal liberty, it has been maintained, is merely an aspect of his humorousness (in the older sense of the word), of his dislike of conformity and regimentation; and so is in a way a denial of standards. But this is not the whole truth. English statesmen at their best have attained to some conception of the liberty that is at the heart of genuine Christianity and have been more successful than the statesmen of any other country in making this conception politically effective.

The lover of personal liberty is inclined to esteem it a fortunate circumstance that the common law never gave way in England, as it did in various European countries, to Roman law. I am not competent to discuss so vast a subject as the influence of Roman law on the medieval and modern world, nor does my present subject require it. It is enough for my purpose to point out that the conception of liberty found in Roman law, even at its best, is very inferior to the Christian conception; it reflects unduly Stoic rationalism and, like all Greek and Roman political philosophy, is ready to sacrifice in a quite unwarranted measure the individual to the state. At its worst Roman law does not deserve to be called Roman at all but Byzantine. One should note the origin assigned in Roman law to the idea of *plenitudo potestatis* or unlimited sovereignty, an idea that can be shown to have had a considerable influence on the absolutists of the late medieval and early modern period. By the *lex regia*, we read in the *Digest*,[1] the Roman people made over its unbounded power to the emperor. The reasons for this renunciation are worth pondering. At the instigation of its demagogues, the Roman people had refused to limit itself and had at the same time tended toward the type of equality that is won at the expense of quality and the due subordination to standards that quality always requires. So far as our modern democracies are pursuing a merely quantitative equality, their fate would seem to be foreshadowed by this Roman development. The moment comes, sooner or later, when the concentration of power in the hands of one man

---

[1] Bk. 1, 4.1; see also *Institutes*, bk. 1, 2.6. So far as it refers to one specific transaction, the *lex regia* is of course a juristic fiction. The concentration of power in the hands of the emperor was more gradual.

is felt as a relief from the irresponsible tyranny of the mob. This is at all events the process by which a radical democracy passes over normally into what I have termed a decadent imperialism.

The genuinely medieval conception of sovereignty is very different from the conception I have been associating with the *lex regia* and Roman law. For the Christian, sovereignty does not derive from the people as in Roman law but from God, who is conceived primarily not as reason but as will. The whole tendency of the doctrine of grace is to make this will seem absolute and irresponsible, a sort of supernatural *bon plaisir*. I have already said something about the historical justification of the doctrine of grace; one may maintain without exaggeration that it saved Western civilization. By historical justification I do not mean that the doctrine is to be regarded as a "useful fiction"; the saving element in it is its truth—its emphasis on the higher will. At the same time I have hinted at the difficulties that the doctrine offers to the individualist. The acceptance of the maxim that man is the measure of all things—and all individualists must accept the maxim in some form[2]—is fatal to every absolute whether of will or reason. Absolute and unlimited will in the religious sense has often run over into a will to power, even when the rulers who asserted it have professed to do so only as the humble recipients of the grace of a divine sovereign. The tendency of a belief in the arbitrary sovereignty of

---

[2] I have discussed the various meanings that this maxim may have in the last chapter of *The Masters of Modern French Criticism*.

God to result imperialistically may be illustrated not only from the history of royalty by divine right but also from that of the papacy.

In my first chapter I attempted to trace the transition through an intermediary period of rationalism from the medieval belief in absolute will to another form of the same belief—the transition, in short, from the sovereignty of God to the sovereignty of the people. The superiority of the person who conceives of the political problem in terms of will in any sense of the word is that he is taking his stand for something vital and primary, something compared with which reason will finally prove to be only secondary and instrumental. It is interesting to consider from this point of view the rationalistic absolute of Hegel. According to Hegel the Idea, after various incomplete historical manifestations, finally found its perfect incarnation in the Prussian state. The absolute reason that is supposed to animate this state has shown itself in practice, most persons would agree, the servant of the will to power.

The rival claims of reason and will may also be studied interestingly in connection with international law. This whole subject is now under the suspicion of being chimerical. If this suspicion should prove to be justified, the explanation is either that international law has given a primacy to reason that does not belong to it or else has been unduly superficial in its treatment of will. The representatives of the so-called positive school of international law have tended to confine themselves to recording the unfolding wills of various sovereign states in their relations with one another. If this record is to deserve the name of law at all, it should surely be distinguishable from mere force, from the will to power of some state or league of states at any particular international crisis. At this point one perceives that the fortunes of international law are closely bound up with the new doctrine of will that has tended to take the place of the medieval dependence on the divine will as well as of the later reign of rationalism. The question as to the quality of will that the sovereign people is likely to display is subordinate to the question as to the truth or falsity of Rousseau's underlying dogma of natural goodness. The tendency of this dogma is to discredit both inner and outer control. With the disappearance of control, popular will becomes only another name for popular impulse. I have already concluded that what manifests itself in a people that has reached this stage of naturalistic expansion is not a will to brotherhood but a will to power. One must admit the imperialistic elements that insinuated themselves into the humanistic and religious traditions of the Occident, especially in connection with theories of absolute and unlimited sovereignty. Yet these traditions were after all in some measure genuine and so did something to set bounds to the *libido dominandi.* For at the heart of genuine religion is a will to peace and at the heart of genuine humanism is a will to justice; whereas, if my analysis be correct, radical democracy and imperialism are in their essence identical.

I have already said something about the other side of the modern movement in its relation to theories of

sovereignty (pp. 322 f.).[3] The utilitarian is tending to
conceive of the state in a more and more absolute fashion.
He feels that its power should suffer no restriction when
it is seeking to promote what is socially useful, the greatest
good of the greatest number. The underlying fallacy of
the utilitarian, I have said, is that he conceives of the
"greatest good" and of happiness in general in terms of
pleasure or else in terms of a merely outer working.
Society is bound to protect itself against the unrestraint
of the individual, but if it is not to push this necessary
assertion of its authority to an oppressive extreme, it
needs to take cognizance not only of outer working but
also of the inner working that is the final source of a
sound individualism. To do so is not to become abstract
but on the contrary to turn from sociological theorizing
to positive psychological observation.

This brief survey of theories of absolute sovereignty
would seem to confirm the passage of John Adams that
serves as one of the epigraphs of this volume. From the
lex regia to the utilitarian-sentimental movement these
theories have been associated with a series of theological
and metaphysical conceits that have, in their ultimate
implications, been subversive of personal liberty.

---

[3] Perhaps the best-known attempt to base a theory of sovereignty on
utility and social expediency is that of John Austin in his *Province of
Jurisprudence Determined* (1832; 2d ed., 1861). See especially chap. 6.

BIBLIOGRAPHY

I have included in this bibliography the more important works mentioned in the body of this volume; also a few others that, for one reason or another, seem especially relevant to the topics I have discussed.

ACTON, LORD:
   Letters of Lord Acton to Mary Gladstone. 1904.
   The History of Freedom and Other Essays. 1907.
ALTHUSIUS, J.:
   Politica methodice digesta. 1603.
ARISTOTLE:
   Nicomachean Ethics. Trans. D. P. Chase. 1847. (Reprint
      in Everyman's Library.)
   Politics. Trans. B. Jowett. 1905.
ARNIM, H. VON:
   Die politischen Theorien des Altertums. 1910.
ATGER, F.:
   Essai sur l'histoire des doctrines du contrat social. 1906.

AUGUSTINE, SAINT:
De Civitate Dei. Ed. E. Hoffman. 2 vols. 1898. Trans.
M. Dods. 1897.
BARKER, E.:
*Political Thought in England from Herbert Spencer to
the Present Day.* 1915.
Greek Political Theory. 1918.
BEVERIDGE, A. J.:
The Life of John Marshall. 4 vols. 1916.

Mr. Beveridge brings out interestingly the irreconcilable opposition between Marshall and Jefferson. He should, however, at some point in his work have discriminated sharply between the unionist and the nationalist of imperialistic leanings. Marshall is very far from being a precursor of Roosevelt.

BOSSUET, J. B.:
Politique tirée de l'écriture sainte. 1709.
BOURGEOIS, E.:
Manuel historique de politique étrangère. 3 vols. 4ᵉ éd.
1909.
BURKE, E.:
Reflections on the Revolution in France. 1790.
Letter to a Member of the National Assembly. 1791.
Works. 8 vols. (Bohn Library.) 1854–61.
BURY, J. B.:
The Idea of Progress. 1921.
CARLYLE, R. W., and A. J.:
A History of Medieval Political Theory. 4 vols. 1903–
22.
CHATEAUBRIAND, F. R. DE:
Essai historique, politique et moral sur les Révolutions.
1797.

Mémoires d'Outre-Tombe (1848). Ed. E. Biré. 6 vols. 1898–1901.

CONFUCIUS:

The Conduct of Life. Trans. Ku Hung Ming. 1906.

   This is the Confucian treatise usually entitled *The Doctrine of the Mean.* A still more literal rendering of the two Chinese words that make up the title, if we accept Mr. Ku Hung Ming's explanation of them, would be the "universal norm" or "center."

The Sayings of Confucius (Analects). Trans. L. Giles. 1907

CUMBERLAND, R.:

De Legibus naturae. 1672.

DANTE ALIGHIERI:

De Monarchia. About 1310. Ed. Moore. 1904. Trans. P. H. Wicksteed in Temple Classics.

DEDIEU, J.:

Montesquieu et la tradition politique anglaise en France. 1909.

DIELS, H.:

Die Fragmente der Vorsokratiker. 2 vols. (in 3). 2d ed. 1906–10.

DUNNING, W. A.:

A History of Political Theories. 3 vols. 1902–20.

FERGUSON, W. F.:

Greek Imperialism. 1913.

FESTER, R.:

Rousseau und die deutsche Geschichtsphilosophie. 1890.

FIGGIS, J. N.:

Studies of Political Thought from Gerson to Grotius. 1907. 2d ed. 1916.

An excellent treatment of the all-important period of transition from a theocratic Europe to a Europe of great territorial nationalities.

The Divine Right of Kings. 1914.

FILMER, R.:

Patriarcha; or the Natural Power of Kings. 1680. (Reprinted together with Locke's *Treatises of Government* in Morley's Universal Library.)

FRANK, T.:

Roman Imperialism. 1914.

FUSTEL DE COULANGES, N. D.:

La Cité antique. 1864. 16th ed. 1898. Trans. W. Small. 1874.

It is difficult to exhibit the relation between ethos and political forms without seeming, and perhaps without being, too systematic. *La Cité antique* has been criticized severely from this point of view. C. Bémont, however, goes too far when he asserts (article on Fustel in the 11th edition of *Encyclopedia Britannica*) that it "has been largely superseded"; on the contrary, it is, in certain important respects, a work of almost definitive excellence.

GIERKE, O.:

Johannes Althusius. 1880. 3d ed. 1913.

A valuable repertory of information on such topics as natural rights and the social contract. Gierke probably exaggerates, however, the influence of Althusius on Rousseau, who mentions him only once (end of 6° *Lettre écrite de la Montagne*).

Political Theories of the Middle Age. Trans. and ed. F. W. Maitland. 1900.

GOMPERZ, T.:

Griechische Denker. 2d ed. 3 vols. 1903–9. Trans. L. Magnus and G. G. Berry. 1901–12.

GOOCH, G. P.:

Germany and the French Revolution. 1920.

GROTIUS, H.:

De Jure belli et pacis. 1625. Trans. Whewell. 3 vols. 1853.

HEARNSHAW, F. J. C. (editor):

The Social and Political Ideas of Some Great Medieval Thinkers. 1923.

In one of the articles of this volume Eileen Power points out that Pierre Du Bois, a lawyer in the service of Philippe le Bel, formulated a plan of European peace that anticipated in some respects the Grand Dessein of Sully. This plan, like that of Sully, would have resulted practically in the French domination of Europe.

HOBBES, T.:

Leviathan. 1651. Ed. W. G. Pogson Smith. 1909.

HOOKER, R.:

Ecclesiastical Polity. 1592. (Reprint in Everyman's Library.)

HUME, D.:

A Treatise of Human Nature. 1739–40. (Reprint in Everyman's Library.)

JANET, P.:

Histoire de la science politique. 2 vols. 1858. 4th ed. 1913.

JEFFERSON, T.:

Works. 10 vols. E. P. L. Ford. 1892–99.

LASKI, H. J.:
  Political Thought from Locke to Bentham. 1920.
LECKY, W. E. H.:
  Democracy and Liberty. 2 vols. 1896.
LOCKE, J.:
  Two Treatises of Government. 1690. (Reprint in Mor-
  ley's Universal Library.)
LOUTER, J. DE:
  Le Droit international positif. 1920.
MacDONALD, J. R.:
  The Socialist Movement. 1911.
MACHIAVELLI, N.:
  *Del modo tenuto dal duca Valentino nell' ammazzare
  Vitellozzo Vitelli,* etc. 1502.
  Il Principe. 1513.
  Vita di Castruccio Castricani. 1520.
      Translations of all three pieces appear in the same
  volume of Everyman's Library.
MAINE, SIR H. J. S.:
  Ancient Law. 1861. (Reprint in Everyman's Library.)
      See especially chap. 4, "The Modern History of the
  Law of Nature."
MAISTRE, J. DE:
  Du Pape. 1819.
  Soirées de Saint-Pétersbourg. 1821.
      The "Premier entretien" contains the celebrated
  "Portrait du bourreau."
MANDEVILLE, B.:
  The Fable of the Bees. 1714. (*The Grumbling Hive,* the
  verses that form the nucleus of this volume, appeared
  originally in 1705.) 5th ed. 2 vols. 1728–29.

MARSILIUS OF PADUA:
Defensor Pacis. 1324. Text in Goldast, *Monarchia S. Imperii Romani.*

MERRIAM, C. E.:
American Political Theories. 1903. New ed. 1920.

MICHEL, H.:
L'Idée de l'état. 1896.

MILL, J. S.:
On Liberty. 1859. (Reprinted together with the essays on *Utilitarianism* and *Representative Government* in Everyman's Library.)

MONTESQUIEU, CHARLES DE SECONDAT DE LA BREDE, BARON DE:
De l'Esprit des Lois. 1748.

OLIVER, F. S.:
Alexander Hamilton; an Essay on American Union. 1907.

PASCAL, B.:
Pensées et opuscules. Ed. L. Brunschvicg. 1917.

PLATO:
Works. Trans. B. Jowett. 5 vols. 3d ed. 1892.

POUND, R.:
The Spirit of the Common Law. 1921.
An Introduction to the Philosophy of Law. 1922.

POWERS, H. H.:
America Among the Nations. 1917.

RENAN, E.:
La Réforme intellectuelle et morale. 1871.

RITCHIE, D. D.:
Natural Rights. 1894. 3d ed. 1916.
> The notion of natural rights is, according to Ritchie, chimerical and leads to an unsound individual-

ism. What he opposes to this unsoundness is not a sound individualism but social expediency, which is itself, in virtue of the doctrine of evolution, constantly changing. A useful feature of this book is the appendix which contains the more important eighteenth-century declarations of rights in France and America.

ROUSSEAU, J. J.:

Oeuvres complètes. 13 vols. (Hachette.)

There is no good complete edition.

The Political Writings. 2 vols. Ed. C. E. Vaughan, 1915.

Vaughan has done good work on the text. In his introductory material, on the other hand, he develops ideas—for example, the idea that Rousseau is politically a true Platonist—which will not bear serious scrutiny.

SAINT-PIERRE, ABBE DE:

Projet pour rendre la paix perpétuelle en Europe. 1712–17.

SCHOPENHAUER, A.:

Grundlage der Moral. 1840. Trans. A. B. Bullock, 2d ed. 1915.

SEILLIERE, E.:

L'Impérialisme démocratique. 1907.

Le Mal romantique. 1908.

Introduction à la philosophie de l'impérialisme. 1911.

Le Péril mystique dans l'inspiration des démocraties modernes. 1918.

Balzac et la morale romantique. 1922.

Vers le socialisme rationnel. 1923.

M. Seillière intends this last volume as a summary of his whole point of view. Among the expositions of his philosophy that have been published by others the best is that by R. Gillouin: *Une nouvelle philosophie de l'histoire moderne* (1921). See also *La Pensée d'Ernest Seillière,* twelve studies by contemporary French writers, 1923 (bibliography at the end). M. Seillière has been criticized for giving an undue extension to the term "imperialism." A more legitimate objection is that to his use of the word "mysticism." On this latter point see Henri Bremond, *Histoire littéraire du sentiment religieux en France,* vol. 4 (1920), p. 566 n.

SHAFTESBURY, ANTHONY ASHLEY COOPER, THIRD EARL OF:
Characteristics of Men, Manners, Opinions and Times. 1711. 2d ed. 1714. Ed. J. M. Robertson. 1900.
The Life, Unpublished Letters and Philosophical Regimen. Ed. B. Rand. 1900.

SMITH, A.:
The Theory of Moral Sentiments. 1761. 6th ed. with critical and biographical memoir by Dugald Stewart, 1790. (Reprint in Bohn's Library.)
The Wealth of Nations. 1776. (Reprint in Everyman's Library.)

SPENGLER, O.:
Der Untergang des Abendlandes. 2 vols. 1919–22.

STEPHEN, FITZJAMES:
Liberty, Equality, Fraternity. 2d ed. 1874.

TAGORE, RABINDRANATH:
Nationalism. 1917.

TROLTSCH, E.:

Augustin, die christliche Antike und die Mittelalter. 1915.

VIALLATE, A.:

L'Impérialisme économique et les relations internationales pendant le dernier demi-siècle (1870–1920). 1923.

WHITMAN, W.:

Leaves of Grass. 1855.

Democratic Vistas. 1871.

ZANTA, L.:

La Renaissance du stoïcisme au XVI˚ Siècle. 1914.

INDEX

The Palatino typeface used in this volume is the work of Hermann Zapf, the noted European type designer and master calligrapher. Palatino is basically an old-style letterform, yet strongly endowed with the Zapf distinction of exquisiteness. With concern not solely for the individual letter but also the working visual relationship in a page of text, Zapf's edged pen has given this type a brisk, natural motion.

Book design by Design Center, Inc., Indianapolis, Indiana
Typography by Weimer Typesetting Co., Inc., Indianapolis, Indiana

Printed in the USA
CPSIA information can be obtained
at www.ICGtesting.com
JSHW082226140824
68134JS00015B/758